The Methuen Drama
Contemporary Japane

JAPANFOUNDATION
国際交流基金

The Methuen Drama Book of Contemporary Japanese Plays

The Bacchae—Holstein Milk Cows

One Night

Isn't Anyone Alive?

The Sun (2016)

Carcass

Published in Partnership with The Japan Foundation

methuen | drama

LONDON · NEW YORK · OXFORD · NEW DELHI · SYDNEY

METHUEN DRAMA
Bloomsbury Publishing Plc
50 Bedford Square, London, WC1B 3DP, UK
1385 Broadway, New York, NY 10018, USA
29 Earlsfort Terrace, Dublin 2, Ireland

BLOOMSBURY, METHUEN DRAMA and the Methuen Drama logo are trademarks of
Bloomsbury Publishing Plc

First published in Great Britain 2022

For legal purposes the Acknowledgments and permissions on p.ii constitute an extension
of this copyright page.

Cover design: Rebecca Heselton
Cover image: Traditional Japanese textile stencil pattern © Giorgio Morara

A catalogue record for this book is available from the British Library.

A catalog record for this book is available from the Library of Congress.

ISBN: HB: 978-1-3502-7837-0
        PB: 978-1-3502-7836-3
        ePDF: 978-1-3502-7839-4
        eBook: 978-1-3502-7840-0

Typeset by RefineCatch Limited, Bungay, Suffolk
Printed and bound in Great Britain

To find out more about our authors and books visit www.bloomsbury.com
and sign up for our newsletters.

Contents

Introduction

The Japan Foundation promotes international cultural exchange through the Japanese language and culture. In the field of performing arts, the Japan Foundation introduces a wide variety of Japanese performing arts to countries around the world. These include classical performing arts, such as *Noh, Kyogen, Bunraku, Kabuki,* and *Nihon Buyo*, as well as more modern Japanese music, folk songs, jazz and classical music, contemporary dance and theatre, and international co-productions.

The Foundation also provides support and subsidies to groups and artists who perform abroad, and operates a website to provide information on Japanese performing arts.

We are pleased to announce that we are publishing with Methuen Drama, an imprint of Bloomsbury Publishing Plc *The Methuen Drama Book of Contemporary Japanese Plays*, a collection of Japanese plays in English translation, which showcases the 'here-and-now' of Japan, focusing on five playwrights who have recently been attracting attention at home and abroad as leaders of the next generation.

Following the declaration of the Covid-19 pandemic, theatrical performances around the world came to an unprecedented halt. As a result, artists and staff lost the opportunity to present their productions and audiences could no longer casually visit theatres as in the past. However, when the pandemic is under control and the theatres regain their former liveliness, the plays introduced in this book may stimulate the imagination of a wide variety of people. Thus, we have decided to publish this collection with the sincere hope that the plays will one day be performed as readings or in full stage performances.

We would like to express our heartfelt gratitude to the many people involved in the editing and producing of this collection for their great support and cooperation.

The Japan Foundation
March 2022

Japanese Theatre by Playwrights of Generation X and on

Hiroko Yamaguchi (*The Asahi Shimbun staff writer*)

Translated by Mari Boyd

This collection contains five plays in English translation for the purpose of introducing contemporary Japanese theatre to the global community. Five early to mid-career playwrights have been selected, and their best works as of 2021 are included in the book.

Four were born in the 1970s, and the youngest, Satoko Ichihara, in 1988. In Japan, many other playwrights of the same generation are also productive, comprising a strong leading force in today's theatre.

Needless to say, these playwrights have different personalities and different creative directions. Their works cannot simply be categorized by generational factors. However, it is possible to find perspectives on their artistic expressivity through reflecting on the state of Japanese society when these artists were developing and maturing.

Coming of age in a time of economic stagnation, natural disasters, and pervasive hopelessness

In 1945, Japan was defeated in the Second Word War and set out to rebuild the nation that had been reduced to scorched earth. Since then, the economy basically continued to grow for more than forty years, although there were occasional fluctuations.

Especially in the late 1980s and early 1990s, when Gen Xers were teenagers, Japan experienced an unprecedented economic boom, known as the "bubble," with land and stock prices skyrocketing. The acquisition of the Rockefeller Center in New York and some major film studios in Hollywood by Japanese enterprises symbolized the exuberance of the times.

Stock prices fell disastrously after reaching a peak at the end of 1989. Land prices also crashed soon after. The bubble burst in the early 1990s, and the Japanese economy entered a long period of stagnation known as the "Lost Decades."

It was around this time that Gen Xers, who were the offspring of the baby boomers, graduated from college. In addition, the rapid economic downturn led companies to reduce new hiring, resulting in the extreme difficulty of finding satisfactory employment during the so-called "ice age." Unable to get the position they desired, many young people entered the workforce as part-time, casual, or temporary workers.

Until then in Japan—this was especially true of fully employed men—their salary would increase incrementally with age. A stable lifestyle was considered the standard: they could get married, buy a house, support their family, and eventually retire. This unique Japanese system of "lifetime employment" and "seniority system" that supported this lifestyle began to collapse.

Many people who started working as non-regular employees during the ice age that followed also entered their forties in unstable positions. The government estimates that as of 2021, there will be one million people needing support to find stable jobs. The unmarried rate is also high.

In this generation, the phenomenon of *hikikomori* (shut-ins), who refuse to get involved in social activities, such as school and work, and who stay at home for long periods of time, began to draw attention.

In the 2010s, the Japanese economy saw a rise in stock prices and other indicators due to large-scale monetary easing and fiscal stimulus, but few people today have a palpable sense that they have become more affluent. With unstable employment, declining birthrate, aging population, and ever-increasing national debt, problems are mounting, and society is overwhelmed with hopelessness.

Since the economy entered a long period of stagnation, two huge earthquakes have occurred.

In January 1995, the Great Hanshin-Awaji Earthquake struck major cities in western Japan, killing more than 6,400 people. Everyone was speechless at the sight of cities destroyed, highways toppled over, and densely populated areas burnt to the ground.

In March of the same year, the cult Aum Shinrikyo conducted a terrorist attack on Tokyo by releasing poisonous Sarin gas in the metropolitan subway and causing thirteen deaths and 6,300 casualties. This cult instigated numerous other vicious incidents and has left an indelible mark on society.

Then came the Great East Japan Earthquake in March, 2011. The massive quake and tsunami killed 15,899 people, and 2,526 people are still missing (as of March, 2021). The meltdown at the nuclear power plant brought about by the tsunami has not been brought under control even after ten years, and approximately 36,000 displaced residents in the surrounding area are still forced to live as evacuees (as of January, 2021).

Witnessing the horrific death and destruction, we were made keenly aware of the fragility of civilization. At the same time, we were reminded of the irreplaceable value of our ordinary lives. This common experience, accompanied by the pain of loss, echoes like a thorough-bass in various artistic forms that have been created since, including theatre.

The "decades that were not lost" for theatre

The "lost decades" for the economy had the opposite effect of improving the environment for Japanese theatre. The various facilities and measures that had been conceived during the economic boom took shape and began to operate efficiently.

A nationwide Japan Arts Council was established in 1990 and enabled the expansion of funding systems for national and local municipalities. To commemorate the 1997 opening of the New National Theatre for opera, dance, and contemporary theatre, Hisashi Inoue (1934–2010), a leading contemporary playwright, wrote and produced *Kamiyacho Sakura Hotel*, set in Hiroshima in 1945, just before the atomic bomb was dropped. Public theatres have increased in number throughout the nation since then, and a system of public support for creative work is now in place.

The 1990s also saw an increase in the number of universities that invited practicing playwrights and directors to teach theatre as performance. The college-level study of arts management has also taken root.

International arts festivals, both large and small, are now held in various parts of Japan, and the opportunities for performing arts events and exchanges have expanded. The ubiquity of the Internet has facilitated information exchange and networking; hence the hurdles to planning and executing global performances and international co-productions have been greatly reduced.

In recent years, the magnetic power of the arts, especially theatre, to draw together a wide range of people has attracted attention, enabling theatre artists to extend their activities into public arenas other than stage performance.

In this way, although there are still many budgetary and systematic shortcomings compared to those in advanced countries, an environment has gradually been created for theatre artists to develop diverse activities. As a result, playwrights born in the 1970s and later have been able to acquire suitable venues and opportunities for their activities, unlike the previous generation that aimed at the single route of developing and sustaining their own theatre company by increasing audience size and performance scale. Encountering a wide variety of talented people and work environments, they are able to acquire opportunities and sites for activities that suit them.

For example, Satoko Ichihara, whose *The Bacchae—Holstein Milk Cows* is included in this collection, had exposure to creative writing at a public theatre in her hometown and later studied theatre at a university in the Tokyo metropolitan area. She has been involved in international performances and international co-productions since early on in her career. Her *Bacchae* was premiered at the Aichi Triennale 2019. The development of her career can be said to symbolize how the contemporary theatre world operates.

Toward a 'quiet real'

Let us conduct a quick review of the trajectory of contemporary theatre in postwar Japan.

Major currents of contemporary theatre emerged in response to the social situation of each period. Each trend did not end as a temporary fashion, but continued in parallel with new ones while transforming and giving birth to fresh artistic expression. We will focus on the early period in the evolution of their various iterations.

From the 1960s to the 1970s, "underground theatre," which emphasized physicality, emerged among young people who rebelled against conventional realist theatre. The word *angura*, short for "underground," had an energy that resonated with the countercultural movement of the same period. The major creators include Shuji Terayama (1935–83), Yukio Ninagawa (1935–2016), Tadashi Suzuki (b. 1939), Juro Kara (b. 1940), Kazuyoshi Kushida (b. 1942), and Makoto Satoh (b. 1943).

In the 1980s, a "little theatre boom" was triggered by young people. First on the list was Hideki Noda (b. 1955), who performed mythical stories with his light, galloping, boyish frame. Another exceptional artist, Shoji Kokami (b. 1958), gained popularity by staging dialogue plays on topics, such as post-nuclear-war life or the desolation of living in contemporary society, but in a bright, playful style, inserting light dance sequences and fun and games.

The 1990s saw a renewed interest in the real. Koki Mitani (b. 1961), a highly skillful writer of comedies, and Ai Nagai (b. 1951), who critiques history and society sharply while creating mature comedic works, both won high acclaim and popularity.

It was also in the 1990s that a group of plays known as "quiet theatre" began to attract attention, by putting everyday life on stage without resorting to raucous voices or violence.

This type of play was not invented in this period, but preceded by the works of a number of playwrights. First, Kunio Kishida (1890–1954) wrote nuanced dialogue conveying with delicacy various normal states of mind. His plays continue to be staged today. Many of the plays by Minoru Betsuyaku (1937–2020) are also about the quotidian. Belonging to the *angura* generation, he started writing drama in the 1960s and, influenced by Samuel Beckett, established absurdist drama in Japan. More recently, Ryo Iwamatsu (b. 1952) is also said to depict a seemingly prosaic Chekhovian world.

Oriza Hirata (b. 1962), the standard-bearer of this new style, named his approach of subtly revealing the complexity of ordinary people, "contemporary colloquial theatre theory." This branding and his publications explicating his theory and its practice made a huge stir.

Hirata has inspired many young eager followers through his Youth Group (Seinendan) and the Komaba Agora Theatre, where he presides as artistic director. He developed numerous educational theatre activities designed for students from elementary school through college. His influence has also reached many Gen X playwrights and directors.

Toshiki Okada (b. 1973), who has made an impressive impact both in Japan and abroad, says that reading Hirata's book *Contemporary Colloquial Theatre* (1995) was a turning point for him. Yuko Kuwabara (b.1976), whose play *One Night* is included in this collection, began her full-fledged theatrical career when, still a high school student, she performed in a play written and directed by Hirata.

In addition, many of today's leading playmakers, including Shu Matsui (b. 1972), Hideto Iwai (b. 1974), Yukio Shiba (b. 1982), and Takahiro Fujita (b. 1985), have enjoyed working with Hirata in various ways.

Facing harsh reality

Today's plays offer no big narrative with catharsis, but rather a sense that even after the play ends, the daily lives of the characters continue as usual. This sense of reality is shared by Gen Xers.

Kuwabara of *One Night*, mentioned above, and Takuya Yokoyama (b. 1977), author of *Carcass*, included in this collection, depict personal entanglements that deepen through daily interactions with a rich sense of lived life; such portrayal is appreciated and supported by a large variety of audiences.

Holding the raw assumption that humans die day by day, Shiro Maeda (b. 1977) avoids seriousness and expresses the living human condition through silly chitchat, slothful movements, and an occasional quirky set-up. His contribution to this collection, *Isn't Anyone Alive?*, is a good example of his dramaturgy.

Tomohiro Maekawa (b. 1974), who is well known for his play *The Sun*, enjoys writing science fiction and horror. The 1980s little theatre playmakers had an affinity for near-future sci-fi, but it is hardly a common trait among Gen X playwrights.

In Maekawa's works, mysterious things occur side by side with normal life. The characters who have to face the unknown are not equipped with special knowledge or heightened sensibility. Without losing hold on objective reality and accepting what is beyond understanding, they are yet caught in a paralyzing dread. Audiences seem to find this convincing.

Gen X playwrights witnessed as adults the onset of the employment ice age after the bubble burst. Facing society and the world without illusion and reflecting on themselves in the midst of harsh reality—this is their commonality and the solid grounding of their artistic expressivity.

Many of their works are set in neither glamorous nor romantic places—an all too ordinary house, a workplace, a city corner, or a dying provincial town. Many audience members appreciate finding in those plays themes that connect with their own lives and reflect on them seriously. Such a relationship between artists and audiences is supported by the social infrastructure of public theatres, which is gradually being enhanced.

Such "honest theatre" certainly reflects society and the times we live in today.

The Bacchae—Holstein Milk Cows

Satoko Ichihara

Introduction to the Playwright and the Play

Kyoko Iwaki (*Lecturer in Theatre, University of Antwerp*)

Translated by Aya Ogawa

At the core of Greek tragedy is agon. In other words, at its foundation is a confrontation between two human beings or between man and god. However, in Satoko Ichihara's play, which radically reimagines Euripides' *The Bacchae*, all conflict is rendered through liquids. In an episode described in the play, the Housewife, as a child, had tried to dissolve a goldfish in water by desperately stirring the contents of a goldfish bowl with chopsticks. As this story symbolizes, in Ichihara's queer version of Greek tragedy, all dichotomy has dissolved and liquefied with the odor of tepid bodily fluids.

Ichihara, who was awarded the 64th Kishida Kunio Drama Award for this play, is the first playwright in Japan to be acknowledged for portraying a queer worldview. Despite that, she has never once used the highly politicized word "queer" and instead, as she does in another one of her plays, uses the endearing term "fairy" to portray all of the things that have been pushed to the fringes of society. In particular, Ichihara places her focus on the types of "lookism" that characteristically plague Japanese women. If a woman is not of a certain age, a certain body type, a certain appearance, she is treated as nonhuman in Japan. The frustration towards this violence lies at the base of her work.

The majority of writers who have adapted Greek tragedy have been men: Seneca, Hölderlin, Hofmannsthal, Voltaire, Gide to name but a few. For much of time the performers and audiences of Greek tragedy were limited to adult men. Judith Butler exposed this reality and her *Antigone* shook the world by declaring that state and family are not oppositional forces but, in fact, complicit. But Ichihara takes it further with her play, which is set against the worldview inherited from the collapse of modern society constructed by the Western white man, where both state and family have fallen into complete dysfunction. In order to represent this postmodern male society, Ichihara makes all of her characters, including the Chorus, sing, dance, and be embodied by women of pernicious charm.

Finally, Ichihara's wordcraft is infused with dramaturgy that queers all conflict. Since the 2010s, the genre of "monologue dramas" has proliferated in contemporary Japanese theatre, but even in this context, Ichihara's works contain soliloquies of extraordinary length. In a prior interview, Ichihara said that "flesh-and-blood conversations between people are usually speckled with lies," so when she sees scenes in theatre where characters are trying to communicate their true intentions with sincerity, she wonders what they're doing and feels disengaged. These are the utterances of modern folk for whom a dual life offline and online is normal, utterances that epitomize the transformation in the rules of dialogue itself. In physical everyday conversations we express nothing of substance, while in digital spaces like social media, we convey our true feelings. In other words, Ichihara's soliloquy dramas skillfully translate to the stage the forcible current-day reversal of public and private space. Her plays are truly pertinent readings of the changes in contemporary Japanese society.

Playwright Biography

Satoko Ichihara

Playwright, director, and novelist. Born in 1988 in Osaka, raised in Fukuoka, Japan. Studied theatre at J. F. Oberlin University. Ichihara Satoko has led the theatre company Q since 2011. She writes and directs plays that deal with human behavior, the physiology of the body, and the unease surrounding these themes, using her unique sense of language and physical sensitivity. In 2011, she received the Aichi Arts Foundation Drama Award with the play *Insects*. In 2017, she was nominated as finalist of the 61st Kishida Kunio Playwriting Prize for *Favonia's Fruitless Fable*. In 2019, she published her first collection of stories, *Mamito no tenshi* (*Mamito's Angel*). Her latest work *The Bacchae—Holstein Milk Cows*, based on a Greek tragedy, premiered at Aichi Triennale 2019 and won the 64th Kishida Kunio Drama Award. She is a Junior Fellow of The Saison Foundation (2020–2021).

For more information please visit: http://qqq-qqq-qqq.com/

The Bacchae—Holstein Milk Cows

Satoko Ichihara

Translated by Aya Ogawa

Characters

Housewife
Beast
Dog
Girl
Unknown Entity
Chorus (The Spirits of Holstein Milk Cows)

This play is a contemporary play that borrows its structure from ancient Greek plays and is based on Euripides' tragedy *The Bacchae*.

As is the structure of Greek theatre, the play is performed by three actors who portray the three primary characters and a Chorus of twelve to fifteen performers.

The Chorus functions as a singing and dancing ensemble that explains the setting and circumstances of the play as well as the inner feelings of the primary characters.

The play begins with the Prologos (introduction) and the Parodos (entrance song of the Chorus), with several repetitions of Epeisodion (dialogue) and Stasimon (song), and ends with the Exodos (final chapter). The audience seating bank is shaped like an earthenware pot surrounding the half-circular acting area.

The set portrays the living/dining room in the home of Housewife. At the bottom of the earthenware pot-shaped audience seating bank is a square dining room where Housewife lives, like a lone square island. Inside the room there is a dining table set, sofa, coffee table, ironing board, and such. Upstage of the dining table set is an open kitchen. The room looks like a replica of an IKEA showroom. Around the room there is space for the Chorus to stand by. All the props that are used in the play (rope, nursing bottle, etc.) are kept in that space. There is a screen in the upper part of the stage where video can be projected.

Prologos

Housewife *enters, holding a teacup. She is wearing a brand-new floral print apron that does not have a lived-in quality. She sits at the dining table. On the table are a hot plate, a box of Corn Flakes, a straw, cooking chopsticks, rubber gloves, and Tupperware.*

She looks out at the audience.

Tonight, we're having barbecue. What are all of you thinking about eating today? I grill meat maybe once a month? So that day is today. Usually I eat the opposite of barbecue or, like, my meals are very close to a cow's diet, I guess? My meals resemble what cows eat. Plain, plant-based meals. And Kellogg's Corn Flakes in the morning.

She indicates the box of Corn Flakes on the table.

Oh, did you know? Corn Flakes were invented to discourage masturbation, apparently. I read that online and was surprised. Corn Flakes were created by a guy named Dr. Kellogg. Dr. Kellogg believed that sexual desire was the root of sickness and he didn't have sex because he believed it was bad for his body. I think it's bad for the body *not* to have sex, but … He did have a wife, but they didn't have sex. They even chose to adopt and raise an orphan. Well, even if he were to tolerate the sex act, masturbation was absolutely bad in his book. I also read this online recently: Skin-to-skin contact releases the "happy" hormone oxytocin, and that's why sex is good for your health, it said. But then I also read another article that said any skin-to-skin contact, like petting a dog, can release oxytocin the same way. So then I thought, maybe Dr. Kellogg accepted sex not in terms of skin, but the liquid enveloped by skin. When you kiss someone, you exchange saliva, right? That can strengthen your immune system, apparently. I happened to read that online too, and I thought, a-ha, I finally get it! Masturbation is bad because there is no exchange of fluid with another person. Of course, there is also the risk of disease when liquids intermingle. And as for kissing, you can do that with a dog, right? Dogs love to lick people anyway. So, the takeaway, if you follow a normal thought pattern is this: It's good to procreate—I think that's the point. I don't know if it's really healthy. My friend looked horribly drained after childbirth with dark circles under her eyes. And also, raising a child well is a whole other issue. These days you hear about child abuse a lot. So many horrifying incidents in the news. What do you think?

She waits for audience reaction.

Hmm. What was I talking about? Oh geez, whenever I talk, I start thinking about all sorts of things and I can't help but say them out loud so I ramble on and on. Where was I? So the birth of a new life is a universally celebrated thing, isn't it? Even Dr. Kellogg conceded as much. Oh, but to his point, nowadays you can sell your sperm to a sperm bank. But Dr. Kellogg advocated against masturbation. He said that meat and other rich diets heightens sexual desire. Oh, they say he was a vegetarian himself. And he wanted to create a plain, simple meal that wouldn't heighten desire, and that's how he came up with Corn Flakes. According to Dr. Kellogg, Corn Flakes purifies the heart and body. I hope that's true, but in reality, Corn Flakes alone can't suppress sexual desire, of course. I eat them every day, but I still masturbate. But I do agree with Dr. Kellogg. I'm not as extreme as him but I eat Corn Flakes every day and hope to have a peaceful day. It's my lucky charm. I still think that humans need restraint. That our baseline should be restraint. If we ate meat every day, we wouldn't feel the joy of meat. Because our baseline is vegetables, we can appreciate meat on rare occasions. I think that's true for everything. Because our baseline is not eating, we can appreciate eating. Because our baseline is working, we appreciate rest. Because our baseline is silence, we appreciate conversation. Because our baseline is not having sex, we appreciate sex. Everything begins because of our baseline. If we were loyal only to our desire, desire, desire—humankind would perish. The opposite is also true: If all we have is restraint, restraint, restraint, humankind would perish. Actually, I'm almost at the point where I want to be vegetarian. I'm beginning to feel joy in what society sees as restraint. But eating only vegetables diminishes my gratitude for vegetables, so that's why I keep some beef in the mix. I also eat cow to reaffirm that I am not a cow but a human. Humans don't eat humans, nor do cows eat cows, right? That's why today is our rare barbecue day.

She drinks tea from her teacup.

Almost all cows are created through artificial insemination. I used to fertilize cows. Not cows for beef but for milk. I worked in a dairy farm and all our cows were female Holsteins. I did some milking of cows, but I was also licensed as a domestic animal inseminator. I was a specialist. I was very good at what I did so most of the time I succeeded in fertilizing my cows. The owner of the farm trusted me deeply and that made me proud. This is obvious, but cows, like humans, don't produce milk unless they've given birth. So I had to work hard to make sure every cow gave birth to a calf every year. And even though these cows were pregnant all the time, they were all virgins, since their pregnancies were through artificial insemination. To be specific, I would observe the cows every day and find the ones in heat.

She goes near the ironing board as if she is a cow in heat.

The easiest thing to recognize is "standing." "Standing" is when a cow is mounted and it just stays standing there, that's what "standing" is. Cows mount each other even when they're not in heat. They mount other cows from behind like this.

She mounts the ironing board.

This is mounting and if the mounted cow stands there without resistance, that is "standing." "Standing" is the certain indication of a cow in heat. Once I decide to go for it, I inject the sperm. The farm I worked on had no bulls. Bulls are big and aggressive—people die trying to keep bulls because they're so difficult. Most importantly, they don't produce milk, so there's no need to keep them. Our bulls were just their sperm, frozen in liquid nitrogen. They're kept in individual frozen straws.

She picks up a straw from the table.

There are some farmers who only raise bulls to collect and sell their sperm. For good cows, like marbled wagyu and other trending brands—since everyone is particular these days—the sperm of such elite breeds can sell for tens of thousands of yen. There's a catalog for sperm and you can choose cows that produce a lot of milk or cows with delicious meat. The prices range widely. Hundreds of yen on the low end. And the frozen sperm has to thaw and then set in a long stick.

She picks up the cooking chopstick from the table and fits it into the straw.

Then I put on a glove and stick my hand into the cow's rectum.

She takes a rubber glove (a common household glove used for dishwashing) from the table and puts it on one hand as if it could cover her entire arm (like industrial gloves used by animal inseminators). She takes her gloved hand and moves it in relation to the ironing board as if sticking it into a cow's rectum.

Even as all this poo comes out, I have to stick my entire arm in there, up to my shoulder. With my other hand I insert that stick into its wrinkly vagina.

She takes her free hand, and using the chopstick-straw contraption, moves it in relation to the ironing board as if she is pushing the stick into a cow's vagina.

When you're putting it in, first there's the vagina, then the cervical canal, and then the uterus. I do aim for the uterus, but the cervical canal is quite hard and twisty so it's impossible unless I reach from the intestinal wall to stabilize it, which is why I have to stick my hand into its rectum, you see. When the stick reaches the uterus, the sperm is discharged.

She launches the straw.

And if that fertilizes the cow, then congratulations! That's what I did for work, in the simplest terms. If a male is born, we'd sell it right away since we didn't keep males, and it would become ground beef or beef jerky for dogs. The value of male Holstein meat is quite low. Sometimes people tell us they feel sorry for our cows. And they might be right to feel sorry. But we do this so everyone can drink milk and eat beef. Don't you all eat beef and drink milk? It's unlikely that people who consume beef will disappear anytime soon. You may say you feel sorry but all of humankind is complicit in this or, like, you can't live in a way in which you don't need to feel sorry for every living thing in the world. And well, I'm close to thirty and have been wondering about procreation myself. It's a common worry—all my friends have married and had kids, so I thought I'd better start thinking about it. If I don't change anything, my life will be over and I will have only helped to proliferate cows. But it's not that I don't have sex. My baseline is that I shove sticks into cows, I am a penetrator, but once in a while I am penetrated by a male human's penis.

She sits on the sofa.

This departs from the topic of baselines, but in the olden days there were festivals. During festival times, everyone would drink together regardless of their class. People would really let loose and go wild, apparently. All formalities were dropped. They say it was a chance for the farmers to relieve their stress and they were used to prevent riots, but they were just these orgies, just total chaos. They used masks so that beauty wasn't even a consideration. They covered their bodies in mud or flour and all of that was part of the festivities. And so I observe these ancient customs myself. I've made it a custom once a year to go to a "happening bar" in December. That way, I feel like I can work hard through the next year without rioting. Oh, "happening bars" are basically sex clubs. Some of you must have been to one, right?

She awaits audience response.

Simply put, they're bars where there might be a "happening," and by "happening" they mean sexual intercourse. One year I went to a hap-bar like I always did in December and I had a threesome. My baseline is two-person sex, but I'd had a few threesomes before. Never more than three. You know, it's rare to achieve chaotic group sex like the old festival days. Everyone comes to the hap-bar with their own feelings and preferences. Reaching an orgy like the olden days is impossible in the hap-bars of today.

Pause.

The threesome was composed of two women and one man. Up until then, I had never done it with a woman before. In previous threesomes, it was me with two men, so this was the first time I got to touch a woman's body. I was drunk and my memory is a bit faulty, but I feel like when we were drinking, she said she'd never done it with a woman before either.

She recreates the conversation she had with the woman by herself. As she continues, it becomes difficult to tell whether she is playing herself or the woman.

"Oh, I've never done it with another woman before."

"Oh really, me neither."

"Oh, don't you think our faces look alike? Of course, you're prettier than me."

"Thank you, you're really pretty too."

"But maybe we really do look alike."

"Am I drunk? I think we look exactly alike."

"I didn't know I was so pretty?"

"I'm so happy. You're so pretty!"

She falls onto the sofa.

I touched her body, not for her pleasure but for the pleasure of my own hand. Why is she so soft, why does she feel so good? She touched me too, for the pleasure of her own hand. There was some unshaved hair around her knees and that was adorable to me. As if we were the same. I shaved my legs in a hurry before I came here too. Knees are difficult to shave because of they're really bumpy. I thought I really, really liked her. The man who went into the playroom with us couldn't find a way in. He was laughing awkwardly as he just watched us. I couldn't understand why I thought I liked men all this time. Perhaps all women actually like women. Perhaps that was what was normal. That was what was natural for us as living creatures. After all, aren't we the most precious things to ourselves? I suddenly understood why men always severed the ties between women.

She gradually slides down the sofa.

To be honest, I couldn't be bothered by the man's existence. The woman's body was so soft and wonderful, we couldn't see anything except each other. We had never used our hands like this during sex before. We had to grasp at penises that we didn't even like. We were always the softer parts, having to deal with harder parts. We never questioned it; we were satisfied by being told how soft we were. I'd developed a lust for my soft self, for being told I was soft. But touching softness directly without the lens of hardness gratified my hands and gratified me directly. This moved me deeply and I was almost in tears. Because our faces were so alike, it was like being embraced so tenderly by myself and embracing myself back so tenderly, and it was just … so …

Unknown Entity *enters. They sit on the sofa.* **Housewife** *sits next to* **Unknown Entity***, with a straight face.*

Housewife   On my way home from the hap-bar, I was on the first bus in the morning. There were only about three passengers on the bus including me, but this weirdo sat right next to me. I was like, oh shit, I might be murdered. I wanted to escape but I was sandwiched between this person and the window, and I couldn't get by the weirdo. I tried desperately to pretend like I was fine, but I really thought I was going to die. I was going to die and yet I was pretending to be fine. I don't know why I was pretending. Once, when a bee flew into my classroom, everyone screamed and fled, but I pretended to be fine. I thought that was the right thing to do. It was the right thing to do, in a sense, because screaming will get you stung. But I also felt embarrassed of running away. Of course, you can get stung if you don't run away too. I was moments from death and yet acting like I was fine. I thought, I'm going to be murdered as I'm pretending I am fine because of some meaningless sense of shame. I guess this is what it's like to be human. Why did I even go to that hap-bar? Was I being punished for having sex with that woman at the hap-bar? I was really into it because it felt so good. Maybe I thought that the punishment was great because of how good the sex felt. Like Dr. Kellogg. Maybe sex truly was a terrifying thing. Maybe sex had power beyond my ability to measure it. Or maybe I had been careless with sex? Maybe it's better not to engage in homosexual sex or unnatural things? Um, I'm not religious but in that moment, I honestly felt I had gravely disobeyed god. And in that moment, I wanted to sprinkle Corn Flakes over myself as if purifying my body with salts.

Unknown Entity *exits.*

Housewife   Nothing happened. Dawn broke on the night of my inner upheaval. But somehow, I felt I had been changed a little. I started to think seriously about having my own child. I just wanted to conceive, and I thought artificial insemination might

be the way. After all, I am a fertilization specialist. I had pride in getting this far in my
profession. Why would I depend on someone else for my own fertilization? That's the
pride of a professional. They say big-name hair stylists all cut their own hair. They
also say the higher-tiered dentists are, the more likely they treat their own teeth too.
So as long as I had some sperm I could actually fertilize myself. Even non-
professionals can do it. Sexless couples for example can use a syringe to squirt sperm
into their uterus. You can easily get these self-insemination kits on Amazon. I guess
the more natural way is to have sex with someone, but how much time would I take to
build a relationship to the point where your partner would ejaculate inside you
without a condom, you know? Condoms are the rule at the hap-bar. Because people
can catch diseases. So there's no chance of impregnation. Besides, getting pregnant
by someone whose face I can see seems strange to me. That may be an occupational
hazard. Cows are injected with unknown sperm from an unknown bull and get
pregnant and give birth. That's what I was used to. So the idea of looking into
someone's face, saying I love you, and having sex to get pregnant—felt foreign to
me. It seemed extraordinary. Or, like, the idea of a real penis scared me. Even if we
washed ourselves clean, I'd still feel resistance. That's why I wanted to buy sperm
like we did with cows. In Japan, it seems like only married people can buy sperm
from sperm banks. I wasn't married yet so I wouldn't be able to. I suppose I could ask
someone for just their sperm and collect it?

*She takes a Tupperware container from the table, removes the lid, and offers it to a
male audience member.*

Just put it in this container.

She waits for the male audience member's reaction.

… and then take it home? It's not like takeout. It was hard to think of any friends I
could ask something like this, but this was when I found out about this mail-order
sperm place in Denmark. They deliver anywhere in the world by air. I thought, oh I
can just buy it, just like from a bull sperm catalog. All the details about the sperm
were online: race, skin color, eye color, hair color, height, weight, shoe size,
education, even recordings of their voices. You can choose whatever sperm you want.
But the most important qualities are sperm count and motility. The better quality
sperm, the more expensive it is. Sperm quality includes the sperm count in semen and
motility which is the sperm's ability to move. Quality sperm in Japan can cost up to
20,000 yen. Like a real estate search site, on this website you can search by entering
all the qualities you're looking for. First of all, I wanted Japanese sperm, since I can
only speak Japanese and I'd probably raise the kid in Japan by myself. When I was in
middle school I had a classmate who was Japanese—like me—and half, like, foreign,
and she was bullied terribly. She had a really big butt, atypical of Japanese people,
because you know Japanese have no butts. But hers stuck out behind her like three
times the size of mine. She really stuck out. For PE we all had to wear the same
shorts. Mine were so baggy on me, but hers were so tight, you could see her panty
line clearly. People would call her Centaur. There was a popular fighting video game
at the time with a character that was a female Centaur. You know how Centaurs' butts
stick all the way back? This character wasn't very strong but was super-erotic. When

it was hit by an enemy it would moan, 'Ahh!' I do think kids are so cruel. Kids would throw erasers at her and say, "Moan, Centaur!" and stuff. And little Centaur's face would be expressionless no matter what. The massive complex had hardened her, she lost her expressiveness completely. So I always thought it must be brutal to live in Japan if you don't look normal. Well, I guess Korean or Chinese might have been fine because you can't tell. But anyway, I checked the box for Japanese because I kind of thought that Japanese sperm might be good. I chose a reasonable balance of height, weight, sperm quality, and including shipping and everything, I decided to buy sperm for about 100,000 Japanese yen. Buying something that is thrown away in a crumpled tissue for 100,000 yen might surprise some of you. But I'm using this to create new life, you know. Cheap or expensive, we have a low birthrate here. The government ought to subsidize these costs. Oh, I have a pet dog. And that Papillon cost about 100,000 yen at the pet store, so it's about the same, I guess.

She notices that the dog isn't there.

Hawaii! Hawaii! Hawaii!

She exits.

Parodos

The **Chorus** *enters.*

Music plays.

Chorus (*singing*)
  Human milk is breast milk
  Cow milk is just milk
  But cow milk comes from a mother's nipple
  So cow milk is breast milk too
  Bulls cannot lactate
  What do they have nipples for?
  If they can't produce milk they're just decoration
  They're useless—so useless

  What happens to bulls since they don't produce milk?
  Bulls are aggressive and difficult
  They're castrated without anesthesia
  They're sold off dirt cheap
  Mixed in with pork to make cheap ground meat, ground meat
  Or beef jerky for dogs
  But cows don't have it easy either
  Grandma cows who stop making milk
  are killed—goodbye!
  Our meat can't be eaten so we're used for leather—your wallet
  It doesn't matter whether we live or die

It's our destiny to be squeezed dry for our blood, milk, and sperm

Ham, shabu shabu, barbecue, sukiyaki, steak
Japanese Black Wagyu at the steak house is laughing
Cheese, butter, condensed milk, soft ice cream
The Holstein at the ice cream shop is laughing
But whatever happens to the Japanese Black Wagyu or the Holstein
Doesn't matter to us at all
We do not laugh—We do not laugh
Is Centaur laughing now that she's grown up?
In the face of extinction, the Centaurs
Do not laugh—Do not laugh
Even if they die, they do not laugh
Even if they live, they do not laugh
Either way Centaurs do not laugh
Do not laugh—Do not laugh

Music stops.

Chorus *remains on stage as witnesses to all the following scenes.*

First Epeisodion

A chime sounds.

Housewife *enters. She makes a gesture as if to press the speaker button on an intercom.*

Housewife   Yes, who is it?

The video of a close-up of **Beast** *and* **Dog***, as if through a home intercom system monitor, is projected onto the screen onstage.*

Beast   Oh, excuse me, is this your doggie?

Housewife   Oh, yes it is.

Beast   It seemed to be lost in the neighborhood so I brought it here.

Housewife   Oh, really! I'm sorry. Please hold on, I'm unlocking the door.

Video disappears. **Housewife** *exits.*

Pause.

Housewife*,* **Beast***, and* **Dog** *enter.* **Beast** *is wearing a long coat and carries a bag.* **Dog** *is dressed in pink.*

Housewife   Please, come in.

Beast   Thank you

Housewife I'm so sorry for your trouble. Thank you so much.

Beast No prob, no prob. I happened to be passing by.

Housewife I was just wondering where the dog was. I'll put on some tea. Please sit down. Can I take your coat? I can hang it up.

Beast No, thank you.

Beast *sits on the sofa and places the bag on the floor.*

Housewife *carries a tray with two teacups of tea and a plate with cookies from the kitchen. She places these on the coffee table.*

Beast Wow. What a nice house.

Housewife Oh? No, no, it's just an ordinary house.

Beast You must have a nice life.

Housewife No, not really. Recently I've just been glued to my phone.

Beast Your eyes will go bad. I hear it affects the depth of your sleep, too.

Housewife Yes, yes, yes, yes that's right, but I can't stop. When there's something I want to find out, I just search for it.

Beast So your eyesight and knowledge are inversely proportional.

Housewife Yes, I'm getting smarter but my eyes are getting worse. I'm taking this supplement called Enkin, by Fancl,[1] for my eyes.

Beast What does it mean to really get smart?

Dog *laughs.*

Housewife *takes a Ziplock bag full of beef jerky out of her apron pocket, takes one out, and throws it far away.*

Dog *goes after the thrown beef jerky.*

Beast Such a cutie.

Housewife Thank you. That's Lil' Hawaii.

Beast Is it female?

Housewife He's a boy.

She pets **Dog**. **Dog** *laughs.*

Housewife (*indicating* **Dog**'s *clothes*) I worried that this get-up was too cute, but he's neutered anyway so I thought it was OK.

Beast Why Hawaii?

Housewife I think the word Hawaii makes people feel happy. Sure, there's a lot of history there, but everyone loves Hawaii, don't they? I see so many celebrities who go to Hawaii for New Year's on TV. That's why. This might seem a little or a lot silly, but I got a small pedigree dog at the pet store and I dress him in clothes and I can tell some people think I must not be too bright. You know all those European-style cafés with terrace seating and such? There's always someone sitting there with a little dog. It's complicated. I think they look stupid, but I sit in the terrace seat with my dog too. I like Hawaii and I like Europe too. I guess I have fantasies about those places. So when I saw this dog's face I was like, Hawaii!

Beast   Oh really.

Housewife   Apparently if you pet dogs like this, it releases oxytocin. Oxytocin is this hormone that's really good for your health.

She pets **Dog** *vigorously.*

Dog *is laughing.*

Beast   Excuse me, but somehow you seem tired.

Housewife   Really? My eyes are, from the phone.

Beast   Your spirit seems tired.

Housewife   What? (*She laughs.*)

Beast   I usually live in the mountains in an all-female commune.

Housewife   What! Wow. That's amazing. How very LOHAS or like feminist or like communal …

Beast   We use artificial insemination to make and raise children.

Housewife   Whoa. Wait. How do you get your sperm?

Beast   We inject sperm that God offers us.

Housewife   God? What do you mean?

Beast   God is always close to me.

Housewife   Uh, um, where?

Beast   Can you not see God?

Housewife   What? No.

Beast   Because your eyes are tired.

Housewife   Oh really? I'm sorry, I do take Enkin.

Beast   You must be healed by God.

Housewife   Well, I don't really know about "God" or religion, I'm sorry.

Beast   We make milk and butter and meat.

Housewife   Ah, you're in dairy farming! "God" must be the name of a cow breed. Oh, and by "women," do you mean dairy cows? Oh dear. You speak as if they're human. I used to work on a dairy farm, so I'm pretty knowledgeable about them. I quit when I got married.

Beast   I see. That is why you are cursed by the hatred of the cows.

Housewife   What. If I'm cursed, you must be cursed too.

Beast   I am on the cursing side.

Housewife   Huh?

Beast   You must take better care of yourself.

Housewife   Oh, I take really good care of myself.

Beast   You do not.

Housewife   How can you tell?

Beast   God told me.

Housewife   Uh, that's just a cow breed, right?

Beast   Can you not see God?

Pause.

Housewife   Wait. What is this about? I can't see anything. Wait. But I do sense something. Are you part of a religion that's disguised as a farm? You're trying to get me to join your religion. I'm sorry, but I am not interested so there's no point. Actually I've been wanting to go to the bathroom. Will you excuse me? Lately I've been having to pee frequently, excuse me.

She exits.

First Stasimon

Music plays.

Chorus (*singing*)
Why are you searching for your mother, oh wounded one?
Your mother abandoned you to look at her phone day and night
Her head is full of dubious information
Being clever is not true wisdom

Beast
I want to let my semen swim in my mother's uterus
I make my mother birth my duplicate
I want to suckle my mother's nipple and drink
That white fluid that spurts out
I want to save my soul

Chorus
Oh, beautiful one, you seek not revenge but healing
Your mother has abandoned you to pet Hawaii day and night
Her material greed is roused but is not satisfied by consumption
Being clever is not true wisdom

Beast
I want to let my semen swim in my mother's uterus
I make my mother birth my duplicate
I want to suckle my mother's nipple and drink
That white fluid that spurts out
That is how I want to save my soul
And then I want to save my mother's soul

Music stops.

Second Epeisodion

Housewife *enters.*

Housewife   Sorry to keep you waiting.

Beast   That's all right. I was singing with the spirits of my many ancestors.

Housewife   Huh? What do you mean by that?

Beast   Exactly what I said.

Housewife   I don't really understand.

Beast   I just told you what I was doing while you were in the bathroom.

Housewife   Uh, so, what is that, what religion is it?

Beast   Ours is a livestock farm.

Housewife   You say cows, so is it an offshoot of Hinduism?

Beast   No, it isn't.

Housewife   Then what is it? Can I look it up on my phone?

She takes her phone out of her apron pocket.

Beast   What are you going to search for?

Housewife   The name of your religion.

Beast   I don't think a search will reveal anything.

Housewife   Um, I'm sorry, I should've asked earlier but what is your name?

Beast   Please give me a name.

Housewife   Uh, what do you mean by that?

Beast   Exactly what I said.

Housewife   What, I mean, I don't understand.

Beast   I do not know my own name.

Housewife   Why are you avoiding the question?

Beast   I'm not.

Housewife   It's fine if you don't want to answer me.

Beast   I'd like to answer but my mother never named me.

Housewife   Is there such a person?

Beast   There is, right here.

Pause.

Housewife   I feel like this conversation isn't going anywhere.

Beast   We are having a conversation.

Housewife   I'm scared.

Beast   It's because you're tired.

Housewife   That's not what I mean—I'm fine.

Beast   You need a butter massage.

Housewife   Wait, what? You mean an oil massage?

Beast   It's something we do on our farm.

Housewife   Does it feel good? I do like massages.

Beast   Yes. Butter massages are the ultimate healing for cows.

Housewife   Oh, it's for cows? You massage cows?

Beast   No, butter massages are for cows or humans. By receiving a butter massage and healing the cows' feelings, you will ultimately heal yourself.

Housewife   Oh, hmmm. But I already have Hawaii for healing, so no thanks.

She reaches to pet **Dog**. **Beast** *blocks her.*

Beast   As I said, the first step is not to heal you, but for you to use the butter massage to heal the cow that curses you. Petting that dog has nothing to do with the cow.

Housewife   What? Healing a cow? Are you blackmailing me into joining your cult? I did work on a farm but I'm not the only person who eats meat or drinks milk. The cows should be cursing everyone.

Beast   That's right.

Beast *take a cookie from the coffee table.*

Beast   Even this cookie contains a lot of butter. I have been hearing voices demanding the healing of the cow this whole time. That jerky is extremely loud as well.

Beast *snatches the Ziplock bag of beef jerky from* **Housewife**'s *apron pocket and tosses it to the side.*

Housewife   Wait. Is this a joke? I don't hear anything.

Dog *picks up the Ziplock bag and begins eating the beef jerky.*

Housewife   Cut it out!

Beast   As you may know, regular livestock are raised at the whim of the humans. The hatred towards humans is passed on through generations. It has reached a genetic level, infecting the meat. That is why, inside the human mouth, meat hardens with hatred and does not release its flavor. That is what god realized one day while eating barbecue. And so began the healing of that hatred.

Housewife   Uh, cows eat barbecue?

Pause.

Hm?

Beast   First of all, for animals, birth is most important. Livestock are bred through artificial insemination. In that process the human hand shoves its way into the anus. That is a moment of deep displeasure for the cows. And that mother's displeasure infects the fertilized egg, you see. As I said before, because we are a collective of women, only god has sperm. The process of impregnation is by artificial insemination, but it's important to go through that insemination process in a state of relaxation. The fertilized egg must want to be born into this world.

Housewife   Huh?

Beast   First of all, before we inject the sperm, we give butter massages. The butter massage is the foundation for everything. We use the butter massage to heal everything. Instead of ordinary massage oil we use butter made from milk for this express purpose. We make this butter ourselves. It has a lovely milky scent. In a warm room the butter melts slowly. We massage as if melting the butter on the body's surface. The butter is absorbed gradually through the skin and pores. The butter sends love to the outside and the inside of the body. The body warms up from within and begins to sweat. We give the body milk to drink in order to quench its thirst. Up until now, the cow has had its own milk harvested by humans, so now we must heal that. This milk is from a cow that has been healed through butter massage. After massage the anus softens and opens up wide, like a mouth. So it isn't unpleasant to have a hand inserted. In fact, it is ecstasy. That is when we inject god's sperm. We become pregnant after being healed through butter massage. The repetition of rebirthing our souls, healed by butter massage, our meat grows surprisingly soft and flavorful. Our milk grows rich and sweet.

Housewife   I might want to try eating some of that.

Beast   But it cannot enter the mouths of outsiders. Because in the mouth, the flesh is chewed, swallowed, digested, and absorbed. If an outsider who knows nothing of our lives consumes us, the milk and meat will be alarmed. After we worked so hard to heal generations on a genetic level that one experience of stress would set us back to square one.

Housewife   Huh, I see, so that's the logic. Um, excuse me, but are you trying to tempt me by arousing my hunger with this tantalizing description, to get me to convert to your religion?

Beast   I am simply saying that only the humans on our farm are able to eat this.

Housewife   I had a friend who was brainwashed by some pyramid scheme. She sold me cosmetics that were supposed to rejuvenate me with hormones or something.

Beast   I have no intention to make you buy anything. We do not need money. We produce our own drink and food, so we don't have the need for things like that. What we want is different from those kinds of things.

Housewife   Then what is it?

She pets **Dog** *vigorously.*

Dog *laughs.*

Beast   By petting that dog and releasing oxytocin into your system, you may think you are being healthy, but if you receive a butter massage you'd know that that is a hoax. Healing with butter massage, butter …

Housewife   Enough with the butter massage! What is this all about? Are you making fun of me?

Dog, *surprised, runs off somewhere.*

Beast   I want to save you at your foundation. Not with a hoax.

Housewife   Foundation? Everything you've said is a hoax. I think everything is a hoax especially on Instagram and stuff. Celebrities go to dog shelters and stuff. That really turns me off. I feel bad for the dogs, but what's the point of spending money to save a dog? I guess rich people feel insecure. They worry someone with a grudge will drag them down. That's why they feel they have to present themselves as do-gooders. They spend all their extra money on animals when there are so many humans who need help. They give money to animals because animals can't talk. People are criticized when their efforts to help miss the mark. But animals can't speak so, regardless, people feel like they've done good because of cute animal faces. They feel good spending their money like that. Cute, helpless animals are a tool for the rich to get some sleep. I hate that the most. Obviously helping humans is more important. But that's how the world is made. Nobody can change that. That's why, instead of doing something backhanded, I bought a dog at the pet store to help the human being who runs the pet store, you know? I bought this Papillon for 100,000 yen at the pet store. The job I had was necessary for humans, don't you agree? I'd like a little more gratitude. Seriously, I served humankind. I want safe meat and milk. I didn't want to be judged in some backhanded way. You make your food to be consumed, don't you? Butter massage is just a pretense.

Beast   Before you bought the Papillon at the pet store, you bought sperm from Denmark for 100,000 yen.

Housewife   How do you know that? That's personal information! You're scaring me.

Beast   I heard from God.

Housewife   What is God? A sperm-producing cow? Does your religion engage in hacking? I was suspicious of my phone because it's Huawei. This is scary. I have to get an iPhone.

Second Stasimon

Beast   What did you do with the sperm you got from Denmark?

Chorus

Made by Japanese National Sperm

Music plays.

A slideshow of what look like portraits of young Japanese men is projected onto the screen.

Chorus   Can you definitively say that your desire does not harm anyone, that it is safe and secure? Are you forgetting that there is a dark power inside you? Can you turn your ears towards what lies inside?

Chorus   A luxury item acquired across the seas from Denmark

Made by Japanese National Sperm

Japanese men in Denmark sell it for 9000 yen

Made by Japanese National Sperm

His name is

Tanaka? Yamada? Suzuki? Sato? Hasegawa? Taro? Kenta? Shota? Ichiro? Yosuke?

His intention is

To help people? To make extra money? To make a living? To conquer the world?

Maybe they all drank their mother's milk and they're repaying the world with semen?

An exchange of fluids. That is an exchange of love.

A man in America donated his sperm to a sperm bank every day. In that town his children from different mothers proliferated abnormally. Those children left that town so as to not fall in love. Incest—because it's dangerous to have children with blood relations.

If it's bad to be close, I ought to have chosen sperm from a faraway country Made by Japanese National Sperm

But I didn't want my kid to suffer like my classmate Centaur

Made by Japanese National Sperm

Housewife   I thawed the 100,000 yen sperm naturally, in my armpit, and thought I'd inject it not into myself but into a cow that was in heat. It cost 100,000 yen— imagine throwing away that amount of money! You might be shocked, but for some reason I thought it might be possible. I didn't think of it as throwing away 100,000 yen. In fact, I thought the cow, being younger and healthier than me, would conceive more easily. It was as if I had found the best way to spend 100,000 yen, or like, the line that distinguishes me from cows had blurred inside me. Also, even though I'd bought from a trusted vendor, the thought of injecting myself with some unknown man's sperm seemed physiologically disgusting at the last minute. I couldn't do to myself what I did to cows. But I didn't want to throw it away in the gutter either. It was precious sperm so it should be sent to a uterus, even if it is a cow's.

Beast   ...

Chorus   Can you definitively say that your desire does not harm anyone, that it is safe and secure? Are you forgetting that there is a dark power inside you? Can you turn your ears towards what lies inside?

Mixed blood little Centaur, Centaur who has lost her expressiveness. Centaur taught me that everyone has to be the same. Centaur was the example I avoided in choosing national sperm.

Made by Japanese National Sperm

But what I've made is a mixed blood child whose mother is a Holstein and father is human. Where can this creature live, anywhere in Japan or in the world?

Made by Japanese National Sperm

But actually, everyone was fascinated by Centaur. Everyone was fascinated by Centaur's body. They feared her beauty because they were so fascinated by her.

Made by Japanese National Sperm

Housewife   If a human and cow could produce a child, I'd like to see it. Honestly, please answer honestly. A human–cow mix. Wouldn't you like to see such a creature? Right?

Beast   ...

Housewife   Yeah, probably everyone would want to see it. Everyone would be interested, the way we want to see scary things. If it existed, it would be super-popular at the zoo. Because a long time ago, there was a mix between a leopard and a lion called a leopon, and everyone lined up at the zoo to see the leopon. Did you know that?

Beast   ...

Chorus   Can you definitively say that your desire does not harm anyone, that it is safe and secure? Are you forgetting that there is a dark power inside you? Can you turn your ears towards what lies inside?

The one who is a virgin is

   Cow

The one who has a hand shoved up its anus is

   Cow

The one who has to keep giving birth is

   Cow

The one who gives fellatio is

   Human?

   Cow

Late one night, she learned of a cow who performed fellatio, something she assumed humans had the patent on.

Late at night in the cowshed, the farmer exposed his erection and shoved it towards my mouth. It looked like my mother's nipple. My mother's nipple should be mine, but it was milked by a machine, and the milk drunk by humans. It belonged to the humans, not to me. Owned by humans. My mother's milk was robbed by humans and I was raised on powdered milk every day. I even dreamt of my mother's nipple. In a frenzy I suckled onto the farmer's penis, I sucked hard, but milk never came. The farmer climaxed. It was not breastmilk, but semen he let out into my mouth.

She buried what she had seen deep inside her, and continued to perform her duty, sticking her hand into cow intestines and injecting sperm into their uteri.

Except now, the sperm was bought from Denmark

   Made by Japanese National Sperm

Housewife   When I was a child I used cooking chopsticks to stir a goldfish bowl. I had watched my mother cooking from behind. She used cooking chopsticks to beat eggs in a bowl. I watched as the egg yolks and whites mixed together. Wow, I thought, I wanted to try that myself. So I got a pair of chopsticks from the kitchen and stirred the goldfish bowl. The goldfish spun around, but didn't mix with the water at all. I thought if I stirred faster they might mix together. So I stirred faster and faster and couldn't stop. I just couldn't stop myself. I wanted to see the goldfish mix with the water. Before I realized it, the goldfish had died. Why did I kill it? Do you know why?

Beast   ...

Chorus   Can you definitively say that your desire does not harm anyone, that it is safe and secure? Are you forgetting that there is a dark power inside you? Can you turn your ears towards what lies inside?

The egg of a Holstein cow and

   Made by Japanese National Sperm

successfully fertilized. A creature with a human upper half and Holstein lower half is born

A centaur

   but the cow version

A creature with a human upper half and Holstein lower half is born

   Made by Japanese National Sperm

Music and projections stop.

Chorus   Can you definitively say that your desire does not harm anyone, that it is safe and secure? Are you forgetting that there is a dark power inside you? Can you turn your ears towards what lies inside?

Beast *takes off its overcoat. It reveals that its lower half is of a cow. Between its legs is a large protrusion.* **Housewife** *screams.*

Beast   My livestock is myself: I must tame the beast called myself.

Housewife *takes the box of Corn Flakes from the table and sprinkles it over her head.*

Housewife   My livestock is myself: I must tame the beast called myself.

Third Epeisodion

Housewife   Maybe my eyes are too tired. I'm starting to hallucinate.

Beast   Are you all right?

Housewife   I even drink Enkin.

Beast   What do you see?

Housewife   If I can see hallucinations, does it mean my eyesight will improve?

Beast   It's hard to distinguish what is a hallucination and what is not.

Housewife   It looks like you have a penis, even though you have a woman's face.

Beast   I understand this to be a giant clitoris.

Housewife   Oh, that isn't a penis?

Beast   An enlarged clitoris is a penis. So this is an enlarged clitoris. It's a useful clitoris that can ejaculate semen.

Housewife   Uh, but.

Beast   If your eyes are altered, what you see is altered. What did you do with the half-human, half-Holstein? I will help you. Use me as you see fit.

Housewife *begins to reminisce. The stage becomes the apartment in a wood building that she lived in when she was single. She takes off her apron.*

Housewife   I tried my best, you know. As soon as it was born, I took it home right away, because calves can walk right away.

The **Chorus** *takes a rope, one end of which is affixed to something and the other end is a loop, and hands it to* **Housewife**. **Housewife** *puts the loop around* **Beast***'s neck.*

Housewife   I tied it to a post in my house like this. I was still single, so I didn't live in a big apartment like this, but in a tiny studio. You might think it was child abuse, but what else could I do? It was a cow, so I tied it to a post with rope.

Beast *cries.* **Chorus** *hands a bottle of formula to* **Housewife**. **Housewife** *takes the bottle and feeds* **Beast** *the formula.*

Chorus   The mother has nipples, but since she was not biologically its mother, she didn't produce milk. She had created and milked a lot of cows up to now but she couldn't squeeze breastmilk from her own nipples.

Beast *begins to grow magazine.*

Chorus   Cows and humans grow at different rates. By the age of three, its human head on the upper half was still a child but its lower half was already mature. The human head could not understand the desire of its lower half, and didn't know what to do.

Housewife *hands* **Beast** *pornographic literature.*

Chorus   The mother thought she had to educate it. She needed some textbooks. She went to the convenience store to buy pornographic magazines. There was a foreign boy working the cash register. He looks at her like she's a horny old woman. Oh no, this is for my son, she couldn't explain. A mother buying porn for her son?! What if he replied, you can watch all you want for free on porn sites.

Chorus *hands porn magazine to* **Housewife**. **Housewife** *shows the magazine to the thrashing* **Beast**.

Housewife   Look. I bought this. It's a pornographic magazine. Isn't it nice? Wow, look at her. Look how big her boobs are.

She reads the magazine aloud as if reading a picture book.

Wow, look at the old guys' towering hard cocks aiming towards that wet pussy that's dripping after coming with a vibrator. How erotic.

She takes **Beast**'s *hand and makes it grip its protrusion and move it back and forth.*

Housewife   There, hold on like this, focus on the magazine and imagine yourself doing erotic things with that erotic person. Good, keep doing it just like that. Good boy. That's very good.

She continues reading the magazine out loud.

Chorus   Did I want this pornographic book? Is that why my lower half was raging? While it screamed for something, it was screaming for something else. But I was taught that my desire was for this porn. The lust in my loins could now only interpret it as desire for porn. He was given this container called porn and he was locked up inside it. To lock up the unknown into a container is what it means to be human.

Chorus *uses bottles and other containers of sauce and dressing to make it look like a milky white fluid has spurted out of* **Beast**'s *protrusion between its legs.*

Housewife   Wow! Amazing! Good job!

Beast *collapses, spent, face-up.* **Housewife** *uses tissues to wipe up the splattered liquid from the floor. Then she lies down.*

Chorus   Did I want to release this liquid? Is that why my lower half was raging? When it was contained inside my body, it was something else, but the moment it was taken out from within my body, I felt a turmoil inside. I was forced to see the shape of my desire. I was taught that that shape was for this liquid. I can only interpret the desire in the lower half of my body as for that liquid. He has learned the shape of this liquid. To know the shape of the unknown is what it is to be human.

Beast *grows aggressive again. It grasps its protrusion by itself and begins to move its hands back and forth.* **Housewife** *rises.*

Beast   Porn porn porn …

Each time **Beast** *says "porn"* **Chorus** *makes the milky liquid spurt out. And each time,* **Housewife** *wipes it up with tissues.*

Housewife   Stop it, stop it. That's disgusting.

Beast *cannot stop itself.*

Beast   Porn porn porn …

Housewife   I said, stop it, so you'd better stop!

She tries to pry **Beast***'s hands away from its protrusion.* **Beast** *grabs the* **Housewife***'s hands, pushes her down and tries to rape her.*

Housewife   Stop it.

Somehow **Housewife** *manages to rebuff* **Beast** *and get away.* **Beast** *cannot chase after her because it is tied to the post with the rope.* **Chorus** *uses the bottles to spurt out the remaining liquid until there is nothing left.* **Beast** *collapses.* **Housewife** *sprinkles Corn Flakes on the collapsed* **Beast***.*

Housewife   You can't actually do what you see in the porn magazines. What's in the magazines stays in there. Porn is not real life. And if Mother says stop, then stop. Stop, get it? Stop. Don't you understand those words? If you can't understand, you're not human. If a human does something another human doesn't want, then they're not human. Humans understand each other's feelings and words. That's what makes them human. We have to work harder as humans, to be more human.

She lies down. **Beast** *weeps.*

Chorus   Somehow I must make children. I must correct myself. I must fertilize myself the way those Holstein females do. The woman had been possessed by an invisible force, but you couldn't possibly say that the child she made was correct. Nobody knew whether it was cow or human. We fear sodomy—We commit sodomy.

Chorus *hands* **Housewife** *a photograph of herself.*

Chorus   We fear sodomy—We commit sodomy

We fear sodomy—We commit sodomy

We fear sodomy—We commit sodomy

Housewife *gets up.*

Housewife   Hey, Mother needs to go out. You aren't human so you won't get lonely, will you? I'll teach you how humans do it. Animals can't do this, you know. Here is a photo of Mother.

She give the photograph of herself to **Beast***.*

Housewife   It's like with the porn magazines. When you get lonely, look at this picture and think of Mother. You'll feel the way you do when we're together. You won't be lonely anymore. That's how humans can be fine by themselves.

Beast   …

Housewife   Say, "Mother."

Beast   Mother.

Housewife   See, you can say, "Mother." You already have Mother inside you.

The stage becomes the happening bar.

Chorus   And so I left you and went to the hap-bar, because I wanted to see that woman again. But you aren't allowed to exchange contact information with people there. I didn't even know her name or her work. If I did, I could have at least looked her up on Facebook. I don't know if she'll be there today, but I just wanted to touch her body so badly.

Housewife *sits on the sofa.*

Chorus   But when I got to the hap-bar, she wasn't there. Chicks think the first creature they see is their mother. Maybe I am just a chick having seen her first and chasing after her.

Housewife   Um, I just want to do it with a woman.

Chorus   Saying that to the hap-bar staff can connect you with the right people. So I was drinking by myself. A guy drinking alone like me said he wanted me to look at his dick so …

Housewife   Oh, OK.

Chorus   I looked at it, and in looking I saw nothing interesting. It was just a regular dick. Why did he need to show me that? I think I made him wonder why he wanted to show it to me in the first place. After we talked a little, I went to the bathroom and didn't go back and went to sit elsewhere. What am I doing, going to a hap-bar at my age? People must take me for a vulgar old hag, I thought—

Girl *enters.*

Girl   Excuse me

Housewife   Hello.

Girl *sits next to* **Housewife**.

Girl   Hi. Um are you a lesbian? I heard from that bar staff with the glasses. He looks like a drummer for an unpopular band. Aren't his glasses weird? Why would he choose those frames? I could never be friends with someone who'd choose those glasses. The plastic part on the sides? What is the point of having a check pattern printed there? I don't get it. The check pattern distracted me so much that I could barely hear what he was saying earlier. And anyway, when you think of check patterns, you think of skirts, don't you? Check equals fabric, right? It has to be fabric. So why print check on plastic? Is that supposed to be fashionable? Ugh, it's lame. Would he think that my idea that "check equals fabric" is old-fashioned? Am I too traditional? Are his glasses supposed to be like a new interpretation of tradition?

Housewife   A-ha, I see, that's interesting.

Girl   Anyway, I have lesbian longings too.

Housewife   Oh really? I don't know if I'm a lesbian, because I'd only been with men.

Girl Oh, I see, are you bi?

Housewife Oh, I don't know.

Girl Oh, are you pan?

Housewife Pan? I don't know about any of that. It's just that I did it with a girl once and it was good so I want to do it again.

Girl Cool. Was it that good? Most men have no idea what gets a woman going, you know? I have a boyfriend and I love him but the sex is bad. That's why I end up coming to the hap-bar. There are a lot of people here who are good at sex. They're just regular people but many of them are better than my boyfriend. Everyone does a lot of foreplay here. I think that is really great.

Housewife Huh. Why don't you tell your boyfriend that you want more foreplay?

Girl I can't. I agree it would be best if I could, but I just can't. It's embarrassing. What if he thought I was perverted? Also, I don't want to hurt his feelings. I act like I'm always satisfied.

Housewife Oh yeah. That's tedious.

Girl But he gets turned on by my acting and I fall into the illusion that I'm really into it as well.

She suddenly bursts into laughter. **Housewife** *doesn't know why she is laughing, but in her drunken state joins* **Girl** *in laughter.*

Girl …

Housewife Ha.

Girl But don't you actually want to feel really good?

Housewife Yeah, yeah.

Girl I have lesbian longings because we women have the same bodies. Women understand better what feels good to us, more than men do. We masturbate and we're used to touching our clits. Honestly, men have no idea about clits. What's up with that? Men totally ignore the clit. They think pussy equals hole. Don't forget the clit, it's right there! After all, the penis is just an enlarged clit. When we were in our mother's womb, before they knew our sex, the penis was a clitoris. Why does everyone forget the clit? We can't ever forget about the penis. It's not fair. That's why women are unsatisfied by sex with men. There's so much data to prove it. That's why women are more capable of satisfying each other.

She and **Housewife** *go to the kitchen. This is the playroom at the happening bar. There is a video camera in the kitchen.* **Housewife** *picks up the video camera and shoots* **Girl**. **Girl** *strips down to her cow-print undergarments and puts on a headband with cow ears.* **Girl** *acts for the camera according to* **Housewife** *following lines. The video* **Housewife** *captures is projected live onto the screen. From the other side of the kitchen counter, the audience has an obscured view of the women.*

Housewife   I went to the playroom with her. She was young and had big boobs. Perhaps that's why five or six men followed us to peek into our playroom window. Oh, the playrooms are made so you can see in from the outside. I've heard that some hap-bars have one-way mirrors for walls but mine just had small windows. From the inside you could see people on the outside peeping in. I don't know whether she meant to arouse people, but she was young and had big boobs so everyone wanted to watch. People crowded around just our window like a rush hour train. After we showered and turned to face each other, she was acting like she didn't notice all the men peeking in but I could tell she was getting off on it.

Girl *snatches the camera away from* **Housewife** *and continues to act for the camera while shooting herself.*

Housewife   She acted like she was looking at me, but she was actually looking at them. The crowd by the window, like a rush hour train, validated her attractiveness to men. She knew how vain it is to revel in being popular in a back-alley hap-bar. She wasn't stupid, but she couldn't help feeling proud. She was acting like she didn't care but she couldn't completely disguise her feelings. She giggled shyly about having her first same-sex experience, but it wasn't a genuine shy giggle. She was acting the cute young girl for the men—it was that kind of shy giggle. I was turned off by her whole act. She moaned when I touched her boobs.

Girl   Ah! Oh, ah, don't!

Housewife   She felt ecstasy in performing for the men. Sure, her boobs really were soft and nice but I couldn't even tell if I was enjoying it. As I touched her I felt as if I'd become a man. The man that I kept inside, the man I had kept inside was coming out, and he was acting like a male porn star for the peeping men. He was remembering how men touch boobs in porn videos. Why do I have to perform for the peeping men? And somehow, she had also turned into a porn actor …

Girl   Uhhhhhh ohhhhh, that feels so good, I'm coming!!!

Housewife   Even though we were two women we approached each other as if in a porn movie, panting like porn stars do …

Girl   We're coming togetherrrrr, three, two, one, zerooooooooo!

She screams, the whites of her eyes showing.

Housewife   I was so disappointed, or rather, I felt defeated. Not by the peeping men, but the man I kept inside me.

Girl *stands up and puts on her clothes.*

Girl   Thank you. That was a good experience. But I think I'm definitely straight. Sorry to have been confused. I feel like I couldn't get to a good place with you. I'm sorry I was on the receiving end the whole time. And also I was faking that last orgasm, sorry. Or, like, I was faking it the entire time, I'm sorry. It didn't feel good at all and I couldn't wait for it to be over, I'm sorry. I had my own fantasy about what it would be like with a woman. But I guess it's a matter of skill, regardless of gender.

Oh, I'm sorry I didn't mean to diss you for being bad at it, but I guess I am, I'm sorry. Sister, you're really bad at sex, you suck at it.

The projection disappears. **Girl** *exits.*

Chorus   Women can get into hap-bars for free and they can get all the free drinks they want. On the other hand, men have to pay over 10,000 yen to get in. I suppose this implies that men are buying their right to look? There's nothing more expensive than "free." I'd pay 10,000 yen or 20,000 yen to not have to experience this.

Inside the first bus of the morning. **Housewife** *adjusts herself on the sofa, sitting tall.*

Chorus   The woman swayed on the first bus. Nobody else was on that bus. Outside it was not yet getting light. Somehow it was so dark, as if she were on the subway. She couldn't tell where the bus was taking her.

Unknown Entity *enters. It sits next to* **Housewife***. A long silence.*

Housewife   Why are you sitting next to me?

A long silence.

Housewife   Are you trying to punish me?

Unknown Entity *exits.*

The stage returns to being the living/dining room.

Housewife   So I didn't go home but wandered around instead, and met the man who'd become my husband and married him. He's kind of a different type than me. He makes an above-average income. I'm telling you this because we're close. He has horrible breath—I thought so when I first met him, but it's much better than cow breath. He doesn't talk at all and he never laughs. He has no sense of humor. But he has bad breath so it's fine that he doesn't talk. I don't mind because I talk a lot. And he does talk, compared to a cow. Anyway, I didn't want to work anymore and I wanted a house. I didn't think my life would suddenly become rosy after marriage. My mother-in-law is old and has dementia. My husband doesn't have siblings so I'll have to take care of her. But as long as I iron his ordinary shirts every day and feed him ordinary meals and have ordinary sex, I can live in a house and have something to eat until I die. I wanted to live in peace within this system. Asides from his bad breath, I'd hit a home run! You understand because you're human, don't you?

Beast   Mother.

Housewife *drapes herself over the ironing board.*

Housewife   I wanted to use my husband's money to send my kid to Kumon, take conversational English classes and piano lessons, get braces for his teeth. I wanted to do what normal human parents do for their kids.

Third Stasimon

Chorus *takes the rope off* **Beast**'*s neck. They place one* tatami[2] *mat and mic center stage.* **Beast** *stands on the* tatami *as if it is a stage and holds the mic.*

Beast   Mother, Mother. Because I am a cow, I ate the *tatami* floor. I was so lonely, I wept. "Mother, Mother," I cried out, but only for three days. After that, I was too hungry to think. Mother, why didn't you teach me about food? Did you want me to spray my semen, weep, and go hungry until I starved to death? I heard that depressed people go on fasts. When they're hungry, they stop wanting to die. All of their worries just disappear. I really understood that, Mother. Because I am a cow, I ate the *tatami* floor. I had never once thought of *tatami* as food. Because *tatami* is part of the house. Ever since I can remember, *tatami* has been under my feet. I never thought I would end up eating it.

Music plays.

Beast (*singing*)
   My hunger awakened my instincts as a cow
   So hungry I couldn't tell if my eyes were open
   I was in a delirious state

Chorus
   Tatami is grass and grass is food

Beast
   That is what my cow's blood said
   That's why fasting is a remedy for depression
   When you're hungry, your mind goes blank and your body takes over,
   Your strength to live is drawn forth

So Mother did not teach me about food because she was trying to make me live, not starve to death. That was her last gesture of love for me. This thought has been the only comfort in my heart. I know this interpretation is wrong, but I want to believe it.

   Humans always need something to believe in
   Like a cow or rather because I am a cow, I use my molars to grind through grass
   I wondered where I learned how to devour *tatami*
   Through I'm filled with self-hatred I can't stop chewing

The dietary fiber in *tatami* gave me huge bowel movements. Massive amounts of feces soiled my lower half and I ate the shit-stained *tatami*. Then I'd soil myself some more and eat the *tatami* soiled with shit. It's disgusting but I can't stop chewing.

Chorus
   Like a cow or rather because I am a cow, I use my molars to grind through
      grass
   I wondered where I learned how to devour *tatami*
   Though I'm filled with self-hatred I can't stop chewing

Music stops.

Chorus   Hey, it stinks. What are you doing in there?

Beast   The neighbor knocked on the door several days in a row. I was terrified and stayed quiet. In the end, the landlord came and discovered me. I can't tell you what happened after that, until I started the dairy farm but to make a long story short: I sold my body to eccentric perverts.

Music plays.

Beast
    I sold my body to eccentric perverts.
    I had no other choice, and I did have those skills
    I was a new kind of trans, half cow, half human
    In my mind I was a human woman who loved women
    My lower half was a cow with a large clitoris that discharged semen
    To put it in terms you'd understand:
    I was a mix half cow, half human, a transgender lesbian, I don't know
    Since I was three, Mother educated me with pornographic magazines
    Based on that porn I became very familiar with human sexual desire
    I could meet the needs of my clients, I brought every pervert to ecstasy

Chorus
    Satisfaction!

Beast
    I made a lot of money, I went to fancy barbecue restaurants
    Yes, I'd feed myself high-quality beef
    To domesticate the cow in me. I am a human, not a cow
    I am not a cow that eats *tatami*, I am human, I am human, human
    That's how I domesticated myself

Chorus
    Once I met a client at an apartment building made of wood
    Different strokes for different folks
    First we chased each other around and wrestled
    The client bit down on my big cow butt
    Was he pretending to be a lion?
    After various modes of contact, in the end he pushed me face-down on the
        tatami and entered my anus
    As he penetrated me, the *tatami* floor scratched my face
    and the smell that emanated from the *tatami* ...

Beast
    Like a cow or rather because I am a cow, I use my molars to grind through grass
    I wondered where I learned how to devour *tatami*
    Though I'm filled with self-hatred I can't stop chewing

I recalled my horrifying cow self. I felt sick, I teared up, I cried. My client seemed more turned on and violently pounded me, pounded me. The *tatami* was roughed up and some particles got in my mouth. The fragrant flavor spread in my mouth. I was overtaken by the urge to devour the *tatami*. But absolutely, no to that horrifying cow! I had domesticated it, domesticated it. Trauma, desire, and restraint all mixed together, and I vomited everywhere. But still Mr. Pervert wouldn't stop. The *tatami* and vomit scratched my face. I prayed and prayed for it to be over quickly. When it was over I went straight to eat barbecue.

> Salted beef tongue, beef skirt steak, beef kalbi, roast beef
> My human brain desperately orders every conceivable part of cow
> I don't even open the other non-meat pages of the menu
> Once the cow blood in me took over
> And I ordered *choregi*[3] salad
> While that cow blood took over, I ate that salad in a few seconds
> My human self detested that part of me, but my cow self was extremely satisfied

Chorus *looks at* **Housewife**. **Chorus** *puts the* tatami *mat away.*

Chorus   I am an ironing board, I am an ironing board, I am an ironing board, I am an ironing board

Beast *mounts* **Housewife** *from behind and begins to mechanically thrust its hips back and forth.* **Beast**'s *protrusion thrusts in and out of* **Housewife**'s *thighs.*

Chorus   I was ironing my husband's shirt when he grabbed me from behind, drunkenly. I thought I was going to burn myself, my heart stopped. He shoved his mouth covered in salt and seaweed towards mine. His tongue tried to slither into mine. He reeked of alcohol and snacks. Desperately I shut my mouth, held my breath, and hid my mouth. But he pulled my panties aside and pushed his penis in. It was thanks to him that I could quit my job and live in this house. Ironing, cooking, and sex are all my duties. That's the path I chose as a stay-at-home housewife. So what can I do?

> I am an ironing board, I am an ironing board, I am an ironing board, I am an ironing board

When harvesting sperm from a seed bull, there's a board like an ironing board that has a hole for the penis. They're called female mounting boards. Bulls mistake these featureless mounting boards for cows and mount them from behind, push their penises into the hole. Bulls are premature ejaculators so once they're in, they ejaculate without any friction. The semen is frozen with liquid nitrogen right away and sold. How many times do they wet the ironing board with semen? Never in their lives will they release their sperm directly in a cow's uterus. The ironing board is their partner; they are virgins for life. Cherry boy with countless children. There is no love in procreation. The body just moves according to the signals it's given.

> I am an ironing board, I am an ironing board, I am an ironing board, I am an ironing board

Music stops. **Dog** *enters from where he has been hiding.*

Dog   I, I have done it with females that were bigger than me, and females whose pussies really stink, I can't hold back. Arf arf arf I stand on a block and I lick lick lick muff muff muff they might put on airs but wham! I put it in. Bow wow wow wow! I'm doing it, wow! I didn't go to hell, I did go to Hawaii, this Papillon. My balls turn upside down. My balls have balls and balls of sperm waiting and balls and balls sometimes I happen to happily squirt all the liquid out. This Papillon will definitely launch tadpoles in the female's belly and I'll definitely leave my progeny behind, 'cause I'm a dog, a Papillon. But once they took my balls balls, I was placed on the receiving end oh no, bow wow. The old man was touching me he he here and it felt so super-yummy and good yeah somehow it felt so so so good. Hawaii loves to have this part rub-a-dub-dubbed, and I was enjoying it ahh ahh ahh—when he suddenly attacked garrr. Hawaii flipped right over, woof woof this little doggie Papillon and he push shove stuck it innnnnn uh whoa oh noooo. He stuck his wiener in the hole where my poop comes out. Rammed crammed bammed his hot dog docking into me, turning Hawaii into his spicy hot dog. Hawaii Hawaii, the old man grabbed my mouth and I couldn't open my mouth but his hand and mouth smelled salty yummy so I lick lick licked and the old man also got into the lick lick licking. I got really into licking and that's what's good about a Papillon, that's a dog for you. A spicy hot dog, hot and spicy, but all things in moderation, I couldn't keep going on and on. Even this Papillon is super in in into it but this wasn't going to last, stop it stop it, whoa waaah, do you have to have it so hot?! Spicy hot spot, let's hit stop, hot spot, this trouble is too too hot, this hot dog too hot, ramming his wiener, ram cram bam, humans cum so fast, too fast, so short and clumsy. Hey this is Hawaii's poophole! Spicy hot spot spicy tingling doesn't stop. I'm so happy, sure I'm just a dumb dog a Papillon, that's a dog for you. I don't know who decided that a dog goes woof? Sometimes there's no dog dog dog food for real real real so I gotta lick lick margarine all pent-up. Let's spread margarine on this woman's pee hole and Hawaii'll lick margarine dog lick without docking just lick lick margarine dog. Lick lick city send this old lady from the city to go to hell oh no Papillon. Lick lick lick lick lick lick lick lick lick. Hawaii's never even really been to Hawaii and us dogs don't know no heaven or hell, not even some stray dog. Stray dogs don't even wonder who decided dogs go woof. But Hawaii ain't no stray, I've got a pedigree. Dogs don't go woof woof woof woof, dogs don't talk in the first place woof. I'm Hawaii, a very cute woof-woof a darling pet Papillon. If Hawaii could talk, the old lady won't be soothed, who cares how a dog feels? Nobody wants to know woof woof, if I made a mistake and shouted "wonderful" they'd kill kill kill me. Please don't kill me waaaaaaaan, waaaaan, one more chance, one more chance, one more chance

One more chance, one more chance, one more chance, one more chance …

Music plays. All the actors and **Chorus** *dance madly, violently.*

Fourth Epeisodion

The music stops. **Chorus** *collapses.*

Housewife   What am I looking at right now?

Beast   You are seeing what you ought to see.

Housewife   …

Beast   There is a woman at my farm who looks exactly like you.

Housewife   A woman who looks exactly like me?

Beast   Yes, exactly like you.

Housewife   What does she do on the farm?

Beast   Our farm is operated by women who love women. Earlier I explained the butter massages before artificial insemination. Obviously it is the female cows that give birth. Cows are women, and as such, they feel resistance when they are suddenly touched by the hands of men. That becomes an obstacle to the healing process. There is a big difference in the fertility rate between when women provide the butter massage and when men do. But it has to be done not just by any woman, but a woman who loves other women. Butter massage is for women, performed by women who love women. Through this ultimate healing process, we are able to turn the knob to the door ahead. Turn the doorknob to the right to open the door, step through and drown in a sea of 360 degrees of pure ecstasy. The woman who looks like you is very skilled at giving butter massages. If she massages you, you will definitely conceive. Her hands were born to give massages.

Housewife   Could I get a massage from her?

Beast   Of course.

Housewife   I'm so very tired.

Beast   But you seem much more lucid than before.

Housewife   Can I make a reservation?

Beast   How about right now?

Housewife   But I have to get home before my husband does.

Beast   It's all right, you have enough time. Let's go.

Housewife   If you're sure …

Beast   Now then, put this on.

From its bag, **Beast** *takes out something shaped like a pole with a string attached.*

Beast   This is proof that you are one of us.

Housewife   Uh, I don't want to …

Beast   It's all right. This is an enlarged clitoris.

Housewife   It's not a penis?

Beast   It's a clitoris.

Housewife   But it looks like a penis, doesn't …

Beast   As you say, yes, it does look like a penis.

Housewife   Yes, it does.

Beast   But this is a clitoris. As I said before, an enlarged clitoris is what a penis is. So if you enlarge a clitoris, of course it will look like a penis. But the clitoris precedes the penis. This was created as a clitoris.

Housewife   I see.

Beast   We are a community of women. The clitoris is an important symbol for us. This is to declare the commitment to never forget the clitoris. Also, there are many dangers to living only with and amongst women. We did not intend it at first, but because it looks like a penis, with such a magnificent penis, men don't dare prey on us. It has the effect of a magical talisman as well. It is convenient that the clitoris looks like a penis.

Housewife   Do I have to put it on?

Beast   Yes, because it is proof that you are one of us.

Housewife   What would happen if I didn't?

Beast   There'd be a distance between us, and your butter massage would be discordant.

Housewife   Does the woman who looks like me wear this too?

Beast   Of course.

Housewife   OK I'll try it on.

She exits with the pole and string.

Beast   Oh ancestors! Soon, I will be saved. Rejoice with me! Congratulate me! I will let my semen swim inside my mother's uterus. Multitudes of me will swim at full speed towards my mother's egg. My luckiest and strongest self will break through to my mother's egg, finally becoming one fertilized egg. I'll await my reincarnation in my mother's uterus as I receive her blood through the placenta. I will be reborn from my mother's vagina. Mother will embrace me and I will possess her nipples as I suck them dry. I'll suck that spurting white liquid that I'd never had, to my heart's content.

Fourth Stasimon

Music plays.

Chorus
You are kind. That is what makes you terrifying
To murder the mother who abandoned you, fueled by the fires of hatred

or to impregnate your mother after soothing her with warm butter love
Which is the more terrible punishment?

Beast
Breastmilk breastmilk I want to drink my mother's breastmilk
My mother's breastmilk, breastmilk from my mother
Breastmilk breastmilk, I can't wait to drink breastmilk

Chorus
You are kind. That is what makes you terrifying
To have your body torn apart while celebrating Bacchus
or to have new flesh planted in you and your blood and milk sucked away
Which is the more terrible punishment?

Beast
Breastmilk breastmilk I want to drink my mother's breastmilk
My mother's breastmilk, breastmilk from my mother
Breastmilk breastmilk, I can't wait to drink breastmilk

Fifth Epeisodion

Housewife *enters. She has donned the pole with attached rope.*

Beast   How adorable! It suits you.

Housewife   Really? Isn't it weird?

Beast   No, not at all. It suits you very well.

Housewife   It's my first time wearing it, so I don't have confidence.

Beast   It's all right. I'll check.

Housewife   Thank you.

Beast   This is a little twisted.

Beast *fixes the twisted part of the rope.*

Housewife   Oh, thank you.

Beast   Let us go, then. I will serve as your guide and see that you get there safely.

Housewife   OK. I'm a bit worried.

Beast *takes a hold of* **Housewife**'*s hand.*

Beast   It's all right. However, you will need to carry something when you return.

Housewife   Wait, what? I'm scared.

Beast   Don't worry. What you carry will likely be happiness.

Housewife   Huh.

Beast *puts on its coat.* **Housewife** *and* **Beast** *exit holding hands.* **Dog** *follows after them and exits. Silence.* **Dog** *enters.*

Dog   Shit shit shit shit

Chorus   What's happened? Speak, dog.

Dog   You ordering me around because I'm a dog? You dissing me, cow? I'm not an idiot, I'm a dog, cow. You reek. Your stink is in my nose, cow. If a cow is threatening, a dog would bark woof woof. Shit! Sit! Shit down, this is what it is to be a dog.

Chorus   Enough, speak, dog.

Dog   The woman with the big clit got stopped by the cops at the station. She explained it wasn't a penis but a big clitoris, woof, but that didn't make things OK, no, that wasn't the sticking point. Woof woof wonder world. Their conversation got twisted and turned, twisted and turned, twisted and turned around. The cops got suspicious that she was carrying some liquid that would emit toxic gas, so they checked her bags but only found milk in them. The cops were troubled even though they weren't dogs, woof woof wo-woof woof wo-woof, the cops stopped, dropped and rolled out. She boarded the train to go to the mountain. Dogs don't need tickets, they ride free, woof. I don't like mountain climbing because I hate getting dirt under my nails. I love asphalt, I'm Hawaii, a cute pet dog Papillon. Waiting there at the farm was a lady #2 who looked identical to lady #1 woof woof, from there it was one wonder wonderful wonderful world. I was licking not butter but margarine, licking, dogging, docking, licking just margarine, dog go to hell, go to Hawaii, the lady was rubbing not margarine but butter, melting butter so smooth and delectable drool drool dripping hotter Harry Potter dog butter beer cheers! I tried to get a taste and moved in close but I was thrown aside yelp help! But I knew how to take it. I stood right back up. Papillon, that's a dog for you. I couldn't tell them apart, lady #2 who looked identical to lady #1. One two identically, which clitoris is whose? Not a dick but a gigantic clitoris. Shiny clitoris transmigrating into a sparkling new, dog Papillon bouillon butter turns to cheese and tangled up in lady #2's arms. Her legs were spread to the day after tomorrow and from her hole flowed condensed milk spurt squirt gush rush splat splash and pee poop splooge glorp bloop splash the rippling rings in the waters fishes swimming round round round …

Chorus   Hey! Speak normally, dog!

Dog   Huh.

Chorus   Could you please speak more clearly?

Dog   Shut up, you stink. The human-cow tried to inject his own sperm with a syringe but the lady abruptly came to and wiped her drool away. "Stop!" she said but the human-cow wouldn't. It turned into a brawl pow smash bang and the human-cow tried to shove its penis straight inside crying, "Mother—!!"

Dog *climbs up onto the table.*

Inu   And in the end, the lady took the human-cow's red engorged rock-hard dick and ripped it to shreds. Human-cow passed out. The other cows were moo moo moo mooing, going wild trying to rush the lady. Shit shit shit that's why I came running away. I can outrun anybody, that's a dog for you.

Sixth Epeisodion

Housewife *enters, holding in one hand the protrusion that she has ripped off of* **Beast***'s crotch.* **Beast** *enters, ripping through the screen. The protrusion between its legs is gone.*

Beast   Mother. That day, I went to a barbecue place again. When they brought salted tongue, I used tongs to pick up a slice. My hands shook. I was working too much every day. My trembling hands dropped the slice of salted tongue onto my thigh. After a few seconds of silence, the eloquent salted tongue started chatting with me. It probably resonated with the lower cow half of my body. Since that day I've heard the cows' voices all the time. As I listened to the cows, I understood what I needed to do. I must fulfill the mission of my body. Mother, I feel like a weight has lifted off my shoulders to have my penis taken away. Had I bound myself to suffer alone? Was I masturbating, Mother? I don't understand myself anymore. Have I been saved? Please tell me, Mother. Is this your love, Mother? Tell me, Mother. Mother.

Beast*'s voice does not reach* **Housewife***.* **Beast** *exits.*

Chorus   Um … Excuse me.

Housewife   What is it? Who are you people?

Chorus   Oh, we are the spirits of cows.

Housewife   Spirits of cows?

Chorus   We were watching this whole time. May we?

Housewife   I'm really tired.

Chorus   It'll be really quick.

Housewife   Well, I guess so.

Chorus   Do you understand what it is you have?

Housewife   It's a penis. The owner of it claimed it was a large clitoris but there's no way. If it's a giant clitoris that produces semen, it's basically a penis, isn't it.

Chorus   Well, you're right.

Housewife   Right? Can you eat cow penises?

Chorus   I don't know.

Chorus   Does anyone know?

Chorus   They aren't eaten much in Japan, but in China they do. It has a slippery texture like squid. It's squid-like but rather fishy on its own, so you have to marinate it in strong flavors. It's full of collagen so they recommend it for beauty purposes.

Housewife   It's fishy, huh? But collagen is good.

Dog   I bet it's great for your skin.

Housewife   Maybe I'll soak it in barbecue sauce and grill it tonight.

Dog   Yeah.

Housewife   I'm starving already. Maybe I'll just eat it right now.

Dog   Yeah, your hubby's going to be late as usual.

Housewife   Yeah.

She heads to the kitchen with the protrusion. **Dog** *chases after her.*

Exodus

Music plays.

Housewife *carries a plate full of thinly sliced meat (what was the protrusion) and sits at the dining table.* **Dog** *follows her and sits at the dining table.* **Housewife** *grills the meat on a hot plate.*

Chorus
> The honor of humans is not the honor of cows
> Humans can only see the world through their human eyes
>
> Centaur grew up and is laughing now
> Centaur ran off naked into the real world
> She's eating grass, running, shouting, drinking, drunk
> Suddenly another Centaur appears—Seeing another Centaur for the first time
> Let's embrace each other, become one, and breathe together
> If we eat, if we're eaten like this, we won't mind
> We do not live in the human world
> With the Centaur, I chew meat and I'm chewed up
> I swallow and am swallowed
> Pant, pant, pant
> I'm the most alive right now
> In the real world, the real world
> Centaur in a loud voice
> Is laughing, laughing out loud
>
> At the same time, at a table on the other side of the Earth
> Everyone is laughing out loud
> As they grill meat and drink milk

Whether they're happy or sad
Whether the food is delicious or bad
From birth to death, from morning to night
They're laughing, laughing out loud
Ha ha ha, ha ha ha

The smell of grilled meat fills the air. **Housewife** *and* **Dog** *are laughing. Music stops.*

End of play.

Notes

1. Fancl is a Japanese skincare brand known for their cosmetics and dietary supplements.
2. *Tatami* is a type of mat used as a flooring material in traditional Japanese-style rooms typically made of rice straw.
3. *Choregi* salad is Japanese-coined Korean-style salad with a sesame oil base dressing.

One Night

Yuko Kuwabara

Introduction to the Playwright and the Play

Hiroko Yamaguchi (*staff writer,* The Asahi Shimbun)

Translated by M. Cody Poulton

For a very long time now in Japan, women playwrights were a marked minority. Of the roughly 1,250 playwrights in the 150 years of modern Japanese drama who are listed in the comprehensive *Nihon Gikyoku Daijiten* (Encyclopedia of Japanese Drama. Hakusuisha, 2016), women amount to only 10 per cent. Even after the end of the Second World War, only nine of the seventy-four who have won the Kishida Drama Prize (established in 1955) for new playwrights have been women. However, a great number of female playwrights have emerged in the latter half of the first decade of the millennium. These women, born in the 1970s, have put an end to the age in which it was rare to be a female playwright. Yuko Kuwabara is one who represents this generation.

Kuwabara's dramas portray with a realistic touch the people who inhabit contemporary Japan's townscapes. She carefully gives shape to each and every one of her characters and weaves them into intricate stories. Motifs common to her plays include "margins," "catastrophes," and "crime and punishment."

The work that brought her to attention, *Sweet Hill* (Amai oka, 2007), portrays a group of women working in a hillside sandal factory. *Upheaval* (Outen, 2011) examines the past and present situation of a group of passengers on an overnight bus that has an accident on its way from Tokyo to the Tōhoku (northeast) region. *Traces—on and on* (Atoato, 2014) covers ten years in the lives of people involved in a hit-and-run accident that occurred on a stormy night by the banks of a river on the fringes of metropolitan Tokyo. *Wasteland* (2017) is a thrilling account set in a declining provincial town where a single woman, forced to evacuate from a fire, spends a night with a man she has been close to and his wife. In *Love You* (2019), an earthquake threatens an idyllic communal way of life on a farm run by a group of ex-cons.

These all sound like tragedies, but the tone of these works is far from dark. The plays are full of vivid characters and rich occasions for humor. Kuwabara embraces her characters' faults and difficulties and affectionately observes their clumsy efforts to redeem themselves even as they go on making mistakes. As she does so, she is also mindful to capture the cruel catastrophes that occasionally befall ordinary life.

Natural disasters are common to Japan. Earthquakes are frequent, and typhoons and heavy rains often leave serious damages.

The triple disaster of earthquake, tsunami, and nuclear meltdown that struck eastern Japan on March 11, 2011 remains for us to this very day a problem that exists in the present tense. It was an experience that reminded us keenly how we live in an absurd world where catastrophe and death can suddenly come calling. I believe that this sensibility lends a certain intensity to Kuwabara's creative stance, one that enables her to embrace humanity, love those eking out a living at the margins of society, and embrace their wounds, the sins that they must make amends for.

One Night (Hitoyo) begins on a cold night in March, with a mother's confession to her children that she has killed their father, a man guilty of hideously violent acts against his family. This prelude is followed fifteen years later, when she returns after having served her time. The first performance was in October 2011. Just as these characters' lives had been upended overnight, so too had the earthquake cast a dark shadow on this play. And yet, the story makes no reference to the current disaster, directing its attention instead to universal problems of love and hate, sin and foregiveness, despair and hope, human foolishness. The play has won a loyal audience with numerous productions, and was made into a film in 2019, directed by Kazuya Shiraishi.

Playwright Biography

Yuko Kuwabara

Born in 1976, Kuwabara is the head of KAKUTA theatre company, and since its founding in 1996, she has written and directed all their plays and performed in most of them. *A Sweet Hill* (2006) was her very first work to be shortlisted for an award—the 2007 Kishida Drama Prize—and the revival of the play won the 64th Agency of Cultural Affairs National Arts Festival Award and the New Artist Award (for script and directing) in 2009. Her *Outen* was shortlisted for the 15th Tsuruya Nanboku Drama Award and the 56th Kishida Drama Prize in 2012, and *Traces—on and on* won the 18th Tsuruya Nanboku Drama Award in 2015. *The Wasteland* (Honokuni Toyohashi Arts Theatre PLAT independent production) won the 5th Hayakawa Higeki Kigeki Award in January 2018. She won the 70th Yomiuri Prize for Literature in the Drama and Scenario division in 2019. Besides plays, Kuwabara writes TV dramas and screenplays, such as *Junior High Student's Diary* (NHK Educational TV) and the film *Rambling Heart*. *One Night* was made into a film (dir. Kazuya Shiraishi) in 2019.

Kuwabara is actively engaged in many areas of performance including acting. Since August 2018, she has been the arts culture advisor for the Honokuni Toyohashi Arts Theatre PLAT in Aichi prefecture.

One Night

Yuko Kuwabara

Translated by Mari Boyd

Characters

Koharu Inamura *(age fifty-six), mother of the Inamura family*
Daiki Inamura *(age thirty-six), eldest son, Fuku-chan's Appliances employee*
Sonoko Inamura *(age thirty-three), eldest daughter, bar employee*
Yuji Inamura *(age thirty), second son, freelance writer*
Yumi Shibata *(age fifty-two), office worker and dispatcher, Koharu's best friend*
Susumu Marui *(age thirty-eight), president of Inamaru Taxi company*
Maki Ushiku *(age thirty-two), daytime woman driver, nicknamed Moe*
Yoichi Utagawa *(age thirty-five), full-time driver*
Mr. Yoshinaga *(age unknown), from a dairy farm in Hokkaido*
Fumiko Inamura *(age thirty-eight), Daiki's wife, in mediation for divorce*
Junya Tomokuni *(age twenty-nine), yakuza, formerly "younger brother" to Doshita*
Hinako Kimata *(age twenty-four), Tomokuni's lover*
Michio Doshita *(age fifty), new taxi driver; former "older brother" yakuza to Tomokuni*

Background

Inamaru Taxi company is located in a mountain town about two hours away from central Tokyo. In 1975, Yuichi Inamura and his wife, Koharu, started a family-owned taxi business under the name of "Inamura Taxi," and gradually increased the number of vehicles and employees. In 1982, it became an incorporated taxi company.

In 1996, business was temporarily halted due to a certain incident; however, when Yuichi passed away suddenly, Koharu's older brother, Shinichiro Marui, took over the management of the business. Inamura Taxi was renamed "Inamaru Taxi" as a joint management company with the Inamura family's eldest son, Daiki, succeeding to the position of company owner.

After Shinichiro's death in January 2011, his son, Susumu, took over as president.

The company currently has about ten employees, a few of them are from the Inamura Taxi days, but the majority are relatively young.

The types of workers are: alternate-day shift drivers, night/day shift drivers, office staff, and dispatchers.

Their main source of income is from dispatching taxis via the booking service, and the taxis rarely cruise for customers. Located in the countryside, they are open twenty-four hours a day, but few call late at night.

There is a private railway station about a five-minute drive away and a national railway station twenty minutes away.

Stage

The office of Inamaru Taxi (formerly Inamura Taxi). Built next to the main house of the Inamura family, it is an old prefabricated and reinforced concrete building.

The entrance to the office is located stage left. By the entrance, there is a counter, equipped with a desktop computer for inputting daily reports and a breathalyser.

On the wall next to the counter is a whiteboard for writing down shifts and colored magnets with employees' family names on them—yellow indicating day shift; blue, night shift; and red, absence.

In the center of the office, there is a large dining table with chairs, where the employees hold meetings and take breaks.

Upstage are two small private rooms. One is a curtained-off nap room with a wooden bunk bed and shelves for uniforms and seat covers.

The other is a dispatch room that takes dispatch calls and contains a phone, a desktop computer, and a bookcase with a local map of the area.

There is a window with a blind between the dispatch room and the main office, so what is going on inside can be viewed without opening the door.

At stage right is a small reception area with an old analog TV, sofa, coffee table, and a kitchenette with a refrigerator and sink.

Behind it is the door to the washroom with toilet and shower.

The glass doors next to the reception area opens up on a small patio that leads to the Inamuras' main living quarters

This patio is so small that even three people would feel cramped in it, and in addition to a washing machine and clothesline, there is a smoking area with an ashtray and stools.

Without recent repapering, the dull wallpaper of the office is peeling away. Various torn traffic safety posters from years ago are attached to it, making the walls look as if they had been like that from the very beginning.

It must be cold in winter and hot in summer in this yellowish building with poor ventilation.

The only item that looks comical and disproportionate is the large, car-shaped sign that has been erected on top of the poorly maintained building. Barely recognizable as a taxi, it has a diamond-shaped lantern on the top with the word "Ina" written on it.

The sign, once painted blue, has been soaked by rain, blown by the wind, and over the years has completely lost its original color. It may have already faded away that night in 1996, when a historic snowstorm hit the town.

What remains is the light of a little lantern. Both tonight and fifteen years ago, its dull, warm orange light has been constantly lit as if to express the force of someone's will.

Signs used in the dialogue

• Indicates that the lines are delivered from offstage (where the speaker cannot be seen).
* Indicates that the utterance is made simultaneously with the lines marked with the same symbol.

Opening: A Night Fifteen Years Ago

March, around 10 pm. Snow is falling on the patio.

The telephone rings, and **Yumi Shibata**, *the dispatcher, picks up the phone as usual.*

Yumi   Thank you for calling, this is Inamaru Taxis . . . Thank you. May I have your name? . . . Mr. Tanaka, let me check your pick-up time; please hold a moment.

At the office, the Inamura family's children are watching a TV drama. The eldest son **Daiki** *is sitting at the dining table writing something. Occasionally, he twists his body as he watches the screen. Fresh bandages are wrapped messily around his head.*

His younger sister, **Sonoko**, *the eldest daughter, sits on a sofa, her eyes gazing vacantly rather than watching TV. From time to time, she picks up a hand mirror and checks the large red bruises on her face and her injured mouth oozing with blood.*

The sounds from the TV drama mingle with the sound of a phone call on hold coming from a speaker in the dispatch room.

The sliding door opens and **Koharu**, *the mother, walks in. She is dressed in a taxi driver's uniform of shirt, vest, and tie, with a jumper over it.* **Koharu** *lightly brushes the snow off her head, takes off her jumper and puts it on a hanger while she checks on the dispatch room.* **Yumi** *notices* **Koharu** *and raises her hand lightly from the dispatch room.*

Koharu   Anything to eat?

Sonoko *gets up and prepares a meal of leftovers in the kitchenette.* **Koharu** *opens the door to the dispatch room and speaks to* **Yumi**.

Koharu   Yumi, that's enough for today.

After ending the telephone exchange, **Yumi** *starts getting ready to go home right away. During that time,* **Sonoko** *puts out on the table a single portion of rice balls and side dishes and then makes a serving of instant miso soup with hot water from a thermos.*

Koharu   Did you have supper here?

Sonoko   I haven't cleaned up the broken glass yet.

Koharu   . . . Show me your head. (*Looks at* **Daiki**'s *face, and reaches out to take off the gauze.*)

Yumi   Is it OK to close the office?

Koharu   Go ahead—(*To* **Daiki**.) I got some antibiotics. Take these and your head won't sting so much.

Daiki *accepts the medicine.*

Koharu   Where's Yu?

Daiki *points to the Inamura house.*

Koharu *goes out through the glass doors, cuts across the patio, opens the door of the Inamura house, and calls out.*

Koharu   Yu, Yu, come over here.

Yumi *finishes her preparations to leave, turns off the lights in the dispatch room, and comes in from the patio. She puts on her coat.*

Yumi   Did you make this supper, Sono?

Sonoko *nods modestly.*

Koharu   Yu, come on.

Yumi   It's prepared nicely.

Koharu   Brrh! Cold, cold, cold. It's going to snow. It's going to snow soon tonight.

She cuts across the patio and comes back inside.

Yumi   But it's spring.

Koharu   Right.

Yumi   Should I stay a bit longer after all? The traffic will be heavy.

Koharu   Not to worry, not to worry. Last time, we took off the snow chains. I've already told the drivers to go home.

Yumi   Really?

Sonoko   Today, we close.

Yumi   That helps. I just had a call from Tsugumi[1] saying she wants a ride home.

Sonoko   Where is she?

Yumi   At the cram school.

Koharu   At this late hour.

Yumi   Cram schools nowadays keep even grade schoolers in till this late.

Koharu   Tsugumi's quite something.

Yumi   She could go home by bus, but can't be bothered to. Well then, I'll go ahead then.

Koharu   Thanks. Take it easy.

Yumi *rushes away.* **Sonoko** *finishes preparing dinner and serves tea to* **Koharu**, *who is seated at the dining table.* **Yuji** *now enters from the Inamura house. In training wear, he has his injured right arm in a sling.* **Yuji** *stands in front of the TV.* **Daiki** *continues to watch TV.*

Daiki   I can't see.

Yuji *sits down on the sofa.*

Koharu   Yu, come over here.

Yuji *moves to a dining chair in reluctant silence.*

Koharu   You did a good job with the cooking.

Sonoko (*sitting across from* **Koharu**)   It's frozen food.

Koharu   Oh really. Let's eat.

She starts to eat energetically. The children watch TV.

Koharu   Dai, turn off the TV. We have to talk.

Daiki *is silent.*

Koharu   Dai.

Daiki *turns off the TV.*

Koharu   Frozen foods aren't bad. Where do you get them?

Sonoko   I don't know. (*Saying that she takes one of* **Koharu**'s *croquettes and crunches into it.*)

Koharu   The corn tastes like it's been frozen.

Sonoko   Um.

Koharu (*eating*)   . . . How was school, Yu?

Yuji *nods his head.*

Sonoko   Uh, you didn't go, right?

Yuji *shakes his head.*

Koharu   Uh-huh.

Daiki (*a beat*)   What?

Koharu   Huh?

Daiki   Uh, you want to tell us something . . .

Koharu   Ahh, yes . . . (*Continues to eat.*)

Daiki (*waits a bit*)   So?

Koharu *gestures to indicate that her mouth is full and so could he wait.*

Daiki *tries to turn the TV on again.*

Koharu   Daiki . . .

Daiki *says nothing.*

Koharu   Sonoko, Yuji, listen up OK? I, I killed Dad today.

The children are stunned and silent.

Koharu   I ran over him.

Daiki (*a beat*)   Uh.

Koharu (*munching a rice ball*)   You all hated Dad and so did I. So I am feeling proud of myself now.

The children are silent.

Koharu   So, yes, yes. I'm going to go to the police now, I'll be away from home for a while, but uncle Susumu will take care of the company, so it's OK. But, you know, just because Mom is a murderer, you can't think that you can do it, too. I did it because of Dad. Yeah, ummmm, I waited. I waited for Dad's father and mother to die. I waited until no one would feel sad when Dad was dead. I waited until Dai got a job offer. I waited for Sono to get a job at a vocational school. I couldn't wait until Yuji . . .

Yuji *raises his head.*

Koharu   . . . graduated from high school. With the new . . . (*some rice gets stuck in her throat*) house . . .

Sonoko *hurriedly offers some tea.*

Koharu (*drinking tea*)   I waited till the construction of the new house was completed, too. Thank you.

Daiki *looks at the house.*

Koharu   That house belongs to Daiki. But if he marries, give it to Sonoko. If Sonoko leaves home, give it to Yuji. Until Yu graduates college, get by on my savings. Daiki must live on his own income.

Sonoko *tries to say something.*

Koharu   And, and now, about the future, I will go to the police and explain that I ran over him by mistake. When I was backing into the garage, I didn't realize Dad was there and unknowingly . . .

Daiki (*stands*)   In the garage?!

Koharu   . . . Right, He's in the garage. He is, well, his body is.

Daiki *is stunned.*

Koharu   That night.

Music.

That night, I had finished work and was trying to back the taxi into the garage. I didn't notice. I didn't notice Dad was behind me and by accident . . .

Her words are gradually erased by the music.

Title: One Night

Koharu, *alone in the music, continues to talk, but it is mostly drowned out and made inaudible by the music.*

Koharu   Because the light bulb in the garage was always out. I guess it wasn't a good idea to leave it there when we knew it had to be replaced. Because it was too dark to see, the oil cans that were left there would, you know, get knocked over. All the time. I didn't even notice Dad squatting down. It was snowing, I had to get back inside.

The children listen to **Koharu**'s *explanation in utter stillness. Time passes.* **Koharu**, *who was absorbed in her story, knocks over her tea cup and spills tea on the table.*

Koharu   Oh, I'm sorry, I'm sorry. I'm sorry.

After a short pause, **Sonoko** *goes to get a dust cloth.* **Koharu** *takes it and wipes the table.*

Koharu (*while wiping*)   Basically, unpremeditated manslaughter? But if I don't get that kind of verdict, we're looking at seven years in prison. Maybe less. Prison? Jail? Release? So even if I do get let out, I don't think I should return right away. Given that I'll need to wait till the whole thing blows over, I'll give you a rough estimate: . . . ten years (*reconsidering*), fifteen years. . . After fifteen years, Mom will be back, I'm sure of it. Until then, you must never come to see me in jail or look for me outside of jail . . . Sono, don't cry. You don't have a father anymore. No one is going to hurt any of you like this again. (*Strokes their faces.*)

Sonoko *cries with abandon.*

Koharu   I'm coming back and will continue the taxi business. Right, Sono.

Sonoko *nods without understanding.*

Koharu   OK? So you see, I'm really, really proud of myself.

Scene One: The Present

1.1 Inside a Taxi

Present time. March. Inside an Inamaru taxi. In the driver's seat is **Michio Doshita**, *a new driver, sitting with his back straight, a tense look on his face, and hands on the steering wheel. In the back seat,* **Yoichi Utagawa** *is sitting slovenly with one leg propped against the back of the assistant driver's seat and making a call on his cell phone.*

Utagawa   I'm going to hang up now . . . So I said, you can't tell even if you stay up all night. (*Looks at his watch.*) Anyways, it's morning already. You get some sleep. (*Clucking his tongue.*) Oh, go right . . . (*To* **Doshita**.) Hey.

Doshita   Yes.

Utagawa   Go right.

Doshita   Go right at the next corner.

Utagawa   Wrong, go right at the place we've just passed.

Doshita   Oh.

Utagawa   The fuck you're doing!

Doshita   Excuse me.

Utagawa (*into his phone*)   No, not you . . . Eh? I'm working right now. Duh . . . I'm not going anywhere at this time of the night. (*To* **Doshita**.) Go left there.

Doshita   Uh, not to the right?

Utagawa   You can do a U-turn from there, OK?

Doshita   Ah, ah. (*Looks around rapidly.*)

Utagawa   That's enough. You suck.

Doshita   I'm sorry.

Utagawa   Hallo.

Doshita   Uh, I'll turn right at the next one.

Utagawa   The next is one-way, shithead.

Doshita   Oh . . .

Utagawa   Do you really know the streets, eh?

Doshita   I'm sorry.

Utagawa   Use the navigator. (*Into the phone.*) So if you're so worried, use a chain . . . You say it's disgusting. Then what should I say? I haven't forgotten. How could I forget you?

Doshita *is bothered by the phone conversation.*

Utagawa   How much are you doing? Cooking meals, listening to her grumbles, cleaning up her messes. (*To* **Doshita**.) Geez—Why take that fucking road?

Doshita   Uh, the navigator indicated it.

Utagawa   Shit, if you want to get to Route 8, you gotta take the next backstreet. That's common sense, asshole.

Doshita *does not reply.*

Utagawa   Sorry, sorry. Hallo? (*The line is dead.*) Oh no—

Doshita *remains silent.*

Utagawa   It's no good getting angry, asshole.

Doshita *says nothing.*

Utagawa   Mr. Doshita.

Doshita   Huh? Nothing.

Utagawa   You're in a bad mood? Hahahahaha . . . Lots of customers are like this, but you know, don't let them bother you. They say all kinds of things to wangle a tiny reduction out of you, like 100 yen or 200 yen.

Doshita   I see.

Utagawa   You don't need to pay a lot of attention to them. Give 'em a break of a meter or so. A kindly-looking man who has no idea of how to rid himself of his daily stress can be the one to fuck you up with his complaints.

Doshita   Yes.

Utagawa   In that case, we are the toilet bowl.

Doshita   What?!

Utagawa   We're the toilet bowl for these guys. We're supposed to put up with the shit they throw up and say nothing.

Doshita   Oh.

Utagawa (*yawning*)   Let's head back.

Doshita   Yes.

Utagawa (*the phone vibrates*)   In the middle of the night.

Doshita   Yes.

Utagawa   My partner's old mother has gone senile and keeps running out of the house.

Doshita   Uh-huh.

Utagawa   Where d'you think she'd go?

Doshita   Where could it be?

Utagawa   What about you, Doshita?

Doshita   Huh?

Utagawa   What are you running away from?

Doshita (*beat*)   Nothing.

Utagawa   Just a joke.

Doshita *is silent.*

Utagawa (*answers the phone*)   Hallo? Yo, so as I said, I haven't forgotten about Tsugumi's granny.

Utagawa *continues talking on the phone.* **Doshita**, *though the driver, looks out of the taxi window.*

1.2 At the Inamaru Taxi Office

At the same time, in other words, at 5 am. At the Inamaru Taxi Office, the telephone in the dispatch room is ringing. **Maki Ushiku**, *a driver, is lying on the sofa reading a magazine, ignoring the call.* **Yuji** *is dozing face down on the dining room table, when the sound of the phone wakes him up. As he gets up to answer the phone,* **Susumu Marui** *comes running out of the washroom in a flurry of activity.*

Marui   Never mind, never mind.

Yuji   Sorry.

Marui (*answers the telephone in the dispatch room*)   Thank you for your call. This is Inamaru Taxis. Marui at your service.

Maki   You have sleep lines on your face.

Yuji   What's the . . .

Maki   Past 5:00 am.

Susumu (*puts the telephone on hold*)   Misaka bus stop.

Maki *spreads one hand wide open and makes a scissors shape with the other.*

Susumu   Our taxi will pick you up about seven minutes from now. (*He continues.*) Please wait in front of the bus stop. Thank you.

Yuji   Still working?

Maki   I was about to finish my shift.

Yuji   You're just a girl.

Maki   Yu, why don't you sleep in your own room?

Maki *gets up and prepares to leave.*

Yuji   I don't have a room of my own.

Maki   Huh? Oh, your niece stole it.

Yuji   My room has a lace canopy.

Maki   You leave the house for long periods of time. It's OK to use the kids' room. The kids are away, anyway.

Yuji   I can't settle down there. That Licca-chan doll and all the other dolls are staring down at me with their glittering eyes.

Susumu (*to* **Maki**)   If you're here, answer the telephone.

Yuji   Sorry.

Susumu   No, no, Yuji, you can relax. You've got to be tired. (*Glaring at* **Maki**.)

Maki   You don't like me.

Susumu   That's not the point. The telephone is the key! Without a dispatch system, we can't run this business.

Maki   Misaka, right? What's the name?

Susumu   Um.

Maki   The name.

Susumu (*beat*)   Oh no, I forgot to ask.

Maki   Really.

Susumu   That's bad.

Maki   Telephones are the key to operation, right?

Susumu   Well, this isn't my job.

Maki   How many years have you been at this?

Susumu   I'm so sorry.

Maki   Hire a new dispatcher.

Susumu   We can't find anyone quickly in times like this, even when we put out a want ad.

Yuji   I'll do it.

Susumu   You don't need to. You're tired.

Maki   Of course Yuji doesn't need to do it.

Susumu   As soon as you got back, we had Dad's memorial service. That was an immense job.

Maki   That's right.

Susumu   Take it easy for a while.

Maki   Take it easy.

Yuji   Thanks.

Maki   No problem.

Susumu   Hey, you have only seven minutes. Get going.

Maki   It's really only five minutes away.

Susumu (*a beat*)   I see you now, your long hair trailing in the breeze. As if you're saying, "I'm Hwasa.[2] I'm here. I am the Inamaru speed racer."

Maki   Oh, Boss.

The telephone rings again.

Susumu (*heading toward the dispatch room*)   Seven minutes.

Maki   It's not a hoax, is it?

Susumu   It's real, it's real. Thank you for your call. This is *Inamaru Taxis. Marui is at your service.

Yuji   *A hoax?

Maki   Sometimes, guys book a taxi for a joke.

Yuji   Humph.

Maki   Does the phone bother you?

Yuji   Hn? Uh-uh.

Maki   . . . How long are you staying this time?

Yuji   Huh?

Maki   You're going to go back again, right?

Yuji   No, I'll be here for a while.

Maki   Uh?

Yuji   So, that's why I want to be the dispatcher here.

Maki (*happily*)   What about your work?

Yuji   I can do that here.

Maki (*very happily*)   So that's it . . . you're not going back.

Yuji   Seven minutes.

Maki   I can get there in three.

She cannot hide her joy as she leaves the building. **Susumu**, *having completed the telephone call, is standing there grinning.*

Susumu   She's easy to understand, our Moe.

Yuji   Huh?

Susumu   She still likes you.

Yuji   It's not like that, OK.

Susumu   Yes, it is. The innocent smile she has at times like that hasn't changed since she was a little girl. I liked her, too . . .

Yuji   Uh, you talking about Moe?

Susumu   That kind of thing happens, you know. You visit your cousin's house frequently. She's a bit of a delinquent. In secret, you feel a delicate love for her. She is slim, small, and strong-willed, but also adorable.

Yuji   You really felt all that.

Susumu   But in no time she turns into a very angry young woman . . . with a sharp knife in her pocket. This is no metaphor, mind you.

Yuji   That's ancient history.

Susumu   Yes, from long ago her heart was yours. It was tragic for me.

Maki (*returning*)   Hey.

Susumu   Yes.

Maki   The garage door is open again.

Susumu   Oh.

Maki   Keep it shut. Or else someone's going to steal the equipment.

Susumu   I will.

Maki *exits again.*

Susumu   She still has the knife.

Yuji   What about the telephone call?

Susumu   That one just now? Huh. (*He shrugs.*)

Yuji   What?

Susumu   Just a prank.

Yuji   A prank.

Susumu   Never mind, never mind. It happens from time to time, especially at this time of the year. (*He catches himself and stops.*)

Yuji   Oh.

Susumu   Sorry.

Yuji   Not to worry. What kind of pranks?

Susumu   Huh? Well, no . . . (*Hesitates to say.*)

Yuji   For example?

Susumu (*hesitates, but cannot stop himself from blurting out*)   Silent calls, calls for taxis asking for Koharu as driver.

Yuji   Really.

Susumu   Oh, but there were some had nothing to do with her, too. Hi, welcome back.

Doshita *returns after finishing work. Bows to* **Yuji** *and goes to the nap room to change out of his uniform.*

Susumu   The other day, there was a really ridiculous jokester, a foreigner.

Yuji   A foreigner.

Susumu   Well, the guy was pretending to be a foreigner, speaking in broken Japanese. He wanted to know how to get here, so I asked him where he was. He said Niseko. Niseko is up north in Hokkaido, you know. I told him to stop joking around as it was impossible to get there.

Yuji   Ahh.

Susumu   For a moment, I anticipated a ghost.

Doshita   A ghost?

Susumu   Um?

Doshita   Come again?

Susumu   Ah, you see, in this industry, a long-distance customer who's to be driven far away or who's to be brought from afar is called a ghost. If we get a fare to Tokyo, we consider that a lucky ghost.

Doshita   Really . . .

Susumu   You'd be happy if you met a ghost soon, Mr. Doshita.

Doshita   Yes.

Susumu   I hadn't introduced the new driver to you 'cause of the memorial service.

Doshita   Oh, right. (*Bows to* **Yuji**.) I'm Doshita.

Susumu   This is Yuji, the Inamura's second son and my cousin.

Yuji   Nice to meet you.

Susumu   Yuji will work here.

Doshita   I see.

Susumu   What you said before is real, right? You're not going back to Tokyo?

Yuji   Remember. I can't drive. I don't have a driver's license.

Susumu   Never mind, being a dispatcher is fine. You can do it at night while you get your other work done.

Yuji   Uh-huh.

Susumu   He's an independent writer.

Doshita   Ah.

Yuji   No, not really. I just do transcription.

Doshita   Transcription?

Yuji   Well, you see, I write out in words the audio recordings of interviews and such.

Susumu   Doesn't that make you a writer?

Yuji   It's totally different. I'm aiming to become a writer, eventually.

Susumu   You are a writer.

Yuji   You may insist, but . . .

Daiki *in PJs comes out of the main building. With a mug of coffee in one hand, he sits on a chair in the patio and becomes abstracted.*

Susumu   Come to think of it, where's Utagawa? He was giving occupied taxi training, right? Or did he slack off?

Doshita   No, he'll be back soon. On the way, Sonoko called.

Susumu   I see.

Doshita   She wanted a ride back from the bar.

Susumu (*beat*)   That's appropriation. Appropriation of taxis. Your sister is always like that.

Yuji   I'm sorry.

Susumu   She can easily walk back, but no, she wants a ride.

Yuji   But the valley road is scary for a woman, and it's dark.

Susumu   If you take the mountain path, you'll get here in no time.

Yuji   Even at night, there's a fair number of climbers going up the mountain over there.

Doshita   Yeah, I saw one. He was shouldering a big mountaineering backpack.

Yuji   In this cold, too.

Doshita   He's probably aiming to catch the sunrise.

Daiki *tries to light a cigarette with a lighter, but his fingers move awkwardly. Unable to get it to work, he rubs the device, which makes a clicking sound.*

Susumu (*referring to the climber*)   Huh, that's a fanciful thing to do.

Doshita   On top of that, today, Sonoko was pretty much . . .

Susumu   . . . plastered.

Doshita   I could barely understand what she said.

Yuji   Well, today is, you know.

He stands up and goes out to the patio via the back door.

Susumu   It's like an annual event.

Doshita   An annual event . . .

He stands, takes **Daiki**'*s lighter, and gets it to work.* **Daiki** *lights his cigarette and* **Yuji** *sits next to him and lights up.*

Susumu   Mr. Doshita . . .

Doshita   Yes?

Susumu   Do you know how the father died?

Doshita   Uh, no.

Susumu   You've heard, haven't you? No faking, no faking. You must know, right? It's famous around here.

Doshita   Well, vaguely.

Susumu   Yes, you have.

Doshita   Ah.

Susumu   The memorial day is a commemoration in many ways. The father died and the mom . . .

Doshita   Uh-huh.

Susumu   About fifteen years . . . gone by. The kids probably can't stand it, you know. Dai in particular, he's the eldest son.

Doshita   Yes.

Susumu   He has to manage the household forever.

Yuji (*pointing at the sky*)   What is that?

Daiki (*still toying with the lighter*)   Which thing?

Susumu   We've finished for the day, right?

Doshita   Yes. Oh, uh . . .

Susumu   Um?

Doshita   The garage is wide open.

Susumu   Oh, whoops.

Doshita   Should I have closed it?

Susumu   My fault, my fault.

Doshita   I thought someone was using it.

Susumu   I'll go and check. I'll go. Oh, here. These are leftover altar offerings. So help yourself.

Doshita   Thank you.

Susumu *exits with the key.* **Doshita** *looks at the brothers out in the patio, while helping himself to the* monaka *wafers*[3] *on the table.*

Yuji   An airship?

Daiki   A-airship it is.

Yuji   This late at night?

Daiki (*stutters*)   It's taking a t-t-t-trial flight. Look at where the l-letters . . .

Yuji   Aha, they haven't been painted in.

Daiki   Uh-huh.

Yuji   A department store? It's going to be a department store.

Daiki   In front of the station at the junction.

Yuji   Oh yeah. Humph.

Daiki   It's gonna be big.

Yuji   Isn't that unusual? It's kinda anachronistic . . .

Daiki   This is . . . (*Showing the lighter.*)

Yuji (*taking the lighter*)   Flick it up and then push down on it, then flick it back.

Daiki   Uh-huh. (*Tries but fails.*)

Yuji   Let's switch. I'll use that one.

Daiki *does not speak.*

The front door opens noisily, and **Utagawa** *and* **Sonoko***, with their arms wrapped around each other's shoulders, enter energetically. Dressed in a flashy black outfit,* **Sonoko***, her face sickly pale, is holding her hand over her mouth.*

Doshita   Welcome ba—

Sonoko (*close to barfing*)   Aaarf.

Utagawa   Hold it in, hold it in. We're almost there.

The two make a run for the washroom. As soon as they are inside, the sounds of retching and running water are heard.

Yuji   She doesn't change.

Daiki *nods and stands up disapproving of the retching sound. He stubs out the cigarette and heads for the office.* **Yuji** *goes back to the office, too, and goes to take a look at the washroom.*

Yuji   She's in a bad state.

Doshita   Well. Oh, excuse me, I'm helping myself to the wafers.

Yuji   Go ahead, go ahead.

Doshita   Would you like some?

Yuji   Kneecaps.

Doshita   Uh? They are Hama *monaka* wafers.

Yuji   Oh, you see, we call them kneecaps. The shape suggests knees, don't you think? (*Looking at his own knees.*) . . . well, maybe not.

Doshita   You gave them that name?

Yuji   Uh-uh . . . Mom did.

●Utagawa   Oh no, don't splutter, stupid.

●Sonoko (*gags*)   Aa haa, blarg . . .

Yuji   I'm sorry. You'll lose your appetite.

Doshita   Not to worry.

Yuji (*to the washroom*)   You OK? Need help?

●Utagawa   No problem, no problem.

Utagawa *comes out of the washroom.*

Yuji   Do you need anything?

Utagawa   How about some beer?

Yuji   Um. What? Beer?

Utagawa   For me.

Yuji   Hey. (*Goes to the kitchenette and gets a can of beer.*)

Utagawa   Doshita, you have one, too.

Doshita   Oh, no thanks.

Utagawa   You've finished work, right?

Doshita   Yes.

Utagawa   It's fine. These belong to the boss. "What belongs to the boss belongs to me" is the correct thinking here.

Yuji   Are you sure it's OK?

Doshita   I'm abstaining.

Utagawa   Uh, no drink?

Doshita   Sorry.

Utagawa   I'm curious. You don't do alcohol, cigarettes, or gambling. You come suddenly to a poky little seaside taxi company, yeah? Come on, man, what have you been up to so far?

Doshita   Not much, really.

Utagawa   What about before you came here?

Doshita   I was a fisherman.

Utagawa   A fisherman! Ah, uh, at Oarai?

Doshita   Uh-uh, on the Japan Sea.

Utagawa   Uh-huh. On the other side, eh. What brought you over here?

Doshita   Oh well . . .

Sonoko *comes staggering out of the washroom.*

Utagawa (*handing her a glass of water*)   You OK?

Sonoko   Um. I feel better.

Utagawa   Sono, the charge is 710 yen.

Sonoko   Eek. You charging fare?

Utagawa   I can't give you a free ride back. Not during work hours.

Sonoko   Stingy—

Utagawa   You can pay later.

Sonoko   What are you going to do with all your savings? Spend it on Tsugumi? Then, you are keeping her, right?

Utagawa   No way, stupid.

Unnoticed, **Susumu** *is standing in the doorway.*

Yuji   Huh, by Tsugumi, you mean that Tsugumi?

Sonoko   That Tsugumi.

Utagawa   No . . .

Sonoko   This is a secret from Yumi, alright? It would be terrible if she found out that her precious daughter was in the arms of a co-worker.

Yuji   They taste awful

Sonoko   Yum, yum. I'm young. (*Eats the* monaka *wafers.*)

Utagawa   So you're dead wrong. You're just an interfering drunk. (*To* **Susumu**.) What the fuck are you standing there for all this time?

Susumu   Oh . . .

Doshita   Won't the garage close?

Susumu (*beat*)   Uh, how many tires were there?

Utagawa   Ah?

Susumu   I mean the tires in the garage. About how many were there?

Utagawa   . . . Geez, there's gotta be lots.

Doshita   Is it a puncture problem?

Susumu   Uh-uh . . . Are they stacked up? Like this, boom, boom, up to a meter high?

Utagawa   Huh?

Susumu   Are they in a pile at the back of the garage? And do they tremble and shake like this?

Sonoko   We're not talking about Jello.

Susumu   Aha, so this isn't about tires.

Yuji   What's up?

Utagawa   What's he mumbling about? Is our boss OK?

Susumu (*beat*)   Maybe it's a person.

Utagawa   Huh?

Susumu   Must be something like a person hiding like in the ba-back.

Utagawa   Something like a person's hiding like in the back?

Susumu   It was too dark to see well.

Doshita   In the garage?

Susumu   Um.

Sonoko   A person? . . .

Utagawa   Must be a thief. (*Stands.*)

Susumu   No, I don't know, I don't know. You may be jumping to conclusions. You are jumping ahead. He looked like he was sleeping.

Utagawa   Sleeping?

Susumu   Like I heard him snoring. Maybe he's homeless.

Utagawa   Here in the boonies?

Susumu   Let's go and take a look together?

Utagawa *is more than ready to go.*

Susumu (*energetically leads the way*)   Over here, over here.

Utagawa   I know the way.

Susumu   Mr. Doshita.

Doshita   Uh-huh—

Susumu   Just in case, just in case.

Doshita   Oh well . . .

Utagawa *takes a broom from nearby and brandishes it, and the three men are about to exit.*

Susumu   Uh, are you taking that stick-like thing with you?

Utagawa   Call them, you . . .

Susumu   You mean the police? That's too hasty. It might be a homeless person.

Utagawa   Shut up. You'd still call them. That's common sense.

Susumu *holds his cell phone to the ready.* **Doshita** *looks back at* **Yuji**, *who shrugs his shoulders and stays put. The three men exit taking each step with utmost care A longish pause.*

Sonoko   Aren't you going to take a look?

Yuji   Nope.

Sonoko *does not speak.*

Yuji   The police . . .

Sonoko   Uh?

Yuji   It might be better to call them.

Sonoko   Let's see what happens.

Yuji   Uh-huh.

Sonoko   Are you thinking it might be . . .? I can understand how you feel. I've been thinking all day today about that.

Yuji   Daiki can't get any sleep either.

Sonoko   And what about you?

Yuji   Uh-huh.

Sonoko   Today is the day.

Yuji (*beat*)   But she wouldn't hang out in the garage.

Sonoko (*beat followed by a laugh*)   That's for sure.

Doshita *returns.*

Doshita   Yuji, could you join us?

Yuji   Huh?

Doshita   Utagawa said to call you.

Yuji (*Beat. High tension*)   Why?

Doshita   It looks like a man.

Yuji   A man.

Doshita   He looks as if he is asleep, but he may get violent. So . . .

Yuji   Oh, so he wants me?

Doshita   I dunno.

Sonoko (*laughing*)   'Cause you're a former juvenile delinquent.

Doshita   Really?

Yuji   No, I doubt I'm in his league.

Sonoko   What is that supposed to mean?

Yuji   Could you take my place here?

Doshita   Sure.

Yuji *exits.*

Sonoko   So it was a man.

Doshita   A homeless guy after all.

Sonoko   It's cold tonight.

Doshita   A former delinquent . . .

Sonoko   You don't think he looks like one?

Doshita   No.

Sonoko   Look closely. He has a cute face but very sharp eyes. (*Plays with the lighter on the desk and hums.*) Such . . . times . . . did exist[4] . . .

Doshita *is silent.*

Sonoko   It doesn't light up.

Doshita   You see, you have to pull it up when you flick it.

Sonoko   Oh, it's so difficult . . .

Doshita   This type is becoming common recently. It's a bother.

Sonoko   Kids would burn themselves trying to learn how.

Doshita (*beat*)   Your elder brother was doing the same thing just a while ago.

Sonoko   Dai?

Doshita   Yes.

Sonoko   Oh, his finger won't bend.

Doshita   Huh?

Sonoko   The index finger of his right hand (*bending her index finger in the shape of a key*) is stuck like this. It won't stretch out.

Doshita   Oh.

Sonoko   He injured himself in junior high school.

Doshita   Oh no.

Sonoko   He should have gone to the doctor right away. But he kept it a secret at home, so it didn't return to the normal position.

Doshita   Uh-huh.

Sonoko   So sleepy . . .

Doshita   Ah please, take a nap.

Sonoko *lies face down on the desk,* **Doshita** *looks vaguely outside from the doorway.*

Sonoko   So it was a man.

Doshita   Uh?

Sonoko (*beat*)   Would it be wacky to raise my hopes?

Doshita   What are you saying?

Sonoko *doesn't answer.*

Doshita *goes to take a look at* **Sonoko**. *She seems to have fallen asleep.*

Unexpectedly, his wristwatch alarm goes off. He shuts it down in a hurry so as not to wake her up. Taking out his cell phone, he begins to write an email, but almost at once puts the phone away in his pocket. Taking a desk board, he starts to write the daily report.

Just at that moment, in mountaineering gear and shouldering a large backpack, **Koharu** *opens the entrance door and enters. Not paying any attention to* **Doshita**, *who is absorbed in writing the daily report,* **Koharu** *looks around the room and spots* **Sonoko**.

Doshita (*noticing* **Koharu**)   Oh.

Koharu *bows politely.*

Doshita (*follows suit*)   Do you want to book a taxi?

Koharu *shakes her head in silence.*

Doshita   Have you lost . . . your way?

Koharu *shakes her head and enters the office.*

Doshita   Excuse me.

Koharu   Shhh . . .

Doshita *falls silent.*

Koharu (*in a low voice*)   I'm sorry.

Doshita   No matter.

Koharu *passes by* **Doshita** *quietly, puts her backpack down and approaches* **Sonoko**.

Sitting in the dining chair next to **Sonoko**, **Koharu** *gently puts her hands around her daughter's shoulders and hugs her.*

Sonoko (*still facing down*)   . . . Oh, I feel sick . . .

Koharu *strokes* **Sonoko**'s *head.*

Sonoko   It hurts . . .

Doshita *watches in amazement.* **Koharu** *puts her cheek against* **Sonoko**'s, *while the daughter is still sleeping uncomfortably, and strokes her.*

Scene Two: The Day after Mother's Return

2.1 Inside a Taxi

The following day before 5 pm. **Daiki**'s *wife,* **Fumiko Inamura**, *is riding in the back seat of* **Maki**'s *taxi.* **Fumiko** *is checking her make-up in a hand mirror while gazing at* **Maki** *in the driver's seat.*

Fumiko   Your hair is beautiful.

Maki   What's that?

Fumiko   Your hair. Is it your own hair?

Maki   Yes, it is.

Fumiko   Last time, I went for a beauty treatment. Oh, not for my hair, but for my eyelashes. Have you ever tried it?

Maki   No, I haven't.

Fumiko   "Take the whole hog for 7500 yen." I don't like the "Take the whole hog" bit as it sounds like a free-for-all.

Maki   It does.

Fumiko   But when you put the extensions on, you look gorgeous. The kind called "premium quality mink 3D volume eyelashes" are just fluttering shojo-manga-style cute. I was thrilled. But when I got home, within an hour, my daughter poked me in the eye.

Maki   In the eye?

Fumiko   She came to give me a hug, and her finger landed right in my eye.

Maki   Ooh, that sounds painful.

Fumiko   I was rubbing my eyes because the pain was so bad, so bad. Then about 3000 yen worth of eyelashes dropped out in a lump. (*Leaning toward the driver's seat.*) Can you see? Does this stand out?

Maki   Uh, ah . . . (*Cannot turn around as she is driving.*)

Fumiko   On top of that, my daughter was looking into my eyes. What do you think she said first thing?

Maki   No idea.

Fumiko   What do you think she said?

Maki (*doesn't know what to say*)   Weeell . . .

Fumiko   Redback spider.

Maki   Uh, what?

Fumiko   Spider, it's a poisonous spider!

Maki   A poisonous spider![5]

Fumiko   She's been reading an illustrated insect guidebook my husband got her recently. So she's strangely knowledgeable. I checked redback spider and found that it has red spots in the middle of its body, and its legs are of different lengths, giving it an untidy look—just like my eye with extensions half gone. You know, kids are really observant.

Maki   Yes, that's true.

Fumiko   Nowadays, you don't give girls illustrated insect guidebooks. What was he thinking of?

Maki   I did enjoy mine.

Fumiko   You mean an illustrated insect book?

Maki   Uh-huh. I did.

Fumiko   . . . Well. What's the point of having extensions when I have no one to show them off to? My hubby probably won't even notice.

Maki   I wouldn't say that.

Fumiko   No, he won't. I wish he had the guts to say, "You're a redback spider!"

Maki   He's uncommunicative.

Fumiko   Huh?

Maki   You know, he was always a poor talker, was Dai.

Fumiko   Was he?

Maki   So even if he had something on his mind, he couldn't articulate it.

Fumiko (*beat*)   You had something to do with my husband?

Maki   Excuse me?

Fumiko   Did you two have a relationship beyond being childhood playmates?

Maki   Oh no, nothing like that.

Fumiko   Oh . . .

Maki   Not at all. (*Forcefully.*) Absolutely nothing like that at all.

Fumiko (*embarrassed*)   Excuse me.

Maki   It's OK . . .

Fumiko (*silent for a while, but starts up again*)   You don't have to be so insistent.

Maki   Huh?

Fumiko   You make it sound as if my husband wasn't popular.

Maki   Wait, that wasn't my intention.

Fumiko *sulks.*

Maki   Oh, are you going home today?

Fumiko   Huh?

Maki   I thought you were going home to your family . . . Oh no, what am I saying?!

Fumiko   I am not going home.

Maki   Oh.

Fumiko   I'm filing for divorce

Maki   Huh? Really? . . .

Fumiko   It's high time I took action.

Maki   Today?

Fumiko   Today is the day.

Maki   Oh no. Today may be impossible.

Fumiko   Why?

Maki   Oh, I don't know, but . . .

Fumiko   Why? Huh, why? What's up today?

Maki   Weeell.

Fumiko   Huh, why? Is somebody coming?

Her interrogation continues and **Maki** *is thrown into consternation yet manages to drive the taxi.*

2.2 The Inamaru Taxi Office

Around the same time, in the office. In the center of the room is **Yumi***, who is hugging* **Koharu** *tightly and having a sobbing fit. Surrounding them are* **Utagawa***,* **Susumu***, with* **Yuji** *standing uncomfortably at a distance.*

Koharu   Please, it's about time to stop crying, Yumi.

Yumi   But, but . . .

Koharu   We're too old to be crying. It's ridiculous.

Yumi   You're right. But still Koharuuu . . .

Koharu   Oh, you are such a crybaby.

Susumu   Once again, Auntie, welcome home. (*Applause.*)

Utagawa   Welcome home! (*Applause.*)

Koharu   Stop the hype. I've only just woken up. Look at this gunk (*She removes some from her eyes to show the others.*)

Utagawa   It's evening already, you know.

Yumi   I hear you arrived at sunrise.

Koharu   Yes, I did. Then I fell asleep for half a day.

Susumu   She came walking all the way from Tochigi prefecture.

Yumi   Why did you do that?

Koharu   Why indeed? Maybe I just wanted to walk.

Susumu   Auntie, I always believed you'd come back.

Koharu   Thank you. You've become a fine businessman. You, too, Uta.

Utagawa   Did you ever imagine that I would be working here?

Koharu   Um, here's one of Yu's bad boys turned into a taxi driver as good as any other.

Utagawa (*happily*)   I said, "I'm gonna be a first-rate taxi driver." Yeah that's what I said.

Yuji *nods vaguely.*

Utagawa   That's right. And I was the one that invited Moe to join.

Koharu   You all kept this company going.

Utagawa (*innocently*)   You went off to Tokyo.

Yuji (*nodding vaguely*)   Yeah.

Susumu   Your dad always said I should keep the company going until Auntie came back. He said that with the Ina of Inamura and the Maru of Marui, we were two families bonded by this company.

Koharu   I am deeply grateful for this.

Susumu (*begins to sob*)   If only . . . when my dad died . . . that's my only regret . . .

Yumi   Susumu.

Koharu   I will give thanks to brother Shin. I'll go right away to pay my respects to him.

Susumu   Never mind. Visiting the grave can be done when we calm down. First, Auntie, please share your stories with us.

Doshita *enters the office. He wants to pay his regards, but seeing that everyone is having a good time, he unobtrusively punches his time card and busies himself with other work.*

Yumi   Right. We haven't heard anything about what Koharu has been doing.

Koharu   Well, yes. After I came back to the outside world, I wandered around from place to place.

Utagawa (*delighted*)   The outside world, she says.

Yuji *continues to smile vaguely.*

Koharu   I worked at a diner in Okinawa and a dairy ranch; had a live-in job at a traditional inn; worked at a dim sum joint in Utsunomiya, then at a bar in Tokyo . . .

Yumi   Oh, I saw that.

Koharu   You're kidding. On TV?

Yumi   I saw it, I saw it. It was on late-night TV.

Doshita *looks at* **Koharu**.

Susumu   That documentary, right?

Utagawa   I saw it, too. On YouTube.

Koharu   Oh no, did you all see it?

Yumi   Me, too.

Koharu   I'm surprised you recognized me. I asked them to blur the pics.

Yumi   We could still tell.

Susumu   Um. The voice had been changed, but we could tell it was yours.

Koharu (*bashful*)   Uh-huh—

Doshita (*opens the nap-room curtain to change into his uniform*)   Oh!

Yumi (*noticing* **Doshita**)   Ah.

Doshita   Oh, excuse me. Good morning[6].

Yumi   Mr. Doshita, this . . .

Doshita   We met this morning . . .

Yumi   Oh, you've already met.

Koharu   You were the first I met, right?

Doshita   Yes. (*To* **Yuji** *in a low voice.*) Not yet? . . .

Yuji *shakes his head and looks worried.* **Doshita**, *concerned about the nap room, is encouraged by the boss to take the breathalyzer. He complies.*

Susumu   Mr. Doshita, please take the breath test, first.

Doshita   Oh, yes.

Utagawa   Did you see it?

Yuji   See what?

Utagawa   The documentary.

Yuji (*shakes his head*)   No . . .

Susumu   And then, and then? After the bar, where did you go?

Utagawa   How did you get that TV job?

Koharu   Let me see.

Yumi   Hold it. You shouldn't fire off so many questions at once.

Susumu (*to* **Daiki**)   Hi, you're back. (*Showing* **Doshita** *the test result.*) Here you are. No problem.

Daiki *has returned home from work.* **Utagawa** *happily runs up to* **Daiki**, *passing his arm around his shoulder and poking him with his elbow without any particular meaning.* **Doshita** *enters the nap room fearfully.*

Koharu   Hi, Daiki. Are you done for the day?

Daiki   No, not really.

Koharu   Aha, foreign companies are more flexible.

Susumu   Um?

Daiki *does not speak.*

Utagawa (*to* **Yuji**)   Is Fuku-chan's Appliances a foreign company?

Koharu   Uh?

Yumi   Now Koharu. What are you going to do moving forward?

Susumu   You're the one that shoots out questions.

Koharu   Moving forward?

Yumi   You're not going off somewhere, are you?

Koharu   Of course not. I'm not going anywhere anymore.

Yumi   Dearest Koharu.

Utagawa (*happily*)   So that's it. Great.

Daiki, *not sure how to respond, laughs.*

Koharu   I'm going back into the taxi business.

Yumi   As a driver?

Susumu   Really, Auntie?

Koharu   Um.

Daiki *gives a troubled laugh.*

Utagawa   Hahahahaha.

Yuji   Why are you so excited?

The telephone rings.

Susumu   Well, Auntie, take a look at my new car. It's a station wagon.

Koharu   A station wagon.

Yumi   Koharu hasn't had a proper family conversation yet. Instead of the new car, family first. (*Takes the phone call.*) *Thank you for your call. This is Inamaru Taxis.

Susumu   *That's right. Family comes first.

Daiki   I, I, I'm going to change.

Koharu   Uh-huh.

Yuji (*to* **Daiki**)   Got smokes?

Daiki   Um.

Daiki *and* **Yuji** *go out to the patio.*

Koharu (*watches* **Daiki** *and* **Yuji**) (*Beat.*)   Can I see your new car?

Susumu   Huh, you want to see it?

Koharu   Um.

Utagawa   I can drive you around.

Yumi (*putting the telephone on hold, announces*)   By the station, male customer, Mr. Mizoguchi.

Utagawa   Excuse me, some other time. (*To* **Yumi.**) In ten minutes.

Yumi (*returns to the telephone*)   In about ten minutes, *a taxi will pick you up, sir. Thank you.

Susumu *(*while leading the way*)   Since we got the station wagon, bookings by groups have increased . . .

Koharu *exits at the urging of the exuberant* **Susumu,** *and* **Utagawa** *goes into the dispatch room, talking to* **Yumi.** *Just as* **Daiki** *and* **Yuji** *are about to light cigarettes,* **Sonoko** *comes out of the Inamura house. She is dressed in a nightie with her hair hanging down slatternly, as if she has just woken up. Her brothers stop smoking.*

Sonoko   Hn.

Her brothers are silent.

Utagawa *takes the deskboard, nods at the two brothers in a thoughtful way, and exits.*
Sonoko *peeks into the washer, looking for the outfit she wore the day before.*

Sonoko   Last night, I . . .

Yuji   Uh?

Sonoko   . . . Did I throw up in my sleep?

Yuji   Yeah.

Sonoko   And my clothes?

Daiki   . . . W-w-were washed.

Sonoko   Sorry, who did?

Daiki   This morning . . .

Koharu *enters energetically. The siblings stare at her entrance. On her way to pick
up the keys,* **Koharu** *spots* **Sonoko**.

Koharu   Late morning.

Sonoko, *instinctively, raises her hand.*

Koharu   Did you sleep well?

Sonoko *nods without thinking.*

Koharu (*toward the outside*)   Key, key!

●Susumu   Thanks.

Koharu *and* **Susumu** *go out again. The siblings watch them exit in a vacant manner.*

Daiki *lights a cigarette.*

Sonoko (*beat*)   It's not a dream.

Yuji *nods and smokes* **Daiki**'*s cigarette.*

Sonoko   She's come back.

Daiki *and* **Yuji** *nod.*

*For a while, the siblings lock eyes with each other. Then they exchange looks. Then,
they burst out in laughter almost at the same time.*

The Three   Hahahahahahaha!

Daiki   Hoho hohoho! She's really come back!

The Three   Ahahahahahahaha!

Sonoko   It's exactly fifteen years.

Yuji   And she's acting just like she never leftl!

The Three   Ahahahahahahaha!

The three continue to laugh. Having changed into his uniform, **Doshita** *comes out of the nap room. For a while, he looks on in amazement. Then making some tea at the dining table, he sits down and starts writing the daily report.*

Yuji   When did you meet her?

Daiki   J-j-j-j-j-j-just as I was about to leave for work.

Sonoko   Did you talk with her?

Daiki   I, I was running late.

Sonoko   I don't remember at all.

Yuji (*to* **Sonoko**)   You were talking with her.

Sonoko   Get real!

The Three   Ahahahahahahaha!

Sonoko   I waited so long, so very long.

The Three   Hahahahaha, ha—hahaha . . .

After a long laugh, their laughter gradually breaks up. **Sonoko** *begins to cry and laugh at the same time.* **Daiki** *becomes serious after his laughter stops, and* **Yuji** *bends his head down.*

Sonoko   Ah—a . . . (*Noticing that her brothers are not laughing, she becomes anxious.*) Are you angry? Are you?

Daiki (*beat*)   No.

Sonoko   Yu, are you crying?

Yuji (*raising his face*)   No, I'm not crying.

Sonoko (*beat*)   Aha.

Yuji (*beat*)   What is it? . . .

Daiki *stands up.* **Sonoko** *grabs his arm.*

Daiki (*smiling, he tries to move away*)   Wh-what? . . .

Sonoko   Where are you going?

Daiki   To ch-ch-ch . . .

Sonoko   Huh?

Daiki   To ch-change, change.

Sonoko   Huh?

Yuji (*peeling* **Sonoko**'*s hand from* **Daiki**)   Why d'you grab him?

Sonoko *lets go. The rebound sends* **Daiki** *staggering. He returns tottering to his own room.*

Sonoko   It's OK to be happy, right?

Yuji *doesn't answer.*

Yumi (*comes out of the dispatch room*)   Where's Koharu?

Doshita   I think she's outside.

Sonoko   Isn't it?

Yuji   Don't ask me.

Sonoko *is silent.*

Yumi   I didn't take off my coat. (*Taking it off as she speaks.*)

Yuji (*beat*)   It isn't anything bad.

Sonoko (*regaining her happy mood*)   Um.

Yumi   Sono, Sono.

Sonoko   Yumi!

When **Yumi** *opens both arms wide,* **Sonoko** *runs over and hugs her.*

Yumi   Great, great.

Sonoko   Uh-huh, uh-huh.

Yumi   You were waiting for her all this time. You wanted to see her.

Sonoko   I . . .

Yumi   You don't feel it's really real, yet.

Sonoko   What should I talk about first?

Yumi   To Koharu? (*Laughs.*) That's true. there are too many things. Oh.

Agreeing with **Sonoko,** **Yumi** *tries to put her coat away and opens the curtain of the nap room. Seeing a half-naked man inside, she closes the curtain in a hurry. The man is* **Yoshinaga.** *But* **Sonoko** *has not noticed him.*

Sonoko   I'll show her my photo album.

Yumi (*the nap room is on her mind*)   Uh?

Sonoko   I was making an album all this while just in case Mom came back and I could show her.

Yumi *is silent.*

Doshita (*about to explain* **Yoshinaga**'*s presence*)   Excuse me . . .

Sonoko   Is that no good?

Yumi   Huh? Of course it's good. The photo album is a splendid idea. She will love it.

Sonoko　I'll go get it.

When **Sonoko** *is about to go, the curtain opens and* **Yoshinaga**, *half-naked, emerges wearing a slightly soiled pair of jeans. Having just woken up, he is still half-asleep and gazes around the office.*

Yoshinaga　The toilet? . . .

Sonoko　Oh. (*Points to it.*)

Yoshinaga *smiles effusively and goes into the washroom.* **Yumi**, **Sonoko**, *and* **Doshita** *watch in great surprise.*

Sonoko　A new driver?

Doshita　Oh no . . .

Sonoko　Smells of sweat . . .

Doshita　He's the dude who was asleep in the garage this morning.

Yumi　I've heard that before.

Sonoko　Oh, you have?

Doshita　Uh, but last night . . .

Sonoko　I don't remember.

Yumi　Didn't you report him to the police?

Yuji (*looking in from the patio*)　He's an acquaintance, Mom says.

Sonoko　Uh?

Yuji　He seems to be her savior. (*His eyes indicate* **Koharu**.)

Yumi　Of Koharu?

Doshita　If I remember correctly, when your mother was working at a dairy ranch in Hokkaido, he helped her. He's from Niseko.

Sonoko　Niseko.

Doshita　He heard that she was going to come back here and dropped by.

Yuji　The ranch failed and he had nowhere to go.

Yumi　He became a tramp and slept in the garage.

Doshita　I don't know how he got here, but he seems to have got lost many times. His strength gave out before he found this place.

Yumi　Even if his strength gave out, the garage is just behind this office.

Sonoko　A lover of Mom's?

Doshita　*No . . .

Yuji　*No, that couldn't be.

Sonoko   He chased after her this far.

Yuji   But still . . .

Doshita   Uh-huh, that dude . . .

The sound of running water. **Yoshinaga** *comes out of the washroom. With a somewhat cleaner face, he looks around the office. When his eyes meet those of the four before him, he smiles.* **Sonoko** *boldly stands in front of* **Yoshinaga.** **Yumi** *stands behind* **Sonoko.**

Sonoko   How do you do?

Yoshinaga *smiles and bows.*

Sonoko   I, I am Sonoko.

Yoshinaga *nods and looks at her encouragingly.*

Sonoko   I am Koharu Inamura's daughter.

Yoshinaga   Oh.

Sonoko   Nice to meet you. You are? . . .

Yoshinaga (*in broken Japanese*)   Yoshinaga.

Sonoko   Uh?

Yoshinaga (*repeats clearly*)   Yo-shi-na-ga.

Sonoko *does not answer.*

Yumi   Mr. Yoshinaga.

Yoshinaga   Um.

Yumi   What is your given name?

Yoshinaga   Ta . . . ku . . . yuki. (*Hesitates.*)

Sonoko   Huh?

Yumi   Takayuki.

Yoshinaga   Um.

Yumi   Ah, I am Shibata.

Yoshinaga   Where is Koharu?

Yuji   Outside.

Yoshinaga   Please excuse me for a moment . . .

Yumi   Oh, please, go ahead.

Yoshinaga *stands at the entrance and waves to* **Koharu,** *who is riding in the car.*

Yoshinaga   A car?

Yumi   A station wagon.

Yoshinaga   Koharu! Koharu! Hahahahaha.

He runs outside. A sharp sound of brakes suggests that he has jumped out in front of the car. **Yumi** *goes to the front door to check the situation.*

●**Koharu**   Be careful Mr. Yoshinaga . . .

Sonoko   Haha.

Yuji   Hehe.

Sonoko   He's a foreigner.

Yuji   But his name is Yoshinaga . . .

Yumi   He speaks broken Japanese.

Doshita   He was tripping over his own first name.

Sonoko   Isn't he joking?

Yuji   I agree.

Doshita   But he's been like that since this morning.

Yumi (*comes back with a serious look*)   I don't understand. How did Koharu survive through the last fifteen years.

Maki *returns. She looks tired.*

Doshita   Welcome home.

Maki *takes a deep breath.*

Yuji   You look really tired.

Maki   Not really . . .

Fumiko *enters, looking back suspiciously.*

Yumi   Oh, hallo.

Fumiko   Oh. . . (*Bows.*)

Maki   Hey, who is that half-naked man?

Sonoko   Probably some foreigner.

Maki   Uh?

Yumi   Dai is back.

Fumiko   Oh, Yuji.

Yuji   It's been a while.

Fumiko   So you're back now? Oh my, I didn't hear about it.

Yuji   Yeah, before the memorial service.

Fumiko   . . . Excuse me, I'm sorry I couldn't attend your father's memorial service.

Yuji   Not at all.

Fumiko   I suppose you have heard of our circumstances. You see, we are at present . . .

Yuji   Uh yes, I got the general picture.

Fumiko   The general picture? . . . (*Dissatisfied with this answer.*)

Yuji   I mean, I have heard it all, uh well some of it.

The telephone rings. **Yumi** *answers it.*

Sonoko   You know, is it alright for that man to be lurking around half-naked?

Yuji   I'll tell him.

Doshita   It's that dude who was in the garage.

Maki   Ah.

Fumiko   My husband is. . . (*Points to the Inamura house.*)

Yuji   Certainly.

Fumiko (*to* **Maki**)   Excuse me, thanks for your assistance.

Maki   Oh, you're welcome.

Fumiko *heads toward the Inamura house.*

Yuji (*goes outside*)   Excuse me.

Brakes screech. Everyone looks toward the entrance.

●Koharu   So sorry.

Yuji (*rushes back to the door*)   Hahahahaha.

Sonoko   What happened?

Yuji (*laughing*)   Mom almost ran over me.

Sonoko   What?

Yuji (*laughing he puts his hands to his head*)   I can't . . . after all . . . I don't get it. I still can't make sense of it. How should I take all this?

Maki   Yu?

Yuji   Huh? I don't know how Mom can drive a car like it was the normal thing to do.

Yoshinaga (*comes back in*)   Are you OK?

Yuji (*laughs*)   Shit, like who the hell are you?

Yumi (*coming out of the dispatch room*)   What's going on?

Sonoko   Umm.

Yuji   Sorry. Maybe I haven't been getting enough sleep.

Sonoko   That's it.

Yuji   Yeah.

Sonoko   Take a rest, Yu.

Yuji   Um. I'll take it easy. Take a nap and see how it goes. Um . . .

Yuji *totters over to the nap room, enters, and closes the curtain.*

Yoshinaga (*cheerfully*)   Everything alright?

Sonoko *doesn't respond.*

Yumi   Oh, uhh, Beach Park.

Doshita *stands up.*

Yumi   Woman. Mrs. Yoshida.

Doshita   Ah.

Yumi   Uh?

Doshita   Ah . . . ah, my stomach hurts. . . (*Is in pain.*)

Doshita *strokes his belly unnaturally and goes off to the washroom.* **Yumi** *is puzzled.*

Maki   Fifteen minutes.

Yumi   Can you? You've only just got back.

Maki   I can. (*Looking toward the Inamura house.*) It'll be a change of scene.

Fumiko *is standing in the entrance way of the Inamura house.*

Yumi   Isn't she going inside? (*Saying this, she returns to the telephone.*)

Maki   I'm go-ing.

Sonoko   Excuse me . . .

Yoshinaga   Hm?

Sonoko   Your clothes . . .

Yoshinaga   Ooh. (*Waves his hand dismissively.*)

Sonoko   Uh? No, you see, that's not quite, you know. . . Please wear something on top.

Yoshinaga (*smiling*)   No nothing.

Sonoko   You may say so. But . . .

Yoshinaga   They're being washed, right?

Sonoko   Uh?

Yoshinaga   You threw up.

Sonoko   Huh?

Yoshinaga   You, this morning, clothes, my bag too. (*Gestures vomiting.*)

Sonoko (*beat*)   Ohh. (*Remembers.*)

Yoshinaga (*sympathetically*)   Not to worry.

Sonoko (*beat*)   Well, in that case, I'll bring some of my brother's clothes.

Yoshinaga   Hm.

He sits on a dining chair and starts to read a newspaper. **Sonoko** *looks back at* **Yoshinaga** *while she heads for the Inamura house.* **Fumiko** *is still standing by the house. When her eyes meet* **Sonoko**'s, **Fumiko** *turns to go back to the office.*

Sonoko   Aren't you going inside?

Fumiko *doesn't speak.*

Sonoko   Should I call Dai for you?

Fumiko (*at first she declines the offer, but . . .*)   Could you please?

Sonoko goes into the Inamura house. **Fumiko** *goes back to the office and is astounded to see* **Yoshinaga**; *she sits down abruptly on the sofa. She takes out the divorce papers from her bag and spreads them conspicuously on the coffee table, frowning.* **Doshita** *comes back from the washroom, and* **Fumiko** *puts away the papers. The sound of the telephone.* **Yumi** *answers.* **Doshita** *sits down on a chair.*

Doshita   Aren't you cold?

Yoshinaga   I am. (*Reads the newspaper.*)

Doshita   Ah . . .

Yoshinaga   Why are you a taxi driver?

Doshita   Uh?

Yoshinaga   Hahaha.

Doshita   Is it strange?

Yoshinaga   You don't look like a taxi driver.

Doshita   Huh, uh, is that right.

Yoshinaga (*smiling at* **Fumiko**)   Don't you think so?

Fumiko *smiles politely and tilts her head.*

Yoshinaga   Hahaha.

Doshita   Uh, why do you say that? . . .

Yoshinaga *turns to his newspaper.*

Yumi (*over the broadcasting system*)   Beach Park, man, Mr. Akai.

Doshita   Ah, yes. I'll take it.

Through the inner window, **Yumi** *has a puzzled look. 'Is he OK?')*

Doshita   Fifteen to twenty minutes.

Doshita *stands up and starts to get ready. He is a little nervous. At that moment,* **Koharu** *returns. She meets eyes with* **Fumiko** *and bows lightly. Then she returns the car key.*

Koharu   Mr. Yoshinaga, aren't you cold?

Yoshinaga   I am cold.

Koharu   Well, how about a hot shower?

Yoshinaga   Uh-huh.

Koharu   Meanwhile, I'll get you some clothes.

Yoshinaga   Clothes are coming.

Koharu   Oh really?

Yoshinaga *stands up, smiles at* **Doshita**, *and goes to the washroom.*

Doshita   Oh, may I have the car key?

Koharu   Are you going to use it?

Yumi (*showing her face at the inner window*)   Doshita, you don't need to put yourself out.

Doshita   Uh?

Yumi   I can call the backup by wireless. As it's your first job, you don't want to come down with a stomachache.

Doshita   I feel alright now.

Yumi   Are you sure?

Koharu   Is this your first assignment?

Doshita   Uh-huh, well.

Koharu   Do your best. Don't get upset if you get landed with a snarky customer.

Doshita   Thanks. I'm going.

He exits.

Yumi   Where's Susumu?

Koharu   In the garage.

The telephone rings.

Yumi   Is he still messing about?

Koharu   No, I think I scratched it up.

Yumi   What?!

She goes back to the dispatch room. **Koharu** *approaches* **Fumiko**, *who is sitting on the sofa.*

Koharu   Are you waiting for someone?

Fumiko   Oh. (*Nods her head.*)

Koharu   Shall I call the boss?

Fumiko   No . . . I, my husband.

Koharu   Ah, he is an employee here?

Fumiko   No, the name is Inamura.

Koharu   By Inamura, you mean?

Fumiko   Daiki Inamura's . . .

Koharu   Are you his wife?

Fumiko   Uh, ah, yes.

Koharu   Oh!—Really. (*Deeply moved, takes* **Fumiko**'s *hand.*) Is that right? So you are . . .

Fumiko   Uh-huh, you know . . .

Koharu   Where did you meet Dai?

Fumiko   Excuse me?

Koharu   Where did you get to know him?

Fumiko (*beat*)   At work . . .

Koharu   At Apple Japan?

Fumiko   Huh?

Koharu   Did you meet at Apple Japan?

Fumiko (*beat*)   We met at Fuku-chan's Appliances.

Koharu   Oh really. My goodness, at Fuku-chan's? . . .

Fumiko   It's my father's company.

Koharu   Aha, you are the daughter of the president of Fuku-chan's Appliances

Fumiko   Uh, yes.

Koharu (*even more deeply moved*)   Really, what a surprise. I see, my son is married to such a wonderful young woman.

Fumiko   Not really.

Koharu   Kids!

Fumiko (*startled*)   Yes?

Koharu   Yuji told me. You have a girl named Miyo. Four years old, right?

Fumiko   Uh, yes.

Koharu   She's not here today?

Fumiko (*beat*)   No . . .

Koharu   Oh, I'd love to meet her. She must be so cute. We have a kids' room, but no kids. Were you travelling somewhere?

Yumi (*from the dispatch room in a low voice*)   Koharu!

Fumiko   . . . parated.

Koharu   What?

Fumiko   We are separated. (*Almost in tears.*)

Koharu   You're not serious, are you? Dai hasn't said anything like that. Well, I haven't talked with him yet.

Fumiko   Are you a relative?

Koharu (*beat*)   I'm . . .

Fumiko (*interrupting*)   He's having an affair.

Koharu   Dai is?

Fumiko *begins to sob.*

Koharu   Oh my goodness. My dear, my poor dear. What to do?

Fumiko (*not listening to* **Koharu**)   I've really been a good helpful wife, you know. I went against my parents and married him. They were really dead set against it.

Koharu   Of course, of course.

Fumiko   But I've tried very hard to get them to understand him, including the past.

Koharu   Uh-huh, uh-huh . . .

Daiki *comes out of the Inamura house with a change of wear for* **Yoshinaga**. *Noticing* **Fumiko**, *he comes to a halt in the patio.*

Fumiko   Instead of his deceased parents . . .

Koharu   Huh?

Fumiko   I wanted to support him as family, but . . .

Koharu Deceased parents?

Fumiko Yes.

Koharu They died? Fuku-chan's . . .?

Fumiko No, my parents are alive.

Koharu Ohh.

Fumiko His . . . um, haven't you heard?

Daiki M-m-mom.

Fumiko Daiki.

Daiki *falls silent.*

Fumiko (*beat*)   That's a horrid way of calling me.

Daiki Huh?

Fumiko Just because I bore you a baby, I don't want to be called "Mom" by you.

Daiki That's not wh—

Fumiko How did we become like this? . . .

Koharu Mom, Mom.

Fumiko Please stop that.

Koharu You misunderstand. (*Pointing at herself.*) Me. I'm the Mom.

Fumiko What?

She does not comprehend the situation. Blackout.

Scene Three: Late That Night

3.1 At the Inamaru Taxi Office

The same day, just after 11 pm. The office, restricted to partial lighting, is generally dim. The blind is closed in the dispatch room. The stifled laughter of a man and a woman comes from the nap room, and eventually the curtains are opened slightly to reveal **Utagawa**. *He looks around and makes sure there's no sign of human presence, then he goes to the kitchenette in his underwear to avoid making any loud footsteps and takes a beer from the fridge.*

●**Utagawa** No problem . . . It's OK. No one will notice it's gone.

At that moment, **Doshita** *enters, talking on his cell phone. The laughter in the nap room fades away.*

Doshita Ah, hallo. . . (*The other party has the answering service on.*) . . . (*After the ringtone, he is about to say something.*)

●**Utagawa**   Mr. Doshita?

When **Doshita** *shuts off his phone,* **Utagawa** *sticks his face out of the curtain.*

Utagawa   Are you finishing work?

Doshita   No, not yet. How about you?

Utagawa   I'm done for today.

Doshita   I was waiting at the station, but I thought I'd take a shower to wash away the drowsiness.

Utagawa   Ah, um, go ahead.

Doshita   Uh-huh.

Utagawa   It's free.

Doshita   Um.

Sensitive to what may be in the depth of the nap room, **Doshita** *takes off his uniform, hangs it on a chair, and goes to the washroom.* **Utagawa** *goes back into the nap room. At that moment,* **Koharu** *comes by from the Inamura house. She is hugging the photo album.* **Doshita** *and* **Koharu** *exchange smiles and bows.*

Koharu   Good job!

She sits on a dining chair and opens the album.

Koharu   Yumi. (*Toward the dispatch room.*) Why not take a break? (*As there is no response, she goes to the dispatch room and opens it.*) Yumi?

●**Yumi**   Over here, over here. Uh?

She comes out of the nap room. The curtain is closed tight. Her hair and clothes are slightly awry.

Koharu   Sorry, were you asleep?

Yumi   All that sitting gets to my back. So I lay down for a bit.

Koharu   Come on, take a look at this.

Yumi   Uh? (*Still worried about the nap room.*) Oh, Sono's album.

Koharu   Strange, isn't it. All this happened when I was absent, but it feels familiar. Want some coffee?

Yumi   Oh, I would.

Fumiko *in tears comes dashing out of the Inamura house and passes by them.* **Daiki** *looks out from the house, does not pursue her, and shuts the door.*

Koharu   Fumiko?

Yumi   What's the commotion about?

Koharu   She's dead, they say.

Yumi   Huh?

Koharu   Me.

Yumi   That's ridiculous.

Koharu   I'm going to investigate.

Chasing after **Fumiko**, **Koharu** *exits.* **Yumi** *confirms that* **Koharu** *has left completely, and then takes a big breath.*

Yumi   Come out of there. Hurry.

Utagawa (*sticking his face out*)   That was a close call.

Yumi   Go home. I can't stand this kinda thing. I don't like being here.

Utagawa   We didn't get found out.

Yumi   Thrills like this, I do not need. For my age group, this kinda thing is bad for the heart.

Utagawa   There's no other way. Your mother-in-law is at your place.

Yumi   Not only that, but also Tsugumi.

Utagawa (*beat*)   They all think I'm with Tsugumi.

Yumi   That could never happen.

Utagawa   What?

Yumi   You aren't a good match for Tsugumi.

Utagawa   Hey, that's rude to you and to me, ain't it?

Another segment. **Fumiko** *comes running and stops at a lamppost a short distance from the house to catch her breath.*

Yumi   We will have to tell Koharu eventually.

Utagawa   About us? No, that's . . .

Yumi   I used to share everything with her. Are you ashamed of me?

Utagawa   Uh-uh, that's not what I mean, but . . .

Yumi   Anyway for now, go home.

Utagawa   You're gonna chase me out?

Yumi   If you don't like it, rent a house.

Utagawa   Kissy-kissy—?

Yumi   Secrecy—is my policy—Go, go.

Utagawa   You remind me of my mother.

Utagawa *leaves disgruntled. At the same time, A young man,* **Junya Tomokuni,** *comes near* **Fumiko** *crouching by the lamppost. He is looking around in search of someone.*

Fumiko (*noticing* **Tomokuni,** *gets up*)   Ohh!

Tomokuni *is silent. He notices but ignores her.*

Fumiko   What is it?

Tomokuni   Huh? No, nothing.

Fumiko *discourages him.*

Tomokuni   Getting cold, huh?

Fumiko   Uh? . . . (*She wraps her arms around her body in a defensive stance.*) Ohh!

She walks backwards bit-by-bit. Giving a low cry, she runs off. At around the same time at the office, **Koharu** *returns to* **Yumi,** *who is looking at the photo album.*

Yumi   Where's Fumiko?

Koharu   I chased after her, but she high-tailed it and disappeared.

Yumi   Don't worry about her. This happens a few times a month.

Koharu   Oh really?

Yumi   Uh-huh, all the time.

Koharu   But Dai is having an affair . . .

Yumi   Do you really think so? That missus acts up whenever she feels neglected. . . . Want some coffee?

By **Tomokuni** *is* **Hinako Kimata,** *a young woman in a flashy outfit, walking leisurely along.*

Koharu *sits next to* **Yumi** *and looks at the album with her.*

Hinako   Come on, aren't we going yet?

Tomokuni   Um, wait a bit longer.

Hinako   Let's go—I'm tired.

Tomokuni   OK, I get it. (*But still keeps phoning.*)

Hinako   It is frigging c-o-l-d!

Tomokuni   Keep your voice low.

Somewhere in the Inamaru office, a cell phone is vibrating.

Koharu   Hn? (*Looks around.*)

Yumi   A cell phone's ringing. (*Looks around.*)

Hinako (*to* **Tomokuni**)   Come on, treat me to a fondant chocolat at a family restaurant.

Koharu   Yours, Yumi?

Yumi (*shakes her head*)   How 'bout you, Koharu?

Koharu   I don't have one.

Tomokuni   The dude won't answer.

Hinako   Fon-dant—

Tomokuni   I know already! (*Closes his phone.*)

Yumi   It stopped.

Tomokuni *and* **Hinako** *look around carefully and exit.*

Koharu (*looking at the album*)   Yumi, what is this snapshot of?

Yumi   Which one?

Koharu   It says, "The day I felt bitter over a green-tea snow cone"?

Yumi   Oh—that? Sono and I went on a little trip together.

Koharu   Just the two of you?

Yumi   Uh-huh.

Koharu   Where did you go? It looks pretty dreary to me.

Yumi   You don't recognize it?

Koharu   Uh?

Yumi   Maybe you should hear this one from Sono.

Koharu   What? Where could it be?

She removes the photo from the album and looks at it up close then at arm's length.

Koharu   I hear Sonoko quit being a hairdresser.

Yumi   She didn't really quit. She never became one.

Koharu   Huh?

Yumi   She didn't finish vocational school.

Koharu   Working at a bar isn't really her thing.

Yumi   She's making it work for her.

Koharu (*beat*)   How is your husband, Yumi? How you getting along?

Yumi   He's gone, gone.

Koharu   He's dead?

Yumi   He died long ago. Almost ten years ago.

Koharu   Is that right.

Yumi   He kept me waiting for a long time and as soon as he finally entered me into his family register, he popped off, leaving his own mom behind. Well, Tsugumi did escape ending up as his mistress's daughter.

Yumi   What about his mom?

Yumi   She has Alzheimer's. But she's in no hurry to die.

Koharu   You loathe her.

Yumi   I do, really. It's a lie that understanding deepens with the years. Year by year, I hate her more. Change my helper. Stay home during the day. Take me to the hospital. The list goes on.

Doshita *comes back from taking a shower in the washroom. The two women are absorbed in their conversation and do not notice him. He gets dressed where they cannot see him.*

Yumi   I don't mind so much being treated like a housekeeper. What I can't forgive is how she still calls me her son's lover, even when she's senile.

Koharu   That's awful.

Yumi   Really, I sometimes want to kill her. I want to strangle her while she's asleep.

Doshita *perks up his ears at* **Yumi**'s *statement.*

Koharu   Don't talk like that.

Yumi   I do. Seriously. At times like that, I think if I had your courage, I'd tackle that bitch head on.

Koharu   Courage?

Yumi   You see, Koharu, however many years pass, I can't get myself to blame you. You protected your kids. You sacrificed yourself to save them from that crazy, abusive husband. Your courage is something . . .

Koharu (*shouts angrily*)   That wasn't carriage?!

Yumi   What?

Koharu (*restating herself*)   I meant, that wasn't courage.

Yumi   It's OK.

Koharu   Um, you shouldn't say such things.

Yumi   . . . Sorry.

Koharu   It wasn't . . . Um.

Yumi   . . . Then what could it be?

Koharu   Huh?

Yumi   If it wasn't.

Koharu *is speechless.*

Fumiko *comes back crying. Again she runs in front of the two women and ends up crashing into* **Doshita.** *She goes out to the patio and bangs on the front door of the house.*

Fumiko   Dai, Dai, why don't you come chasing after me?

Doshita (*to* **Koharu**)   What is the matter?

Fumiko (*to the front door*)   It's always like this. You don't talk about what's important. You lied about your mother's death, but then when I leave, you don't look for me. You have no interest in bringing me back. (*Collapses.*)

Koharu   This happens a few times a month?

Fumiko   I was almost assaulted!

Yumi   Good thing there are no neighbors nearby.

Fumiko   Why don't you come out? Dai. Are you trying to keep me shut out? (*Wails.*)

Yumi   The missus must be really into Korean melodrama.

Koharu *laughs.* **Fumiko** *glares.* **Koharu** *falls silent.*

Fumiko   Dai?

The door knob of the front door turns, indicating the presence of someone about to come out. **Fumiko,** *with hope rising in her, looks up only to see* **Yoshinaga** *come out.*

Yoshinaga   What's going on?

Fumiko   Uh.

Koharu   Mr. Yoshinaga. (*Waves for him to move on.*)

Yoshinaga   Hn?

From behind **Yoshinaga** *comes* **Daiki.** *Bowing his head several times as if in apology, he moves* **Yoshinaga** *out of the way and stands in front of* **Fumiko.** **Yoshinaga,** *beckoned by* **Koharu,** *enters the office. The others besides* **Yoshinaga** *try not to watch the married couple.*

Daiki *takes* **Fumiko**'s *hand and tries to raise her up.* **Fumiko** *brushes away his hand.*

Daiki   L-let's go back inside. (*Reaches out to her.*)

Fumiko   No . . . (*Pushing his hand away.*)

Daiki *falls silent.*

Fumiko   You don't want me to return to you.

Daiki N-n-n-n-n-no, that's not it.

Fumiko I know. You didn't marry me because you liked me. You just wanted the family business and little Miyo.

Daiki Not true. I . . .

Fumiko What?

Daiki Th-th-th-that's not it. Y-y-y-y-y-you . . .

Fumiko Y-y-y-y-y-you . . . what?

Daiki Y-you, you.

Fumiko You stutter because you have nothing to say.

Daiki That's enough.

Fumiko Huh?

Daiki Do what you like.

Fumiko See, now you don't stutter. When you're angry, you don't stutter. That's when you can dump whatever you don't want.

Daiki *falls silent.*

Fumiko When someone hits the mark, y-y-you start stuttering. What is it with you?

Koharu *throws* monaka *wafers at* **Fumiko**.

Fumiko Ouch, what?

Koharu You bitch. (*Throws* monaka *wafers.*) Y-y-y-y-you . . . How dare you make fun of Dai.

Fumiko Now look.

Doshita Ms. Koharu. (*Stops* **Koharu**.)

Fumiko Mrs. Inamura. Hey stop! That's dangerous.

Yumi Koharu.

Koharu You bitch. You bitch bride.

Doshita You bitch bride?

Yumi Koharu.

Koharu (*to* **Fumiko**) Your Dai's wife, aren't you? If you're his wife . . .

Yoshinaga (*picking up the* monaka) If you're his wife . . .

Koharu If you're his wife . . . (*Overwhelmed.*)

●**Yuji** I'll die. Seriously.

●**Sonoko** See. Just take one more step, then another step.

Yuji *enters with* **Sonoko** *on his back.*

Yuji   Oh shit, I'm exhausted. Seriously.

Sonoko   So I said to bring the car.

Yuji   I can't drive . . . (*Sensing everyone's eyes on him.*) What're you all looking at?

Yumi   Nothing.

Sonoko   I'm back.

Yoshinaga (*cheerfully*)   Welcome home.

Sonoko   When I asked for a ride home, Yuji came. On foot!

Yuji   If you hadn't been drinking, you could've driven home yourself . . .

Sonoko   I don't have a driver's license, either.

Daiki   Let's go inside.

Fumiko *does not respond.*

Daiki   L-let's go back.

Fumiko, *heaving with sobs, goes back to the Inamura house led by* **Daiki**.

Yuji   What's up?

Sonoko   Ohh, again?

Yumi   Um.

Yuji   Huh?

Sonoko   Fumiko's persecution complex. Her take-care-of-me-or-else syndrome.

Koharu   Excuse me.

Doshita   Nothing.

Koharu   I'll go wash my face.

Yumi (*goes with her*)   Sorry. When I talked about courage, I pissed you off, didn't I?

Koharu   I guess I'm on the list of "favorite mothers-in-law to kill" now.

Yuji *goes to the Inamura house to check out the situation there, while* **Yumi** *and* **Koharu** *enter the washroom.* **Yoshinaga** *is looking at the photo album.* **Doshita** *takes his cell phone from his uniform pocket and hurries out of the office.*

Doshita   Excuse me, I'll go out for a bit.

Yumi   Gotcha.

Sonoko (*to* **Yoshinaga**)   Excuse me . . . but could you not look at that without permission?

Yoshinaga   Whose is this?

Sonoko   It's mine.

Yoshinaga   Oh it's yours? So cute. (*Showing the picture* **Koharu** *had removed.*)

Sonoko   Hey, why did you take it off?

Yoshinaga   It came off.

Sonoko   Um, is it cute?

Yoshinaga   So cute—How old were you?

Sonoko   Twenty-six or twenty-seven?

Yoshinaga   So cute, just like a Chow-Chow.

Sonoko *falls silent.*

Yoshinaga   Why are you crying in the photo?

Sonoko   I'm not.

Yoshinaga   You are.

Sonoko   No, I'm not.

Yoshinaga   Yes, you are. Your face is a bit swollen.

Sonoko   That is how I am! Are you being rude? (*Even as she speaks, she realizes.*) Oh—

Yoshinaga   See? . . .

Sonoko   Right. I am surprised you noticed.

Yoshinaga (*sympathetically*)   College examination hell?

Sonoko   Uh-uh, oh, you know such expressions.

Yoshinaga   Why?

Sonoko   Why, why?

Yoshinaga   It's a school, isn't it?

Sonoko   This? (*Shaking her head.*) I was in front of the prison.

Yoshinaga   Prison.

Sonoko   The day Mom was released, Yumi and I went to meet her.

Yoshinaga   Ohh.

Sonoko   But we didn't know the time of her release, so we waited from early morning. It was a really hot day and I came down with anemia.

Yoshinaga   So you cried?

Sonoko   Uh-uh. Yumi took me to a café to have snow cones.

Yoshinaga   So you cried?

Sonoko   Wait! So while I was eating the snow cone, Mom was released.

Yoshinaga (*cautiously*)   So you cried?

Sonoko   So I cried. (*Puts the photo back.*) Because I thought I'd never see her again.

Yoshinaga   Have you ever kept a cow?

Sonoko   Why do you change the subject?!

Yoshinaga   A cow.

Sonoko   NO! It's not normal.

Yoshinaga   I cried when I was stomped on by a cow.

Sonoko   Oh yeah . . . That must have hurt.

Yoshinaga   It didn't hurt. If it hurts, you don't cry.

Sonoko   Your way of talking is a bit off.

Yoshinaga   Ababa[7] . . . you can't move. If a cow stomps on you, you cannot move your leg. Because it'll break.

Sonoko   Why didn't you move the cow out of the way?

Yoshinaga   It wouldn't move!

Sonoko   Ohh, get on with it.

Yoshinaga   I couldn't move. So I cried. I cried all night.

Sonoko   Hm.

The telephone rings. **Sonoko** *heads to the dispatch room.*

Sonoko   Look, your cow has nothing to do with my mom.

Yoshinaga   Hahaha.

Sonoko   Hallo, Inamaru Taxis* . . . Oh, could you wait a mo. Yumi, it's Tsugumi.

Yoshinaga   *If it hurt . . . it hurts . . .? Even if hurts?

Yumi (*returns*)   Sorry, sorry. (*Enters the dispatch room.*)

Sonoko   Give it back.

Yuji *has returned. He is standing in the patio.*

Yoshinaga   Even it hurt? . . . don't cry even if it hurt?

Sonoko (*nods*)   "Even if it hurts, you don't cry."

Yoshinaga   Oh yeah, that feels right, thanks.

When **Sonoko** *goes to the washroom, she sees* **Koharu** *wiping her face and hugs her from behind.*

Koharu   What's up?

Sonoko   . . . Let's go have some snow cones some time.

Koharu   What? It's still too cold, you know.

Yoshinaga *attempts to go back to the Inamura house.*

Yuji   Better not go now.

Yoshinaga *thinks a little but opens the front door.*

Yuji   So I said . . .

Sonoko   I'm going to the convenience store. (*Moves away from* **Koharu** *and changes her shoes in the patio.*)

Koharu   It's very late.

Yoshinaga   I'll go, too.

Koharu   Oh, could you go with her?

Sonoko   It's OK.

Yoshinaga   You can back out, you know.

Sonoko   That's what I'm trying to do.

Sonoko *and* **Yoshinaga** *go outside and almost bump into* **Doshita**, *who is busy with his cell phone.*

Doshita   Oh, excuse me.

Yuji   Is that dude right in his head?

Koharu   Yoshinaga? He's OK.

Yuji *goes out to check on* **Sonoko** *and* **Yoshinaga**. **Doshita**, *left alone, starts calling someone. From his inner pocket, he takes out an envelope stashed with banknotes and looks at it.*

Doshita (*into the voicemail*)   Hallo, it's me, Dad. How are you doing? I don't have anything in particular to discuss . . . Oh, I watched the midnight comedy program on TV you mentioned last time. It was interesting. I don't remember what it was called.

Yumi (*coming out*)   Koharu, oh.

Doshita (*bowing lightly to* **Yumi** *and putting his envelope away*)   So, anyway, I'll send you some this week.

Koharu   What's up?

Doshita   Call me when you feel like it. See you.

Yumi   May I go out for a while? Tsugumi's granny has disappeared again.

Koharu   Go home. We are doing fine, here.

Yumi   Sorry. What a nuisance. Where is she off to at this late hour? Mr. Doshita, I am very sorry to bother you.

Doshita   No problem.

Yumi   So very sorry. I'll see you tomorrow.

She prepares noisily to leave and hurries out. **Doshita** *hurries to go, too.*

Doshita   I'll go back to the train station.

Koharu   Do you have children?

Doshita   Huh? Oh yes.

Koharu   I overheard. Excuse me.

Doshita   I have a son. He's seventeen years old.

Koharu   Seventeen. That sounds like time to become independent from the parents.

Doshita   Oh no, it's not about that. You see, we hardly ever meet.

Koharu   Oh?

Doshita   I got a divorce when he was very young.

Koharu   Ohh.

Doshita   But you see, this year he suddenly contacted me. He wanted to prepare for college entrance exams and wanted advice.

Koharu   You must have been happy.

Doshita   Oh, of course. The other day, we met up for the first time in a long time. I was afraid of what to do if I couldn't recognize him at the meeting place.

Koharu   Did you recognize each other?

Doshita   Uh-huh, he looks exactly like me.

Koharu (*laughs*)   Aha.

Doshita (*laughs*)   I was so happy. All we did that night was have dinner together, but I felt we had shared something solid and unchanging.

Koharu *is silent.*

Yuji *returns. He passes between the two and goes out to the patio.*

Doshita   Excuse me for blabbering.

Koharu   Not at all. I can understand very well. In my case, I was prepared to see everything changed when I came back. But the company remained, and, see, Yu's porn mags are still here (*taking out a copy from the under the bunk beds in the nap room*).

Doshita (*sensitive to* **Yuji**'s *presence*)   Better not touch them.

Koharu (*bursting with joy*)   He must have forgotten about them, I'm sure.

Doshita   . . .You must have had to screw up some courage, right? To come back here.

Koharu   . . . I'd decided on that, to begin with.

Doshita (*nodding*)   You'll have lots to share with them.

Koharu   Um.

Doshita   I envy you.

He lowers his head and heads out to work. **Koharu** *opens the glass doors to the patio.*

Koharu   Is Dai all right?

Cocking his head, **Yuji** *looks quizzically at* **Koharu**.

Koharu   Yu, Yu. (*Beckoning to him.*) Let's look at the photos, together.

Yuji *shakes his head.*

Koharu   Come on.

Yuji *does not reply. Hapless, he comes inside, but doesn't approach the photos.*

Koharu   When were you in Tokyo?

Yuji   Uh? Until recently.

Koharu   So, when did you leave?

Yuji   I was nineteen or twenty.

Koharu   Why did you come back?

Yuji *falls silent.*

Koharu   Tell me. I don't know anything about you all.

Yuji   . . . It was just a passing thought.

Koharu   Just a passing thought?

Yuji   Dai said he was going to get a divorce . . .

Koharu   Ahh, Fuku-chan's Appliances. I thought he was working at a foreign company.

Yuji (*laughs*)   That's hardly likely?

Koharu   Uh?

Yuji   After that kind of incident, usually an applicant wouldn't reach the preliminary offer of employment. If Dai hadn't met his wife at his part-time work, he still wouldn't know what to do.

Koharu   . . . Really?

Yuji   Sis went to vocational school, but couldn't stand the gossip and quit. I got bullied at school and left town.

Koharu   Um . . .

Yuji   Neither Dai's finger nor stutter will heal. Sis is hanging out with alcoholics like Dad. None of us three know how to drive a car. Even now, on Dad's memorial day, we get harassed by phone. That's how it is.

Koharu *is silent.*

Yuji   How about you, Mom?

Koharu   Uh?

Yuji   What were you doing then?

Koharu   I was . . .

Yuji   . . . Sorry, I gotta sleep. (*Heads toward the nap room.*)

Koharu   Um.

Yuji   Mom, you should . . .

Koharu   I am not wrong.

Yuji *falls silent.*

Koharu   I am not wrong.

Koharu *goes back to the house.* **Yuji** *flips the pages of the album, but quickly closes it. Blackout.*

Scene Four: One Month Later (April)

4.1 Inside a Taxi

Hinako's Voice   Could you change the tune?

Utagawa's Voice   Uh?

Hinako's Voice   The tune!

Utagawa's Voice   Yes, miss!

Before noon on an April day, **Utagawa** *is driving the taxi. In the back seats,* **Hinako** *is playing with her cell phone; next to her,* **Tomokuni,** *with one leg on the back of the driver's seat, is sunken slovenly into the padded seating.*

Tomokuni   Go right.

Hinako   Next, your turn, Tomo.

Tomokuni   Go right. Go right at the corner we just passed.

Utagawa   Yes, uh?

Tomokuni   What the fuck are you doing, you shit? (*Kicks the seat.*)

Utagawa   Excuse me.

Hinako   It's your turn, Tomo. (*Thrusts the video game they've been playing in front of him.*)

Tomokuni   I'm going to get car sick. How many times have you fucking turned at the wrong street?

Utagawa   Excuse me, but you see . . .

Tomokuni   You new?

Hinako   It's your turn, Tomo! You said we'd take turns.

Tomokuni   Keep your voice down.

Hinako   If you don't take your turn, we can't advance.

Tomokuni   OK, I just have to knock down the bird?

Hinako   No, we use the birds to knock down the pigs in this game.

Tomokuni   What kinda world is that?

Utagawa   Excuse me—

Tomokuni   I'm really getting car sick. Seriously.

Utagawa   I'm sorry.

Hinako   Hurry, I want to call a friend.

Tomokuni   Go ahead and call.

Hinako   I want to clear the game.

Utagawa   Excuse me—

Tomokuni   Shut the fuck up. Whaddaya want?

Utagawa   Which way should I turn?

Tomokuni   Think it out yourself.

Utagawa   But . . .

Hinako   Ahh, wrong, wrong.

Utagawa   You still haven't told me the destination.

Tomokuni   Huh?

Utagawa   The destination. You just said to get started . . .

Hinako   Give it here.

Tomokuni   Is that real? I haven't told you?

Utagawa   No, you haven't.

Tomokuni   Then of course you can't tell how to get there. Hahaha.

Utagawa (*smiling*)   That's right.

Hinako   Give it here.

Tomokuni   You really piss me off. Why didn't you ask me earlier?

Utagawa   Uh?

Tomokuni   Usually the driver asks for the destination.

Utagawa   Excuse me.

Hinako   Crap, zero skills.

Utagawa   Where are you going?

Tomokuni   Your place.

Utagawa   Excuse me?

Tomokuni   Inamaru Taxi Office.

Utagawa   Wait a moment, sir.

Tomokuni   Go.

Utagawa   Please give me a break.

Tomokuni   Never mind, just git going, will ya!

Utagawa   Come on, sir.

Tomokuni   You got a problem with the destination?

Utagawa   I haven't done anything wrong.

Tomokuni   Hurry up and go, I tell ya.

Hinako   Tomo, shut up.

Tomokuni   Sorry.

Hinako   Oh—Look. Cherry blossoms.

Hinako *and* **Tomokuni** *look outside at the view.*

4.2 Inamaru Taxi Office

Fumiko *is hanging her futon out to dry in the patio, where the cherry blossoms are dancing here and there. She seems to be in a good mood and occasionally peeks inside the office, but when* **Maki** *comes in,* **Fumiko** *returns to the Inamura house, looking offended.*

Maki, *dressed in a helmeted biker outfit, doesn't notice* **Fumiko** *and walks over, taking off her helmet with a cool, dashing gesture, and shakes out her hair. Placing* *her feet on the chair, she takes lipstick from her pocket and applies it, smiling contentedly into the hand mirror.* **Hinako** *watches her from the washroom door.*

Hinako   That's cool . . .

Maki (*startled, she straightens up*)   Oh, oh.

Hinako   Are you a biker?

Maki   Huh?

Hinako   Are you bikers having a meeting?

Maki   No . . .

Hinako   You look like you came from Texas.

Maki (*embarrassed*)   Excuse me. I thought nobody was around.

Hinako   Is this the Texas of Japan?

Maki   What are you saying? Please stop.

Hinako   Well. it seems like . . . (*Looks over at the entrance.*)

Unnoticed, **Yoshinaga** *is standing in the doorway. Dressed like a cowboy, he is drinking milk.*

Maki   Oh.

Yoshinaga   I was waiting for you.

Maki   Uh?

Hinako   Are you going off on a date?

Maki   Not really. He has nothing to do with me. What do you mean you were waiting for me?

Hinako   Umm. His outfit isn't for dating, I guess.

Susumu *comes running in with a convenience store bag.* **Hinako** *begins to read a magazine.*

Susumu   Sorry to have kept you waiting. Mr. Yoshinaga, please don't walk around in that outfit.

Maki   Boss . . .

Susumu   Moe, you came to help out? So glad you're here.

Maki   Who is that girl?

Susumu   Oh, I don't know really. I bought some stomach medicine. Just wait a moment.

Hinako   Oh, thank you. (*Continues to read the magazine.*)

Susumu   Please hurry up and get changed.

Maki   Uh?

Susumu   We are getting swamped.

Maki   This is my day off.

Susumu   Huh, you're not here to help? Come on. We have cherry blossom viewers and shoppers at the new department store . . .

Maki   Today is opening day?

Susumu   . . . and the news reporters on Auntie Koharu . . .

The telephone rings. **Yoshinaga** *goes into the dispatch room.*

Susumu   Anyways, we're swamped with work.

Yoshinaga   Hallo, hallo, this is Inamaru Taxis . . .

Maki   Is it alright to let that dude take the calls.

Susumu   Well. we're short of staff. Yumi is AWOL on this day of days.

Yoshinaga (*using the wireless system*)   Airport, male, Mr. Yamashita.

Susumu   He's surprisingly capable, too.

Hinako (*going toward the washroom*)   Tomo, are you all right?

Susumu   Just when we are busy, we're saddled with complaints

Maki   Complaints?

Susumu   At any rate, help out now. You'll get overtime pay.

Maki   No way. I have a private matter to take care of.

Susumu   What's that?

Yuji *comes out of the nap room. He has just woken up.*

Yuji   Oh, you're here already.

Maki   Ah, um.

Yuji   Sorry, you wanna go right away?

Susumu   What?! We are swamped with work and you two are going on a date?

Yuji   I don't know if it's a date, more like going for a drive.

Susumu   This is how it is. The boss and the foreigner are working their butts off, but the young ones are going for a drive! You drive everyday, don'tcha?

Maki   Shut up. I deserve an occasional day off.

Hinako   Are you going on a date?

Maki Not really . . .

Susumu I can't take this anymore. I really cannot take this anymore. (*Grumble, grumble.*)

Yuji (*beat*) I'll go change. (*Goes to the nap room.*)

Maki Do you think this is strange?

Hinako Uh?

Maki . . . Is this outfit not good enough for a date?

Hinako Not for a date. (*Smiles cutely.*)

Maki (*beat*) Aaaah.

She goes running off to the Inamura house.

Maki (*knocks on the door of the Inamura house*) Sono, halloo. May I?

Susumu Now what?

Sleepy **Daiki** *emerges from the nap room.* **Maki** *goes into the house.*

Susumu What's this. Dai? You sleep over here as well?

Daiki, *without speaking, heads for the washroom.*

Yuji (*sticks his head out of the nap room and in a low voice . . .*) Living apart but still together

Susumu Uh?

Yuji Now that Fumiko is back, Dai is uncomfortable.

Daiki *tries to open the washroom door, but it will not open.*

Susumu But recently, the missus has been in a good mood.

Yuji That's what upsets him.

Daiki *knocks on the washroom door.*

Susumu (*to Daiki*) A customer is in there. (*To* **Yuji**.) Is it because of that magazine?

Yuji Right, right, a fucked-up love story about a couple. On top of that, today . . .

Susumu (*looking at the Inamura house*) Ohh, it's started.

Yuji Already?

The washroom door opens and **Utagawa** *emerges.*

Utagawa (*to Daiki*) Oh, I'm sorry, sorry. (*To* **Susumu**.) Boss—

Susumu They've arrived . . . (*Changing his tone.*) Yes, yes. Just a moment, just a moment.

Following **Utagawa** *is a sickly-faced* **Tomokuni**. **Daiki** *goes inside the washroom, and* **Yuji** *goes back to the nap room.*

Utagawa   He has recovered

Susumu   I apologize for the driver's unruly conduct.

Utagawa   I didn't intend any harm.

Tomokuni   You know, I was knocking out the pigs with the birds . . .

Susumu   Ex-excuse me?

Hinako   You OK, Tomo?

Susumu   Oh, please take a seat. Uh, there's stomach medicine.

It is just an over-the-counter drug.

Hinako   Do you want to put your head in my lap?

Tomokuni   Later on.

Utagawa   Then, I'll go back on duty. (*Heads toward the entrance.*)

Susumu (*chases after him and in a low voice . . .*)   Hey, where do you think you're going?

Utagawa   I haven't done anything wrong.

Susumu   But he registered a complaint.

Utagawa   That has nothing to do with me. I was just ordered to bring him here.

Tomokuni (*with his head on* **Hinako**'s *lap*)   That game was seriously addictive.

Hinako   It totally grabs your attention, right?

Yoshinaga   Utagawa.

Utagawa   Yes, uh?

Yoshinaga   Where's Yumi?

Utagawa   Wh-why are you asking me?

Susumu   She's AWOL.

Utagawa   AWOL?

Yoshinaga   Try calling her.

Utagawa   No, why should I have to do that . . .

Tomokuni   Hey.

Susumu   Oh, yes, I'll be with you in a moment.

Utagawa   I'll call her then.

Yoshinaga   Yeah, you do that.

Utagawa   Um . . . What's got into you? Talking like you own this joint.

He exits. **Susumu** *reluctantly sits in front of* **Tomokuni**. **Maki** *in a flashy bar girl dress comes out of the house.*

Tomokuni   Now . . .

Susumu   Is it too cold for you?

Tomokuni   Huh?

Maki *catches* **Hinako**'*s eye from across the patio and vaguely displays her dress.*

Hinako *cocks her head and looks puzzled.*

Susumu   The taxi can get hot or cold.

Tomokuni   Not really . . . It seemed all right.

Susumu   I see.

Maki *makes a face indicating, "Is this dress no good?"* **Hinako** *gestures, "Wrong."* **Maki** *goes back into the house.* **Hinako** *begins to read a magazine in front of the table.*

Tomokuni   To begin with . . .

Susumu (*tense*)   Yes.

Tomokuni   My inner ears bother me.

Susumu   Ah, is that so.

Tomokuni   Even when I was a kid, you know that galleon ride at amusement parks? . . .

Susumu   Oh, the Viking ride.

Tomokuni   The Viking ride. That made me feel seasick . . .

Susumu   I see, I see.

Tomokuni   . . . One swing and I'm going "blargh."

Susumu   With one swing.

Tomokuni   Yeah. (*Stops talking.*)

Susumu   I see . . . (*He doesn't know how to develop the conversation.*)

Tomokuni   So, you see, here . . .

Hinako   Yeah, this.

Susumu   What is it?

Hinako   Is this article about this taxi company?

Susumu   Let me see, oh no, it isn't.

Hinako   But there's a post-it on it.

Susumu   . . . Excuse me, I don't know who left it here.

Hinako   "The murderer became a Madonna. A mother's dream is granted after fifteen years." . . . A murderer?

Susumu   That can be explained.

Tomokuni   Oh I know about it.

Susumu   Huh?

Tomokuni   It's a sad story, right.

Susumu   Oh, is it?

Hinako   I don't know about it.

Tomokuni   Well, I can understand how the mother felt.

Susumu   I'm glad you think so.

Hinako   Come on, what's this about?

Tomokuni   You'll understand when you read it. Well, I heard about it from someone else. But it's not a thing anyone can easily do. Well, it may be against the law. But she put her own life on the line.

Daiki *comes out of the washroom.*

Hinako   Oh, that's the guy in the magazine.

Tomokuni   Huh?

Susumu   He's the son.

Hinako   "The eldest son and his devoted wife took care of the family."

Tomokuni   That's it.

Daiki *grabs a cigarette and hurries outside as if trying to escape.* **Yuji** *shows his face from the nap room and chases after* **Daiki**.

Tomokuni   Maybe, your company is raking in the cash from this news.

Susumu   . . . Indeed, we do well.

Tomokuni   Yeah, it's an inspiring story.

Hinako   I'm so hungry!

Tomokuni   Just hold it there. So about your family's . . .

Susumu   Snacks. I'll bring something to munch on.

Tomokuni   No, thank you.

Hinako   Yeah!

Susumu   No need to hold back. I think we have some *monaka* wafers.

He runs off to the house.

Tomokuni   I don't know why but it's so effing hard to get my message across to these people.

Hinako   Yikes, this auntie is a murderer. She sure doesn't look like one.

Yoshinaga   She really doesn't look like one, right.

Hinako   Um.

Yoshinaga   How do I look?

Tomokuni   What?

Yoshinaga   How do I look?

Tomokuni   How the fuck should I know?

Hinako   Reggae?

Yoshinaga   Ah!

Hinako   Did I get it right?

Yoshinaga   I'm a cowboy.

Hinako   What! (*Laughs together with* **Yoshinaga**.)

Tomokuni   Don't talk to him.

Doshita *enters the office.*

Doshita   Good morning.

Tomokuni   Ah.

Yoshinaga   We were waiting for you.

Doshita   I heard the boss needed more staff. I'll change right away.

Yoshinaga   Um.

Doshita   Where's the boss?

Yoshinaga   Looking for snacks.

Doshita   Um, are you really so busy? (*He starts to go toward the nap room.*)

Tomokuni   Big bro.

Doshita   Huh?

Tomokuni *stands up and bows his head.*

Doshita   Tomo.

Yoshinaga   Oh, brothers?

Doshita   Ah, well . . .

Yoshinaga (*looks at* **Tomokuni** *straight and long*)   You look alike. You look alike. (*Pointing at the two.*) You both have big, horsey faces.

Tomokuni (*loses it*)   Who the fuck are ya?

Doshita   Tomo.

The telephone rings, and **Yoshinaga** *goes to the dispatch room. Just after that,* **Susumu** *comes back from the house with* monaka *wafers. Following behind him is* **Maki** *in a different flashy outfit.*

Yoshinaga (*answers the phone*)   Yes, Yes, this is Inamaru.

Susumu   Mr. Doshita, you've come to save us.

Maki *gazes at* **Hinako** *with a "What about this dress?" look.*

Hinako   Totally wrong.

Maki   Totally wrong! (*Is devastated.*)

Susumu (*is worried about the patio*)   Sorry to have to call on you when you are on the night shift.

Doshita   No problem.

Hinako   Is it OK? (*Stands and goes toward* **Maki**.)

Tomokuni   Hey, where are you going?

Susumu   Oh, the snack?

Tomokuni   Never mind.

Susumu   Huh? But . . .

Doshita   Oh, uh, this is uh . . .

Tomokuni   I'm his kid brother.

Susumu   Mr. Doshita's? Oh really? You don't say . . .

Hinako   Come on, big sis, your sense of fashion is totally off the wall.

Hinako *goes with* **Maki** *into the Inamura house.*

Doshita   I'll be back right away. So, please let me go. (*Tries to exit.*)

Susumu   Aah.

Tomokuni   But where's Hinako gone?

Doshita   Uh?

Susumu   Oh, if you like, please make yourselves comfortable here.

Doshita   Well, but . . .

Susumu It's alright, it's alright. Your young lady seems to have made friends with our employee, Maki.

Doshita . . . Excuse me, let me talk with . . .

Susumu Of course, of course.

Staring at **Tomokuni**, **Susumu** *enters the dispatch room, where* **Yoshinaga** *is working.*

Tomokuni Are you working today, too?

Doshita . . . What was that about being my younger brother?

Tomokuni Hehe.

Doshita (*kicking him lightly with his tip of his foot*)   I told you not to come to my place of work, stupid.

Tomokuni I apologize. It just turned out that way.

Susumu *and* **Yoshinaga** *observe* **Doshita** *from through the open blind.*

Doshita (*beat*)   Can't do it here.

Tomokuni What?

Doshita Not here. I can't make a delivery here. (*Looks at the dispatch room.*)

Susumu *and* **Yoshinaga** *close the blind.*

Tomokuni Oh no, it's not about that. The system is going to be changed.

Doshita Huh?

Tomokuni About the delivery, that is. Up till now, I had to be the go-between, so it became double trouble.

Doshita How's it gonna be?

Tomokuni Yes. First, there'll be a booking for a taxi by Akazawa, Aoyama, or someone with a name of color. That's just as before. When you pick up the customer at the destination, he'll deliberately forget the goods.

Doshita . . . You take another customer and get him to deliver the goods.

Tomokuni Yes, we'll have him picked up at a set place or have him book a taxi.

Doshita That takes some trouble, doesn't it?

Tomokuni It means that the deliveries will get bigger.

Utagawa *returns. He has a strangely meek look on his face.*

Doshita Good morning.

Utagawa Where's the boss?

Doshita *points to the wireless room.*

Utagawa   I'll take a break then.

Susumu (*comes charging out*)   Huh? No, you can't yet.

Yoshinaga   Going to Yumi's?

Utagawa   Who said anyone was going there? (*Nonetheless, he leaves.*)

Susumu   Wait, wait, wait. Why are you all walking out on me?

Yoshinaga, **Utagawa**, *and* **Susumu** *all exit.*

Doshita   Go home.

Tomokuni   Uh?

Doshita   This kinda thing, we can talk over the phone, right?

Tomokuni   I wanted to see you at work.

Doshita   Oh?

Tomokuni   You know . . . remember that movie, *Taxi Driver*?

Doshita   De Niro?

Tomokuni   De Niro. I was a fan of his, and watched his movies when I was young. But he's turned out to be more of a boring dude than I thought. Kinda lost, you know. I wouldn't want to be like that. If anything, I'd rather be like that weapons merchant who appears half way through. The one with the flashy tie and always looking super-cool. I wanted to become like that one.

Doshita   You are like that now. Come on, I'm ready to go. (*Stands up.*)

Tomokuni   Big bro, are you really gonna stick with this job?

Doshita   Huh?

Tomokuni   You've moved all the way to this lousy place.

Doshita   It's convenient here—being close to the harbor and the airport.

Tomokuni   So what I mean is—you went to the trouble of cutting ties with the gang, but now you are back to being the mule.

Doshita *is silent.*

Hinako *returns.*

Tomokuni   If you need cash, I can lend you some. You were able to make do on your own as a fisherman, right?

Hinako   Tomo—

Tomokuni   To be frank, I really don't like this. You were the personage who sat in the back of the car. You were the one that kicked the back of the seat I was driving in. Don't you feel bad, being used by me?

Doshita   I'm not alone anymore.

Tomokuni   Is it your son? He hadn't seen you in more than ten years and then suddenly wants cash. To me, he's just a fucking freeloader . . .

Doshita *grabs* **Tomokuni** *in a neck hold.*

Hinako   Tomo?

Tomokuni   I apologize. I apologize.

The front door of the Inamura house opens and **Fumiko** *and* **Sonoko** *come out in high spirits.* **Doshita** *lets go of* **Tomokuni** *in a hurry.*

Fumiko   How about watering the flowers?

Sonoko   Sounds great. The office will be in the background like scenery.

Fumiko   Should we have the office staff in the picture?

Sonoko   Yu!

Yuji *returns, and* **Sonoko** *runs up to him.* **Fumiko** *is sensitive to the presence of* **Tomokuni** *and others.*

Hinako   You wanna go?

Tomokuni   Ah . . .

Doshita   He wants to go.

Tomokuni   Big bro—

Doshita *walks away from* **Tomokuni** *and goes to the nap room to change.*

Sonoko   Where's Dai?

Yuji   In a taxi

Sonoko   What?

Yuji   He doesn't have anywhere to be, so he's resting in a taxi.

Sonoko   Humph.

Tomokuni   What were you up to?

Sonoko (*dispirited*)   It didn't come to anything.

Tomokuni   Huh?

Sonoko   Yo, Yu. Could you come with me? It won't take long. (*Guides him to the patio.*)

Utagawa *comes back led by* **Susumu**. *Meanwhile, in the parking lot,* **Yoshinaga** *approaches* **Daiki***, who is sleeping in the driver's seat, and gives him some milk to drink.*

Utagawa   I'm just going to check on her.

Susumu   Why do you need to check on Yumi? (*Harshly.*) On top of AWOL, you're going to take a break without permission.

Utagawa   That's not . . . Hey, was there any message from Yumi?

Sonoko   Uh-uh. You haven't got any?

Utagawa   None.

Sonoko   Call Tsugumi.

Utagawa   I don't know her number.

Sonoko   That's a lie.

Susumu   You don't need to hide it.

Utagawa   I'm serious.

Yuji (*to* **Sonoko**)   What is it?

Sonoko   You know, the reporters are here now, right?

Yuji   I know.

Hinako (*to* **Tomokuni**)   Yeah. I saw the TV crew at the house!

Sonoko *is silent.*

Hinako   Because there's a murderer?

Tomokuni   Thank you—

Hinako   Yo, the TV.

Tomokuni   Big bro . . . (*As there is no reply, he turns to the others.*) Thanks, 'bye.

Susumu   Sorry we couldn't help you out.

Utagawa   Not at all. (*Bows.*)

Tomokuni   Bye now, De Niro.

Utagawa   Oh, thank you.

Tomokuni   I'm not praising you.

Hinako   She was cute, you know . . .

Tomokuni   What were you doing?

●**Hinako**   Being fashion coordinator.

●**Tomokuni**   Huh?

●**Hinako**   It didn't get anywhere, though.

Tomokuni *and* **Hinako** *exit.*

Susumu   That's Doshita's kid brother.

Yuji   Really.

Fumiko   Sonoko. (*Beckons to her.*)

Sonoko   Ah, yes. And about the TV . . .

Susumu (*explaining to* **Utagawa**)   It's a news item on Auntie.

Sonoko   It's from a small local channel. They want the family to be present.

Yuji   What? No way.

Sonoko   It's not a nasty program. The producer is the same as for that documentary Mom was in long ago. He's going to interview Mom briefly.

Yuji   Why?

Sonoko   Fumiko is appearing, too.

Fumiko *waves.*

Yuji   Haven't you learnt the hard way with that magazine?

Sonoko   Why? They did a good job.

Yuji   Where? We've been exposed to public humiliation.

Sonoko   What are you saying? The public has changed their view of us.

Susumu   That is true. Yes.

Yuji   Dai would absolutely hate it.

Sonoko   But Mom wouldn't be misunderstood, right?

Yuji   Misunderstood?

Sonoko *falls silent.*

Yuji   It's not a misunderstanding.

Sonoko (*beat*)   If Dai doesn't want to, you alone would be fine.

Yuji   I have to go out. Got stuff to do.

Maki *comes out of the house. She has changed back into her first outfit.*

Maki   Auntie is calling for you.

Fumiko   I'll go ahead. (*Goes into the house.*)

Sonoko   Please.

Yuji   Let's go.

Maki   I'm OK here. You go by yourself.

Yuji (*beat*)   No, I really don't want to hang around. (*He heads for the door.*)

Sonoko   Yuji.

Yuji *tries to leave, but at that moment,* **Yumi** *arrives and bumps into him at the doorway. She wobbles.*

Yuji   Oh, sorry. Yumi, I'm sorry, sorry.

Yumi   Never mind. Oh, I'm sorry. I wasn't paying attention.

Susumu   Yumi, What happened today? You didn't even message me.

Yumi (*beat*)   I'm sorry. Today, I'd like to have the day off.

Susumu   But you're here.

Yumi   I know . . . but you see . . .

Utagawa   Has something happened?

Yumi   . . . Uta . . . (*Crying, she clings to him.*)

Susumu   Huh? Huh?

Utagawa   Just now, I was thinking of going to check you out . . .

Yumi   I killed her.

Utagawa   What?

Yumi (*beat*)   I killed my mother-in-law.

Hanging onto **Utagawa**, **Yumi** *cries.* **Doshita** *shows his face from the nap room. They all stand aghast.*

Scene Five: Several Days Later

Several days later. **Doshita** *in mourning is sitting alone on a dining chair. On the table, there is a jacket and a paper bag with a gift in thanks for a funeral offering. At that moment,* **Koharu** *comes back by the front door from the memorial ceremony.* **Doshita** *welcomes her back and sprinkles purifying salt lightly over her. The two then sit down in silence.*

Koharu   Mr. Doshita, I thought you had left long ago.

Doshita   I have work to do.

Koharu   Work?

Doshita   Uh, well, as we had a business holiday due to the vigil, I thought I should do some car maintenance.

Koharu   I can help.

Doshita   Uh-uh, please take it easy. You must be tired.

Koharu   . . . Afterwards, I'll see how Yumi is doing.

Doshita   Please do.

Koharu   Why on earth? . . .

Doshita   Huh?

Koharu   Yumi's mother-in-law. Why did she go to such a place?

Doshita   The riverbed?

Yoshinaga *comes out of the house.*

Koharu (*nods*)   But it was already happening many months ago. Yumi was always going home to search for her.

Yoshinaga   I'm back. There's food.

Koharu   Um. At night, she'd go out aimlessly to various different places, Yumi said.

Doshita   She did.

Koharu   Yumi felt responsible because she hadn't been paying attention . . .

Doshita   She and her daughter searched all night, they say.

Koharu   Exactly. No one would search that kind of a place. It's almost as if she didn't want to be found.

Yoshinaga   It's the same with cats.

Doshita   That's a bit . . .

Yoshinaga   She was looking for a place to die. She was a wild animal, too.

Doshita   She wasn't a wild thing. That's not very nice of you.

Koharu   I'm going to change.

Yoshinaga   You were like her, too?

Koharu   . . . Yes, I was.

She goes into the house.

Yoshinaga   Do you want something to eat? There's food.

Doshita   It's all right. I have work to do.

Yoshinaga   Is it a puncture? Hahaha. You can fix it in a jiffy.

Doshita   . . . You sure are cheerful all the time.

Yoshinaga   Huh, I cry, too!

Doshita   . . . Yes, yes, I am sure you cry at times, too. Oh, by the way . . .

Yoshinaga   Hn?

Doshita   Mr. Yoshinaga, what kind of person are you?

Yoshinaga   I'm a Japanese!

Doshita   . . That's not what I meant. When you first arrived here, you were saying that you were Koharu's savior.

Yoshinaga   Ahh, yeah

Doshita   What are you to her?

Yoshinaga   The cow bore a calf.

Doshita   . . . Uh, I don't follow.

Yoshinaga   Koharu came to my place, right? In Niseko!

Doshita   The dairy farm, you mean. Uh, did I make you angry?

Yoshinaga   She was almost dying at that time.

Doshita   The cow was?

Yoshinaga   Koharu was!

Doshita   Huh?

Yoshinaga   Every day, every day, she said she'd die and she'd jump into the hay.

Doshita   Into the hay?

Yoshinaga   The hay . . . from? From above the hay? Huh?

Doshita   Never mind the grammar.

Yoshinaga   Out of prison, she came to my place, she jumped from . . . above the high hay. Thud. She was shouting, "I'll die, I'll die." But from some point, she got better.

Doshita   Why?

Sonoko *returns. She is dressed for the memorial service.*

Yoshinaga   The cow gave birth! (*Stands up and goes to the kitchenette.*)

Sonoko   Wow, what a surprise

Yoshinaga   Koharu pulled it out by the legs!

Doshita   Ohh, you mean the calf.

Yoshinaga   I cried! (*Sprinkling table salt on* **Sonoko**.)

Sonoko   Wait, uh, what are you talking about?

Doshita   How Koharu helped the cow give birth.

Yoshinaga   That's it!

Sonoko   Why are you so angry?

Utagawa, Susumu, *and* **Maki** *return and* **Yoshinaga** *sprinkles table salt on them one after another.*

Susumu   Th-thanks. Thanks. The kind that doesn't have MSG in it would be better, tho . . .

Utagawa   Ahh, I'm done in . . .

Maki   You could have stayed over there.

Utagawa   We have to fix the cars.

Sonoko   Sorry.

Maki   All eight of them?

Susumu   Um.

Utagawa   Do we have tires?

Maki   This morning we used some for the station wagon. So, there may not be enough.

Susumu   Oh no, the expense.

Utagawa   Shit. Who the fuck did it? Seriously.

Yoshinaga (*to* **Utagawa**)   Did you?

Utagawa   This is not the time for making jokes like that.

Yoshinaga *sticks his lower lip out.*

Sonoko   Yoshi, where's Mom?

With his lower lip still sticking out, **Yoshinaga** *points to the house.*

Maki   Well, let's use up what's left in the garage.

Doshita   You're right.

Susumu   I can get supplies tomorrow for what's lacking today.

Utagawa   Hn—

Everyone stands up.

Maki   Aren't you going to change?

Utagawa   When we finish, I'll go back.

Doshita   I'll stay as I am, too.

Sonoko   I am really sorry about this.

Maki   You don't have to apologize, Sono. (*To* **Utagawa**.) Wanna change?

Utagawa   Well, no point in complaining. Let's get it done quick, quick, quick.

Susumu   Thanks a bunch.

Utagawa *exits.* **Doshita***'s cell phone on the table starts to vibrate. When* **Doshita** *returns to pick it up, the vibration stops. Looking at the call register, he smiles inadvertently.*

Doshita   Hal—. . . oh.

Susumu   Hn?

Doshita   The line went dead.

●**Utagawa**   Mr. Doshita.

Doshita   Yes. (*He hesitates, but turns to go outside.*)

Maki   It's alright. Go ahead and call.

Doshita   No, it's OK . . . I can call later when I got time.

Doshita *goes outside.* **Maki** *enters the nap room.*

Yoshinaga   Sonoko.

Sonoko   . . . hn?

Yoshinaga   Can you cheer up?

Sonoko   Uh?

Yoshinaga   Good cheer.

Sonoko   How?

Yoshinaga   Can you cut my hair?

Sonoko   What?

Yoshinaga *shakes his hair.*

Sonoko   Sure thing.

Yoshinaga *and* **Sonoko** *go toward the patio. He waits by the stools.* **Koharu** *emerges having changed her outfit.*

Koharu   Hi, you're back.

Sonoko   I'll get the haircutting shears. (*To* **Koharu**.) Yep, I'm back.

Koharu   What are you doing?

Sonoko   I'm going to cut Yoshi's hair. (*She goes into the house.*)

Koharu   Really? Is that OK?

Yoshinaga *sticks his lower lip out.*

Susumu   Oh, I'm back.

Koharu   Oh Susumu, you're back here, too?

Susumu   Yeah, well.

Koharu (*noticing the baggage on the table*)   Everyone else, too? You could take today off, you know.

Susumu   . . . You see, Auntie.

Koharu   Hn?

Susumu   I don't know how to say this. It's difficult to say, but . . .

●**Maki** You don't need to tell her.

Susumu It's strange to keep it a secret, right?

Koharu ... What is it?

Susumu You see, all of our taxis have punctures.

Koharu What?

Susumu Last night, because of the vigil, no one was here until late at night, you see. The staffers were all at Yumi's place.

Koharu Um.

Susumu During that time, someone was up to mischief. Maybe not mischief, more like harassment.

Koharu Harassment.

Susumu This was pasted on the windshield of the station wagon.

He shows her a page torn out of a magazine from their office shelf. Ugly slurs are written on it in red felt pen.

Koharu Ohh.

Susumu This morning, I noticed it when I got in the station wagon.

Koharu (*beat*) Is it my fault?

Susumu It's not your fault, Auntie. You know, really Auntie, it's not your fault . . . But maybe you should go easy on the magazine articles and TV program appearances.

Koharu *nods.*

Susumu Of course, we'll be more careful from now on. Like today, I had Yoshinaga stay here. I'll make sure someone is always around . . .

Koharu Uh-huh, Thank you.

Sonoko *comes back.*

Sonoko Ready?

Yoshinaga Um.

Susumu It's really bad. There are people who do things like this. Some idiot somewhere.

Sonoko (*sensing the atmosphere in the office*) Are you talking about the taxis?

Yoshinaga Um.

Koharu I'll work on the tires.

Susumu No, no. It's OK.

Koharu But . . .

Susumu   Auntie, you go to Yumi's place, please.

Koharu *falls silent.*

Susumu *goes to the dispatch room.* **Maki** *comes out of the nap room having changed into work clothes.*

Maki   Don't worry about it.

Koharu   Did they all know about it?

Maki *doesn't answer.*

Koharu   My kids as well?

Maki   Well, it happened before the memorial service.

Koharu (*cheerfully*)   I am sorry you had to worry about all that.

Yoshinaga   You gonna cut my hair or not?!

Sonoko   I will cut your hair. I will, I will.

Yoshinaga   Hurry up.

Doshita *comes back. He takes off his workman's gloves and is about to pick up his cell phone.*

Doshita (*bashfully*)   Oh, do you mind if I make a phone call after all?

Maki   Go ahead.

She heads out. At that moment, **Daiki** *hurries in, almost bumps into her, but agilely avoids her. Following* **Daiki** *enters* **Fumiko** *in tears. After her comes* **Yuji.** **Daiki** *crosses the patio and enters the house.*

Maki   What's the matter? (*With a doubtful look, she exits.*)

Fumiko   Dai, wait for me.

Yuji *says nothing.* **Fumiko***, getting attention, smiles evasively.*

Sonoko   Fighting again?

Yuji   No, this time is . . .

Fumiko (*in a silly manner*)   I'm sorry.

Yuji   Even I think this time is problematic.

Fumiko   I . . .

Maki *comes back from the house.*

Daiki (*violently pushing* **Maki** *away*)   Get outa the way.

Sonoko   That's dangerous.

Koharu   Dai?

Dai *stands in front of the wilting* **Fumiko**, *spreads out on the table the divorce papers he brought from his room, seizes a ballpoint pen from a pen holder, and starts to sign it. Feeling the tension in the air,* **Susumu** *looks on from the dispatch room.*

Fumiko   Dai.

Daiki   I'm signing this, so wait.

Susumu   Huh, are you filing for divorce?

Fumiko   Please wait.

Daiki   *You* wait! Then you can g-g-g-go around and show it to everybody

He takes a magazine from nearby and throws it.

Koharu   Hey . . .

Sonoko   What did she do?

Fumiko   I . . .

Yuji   During the funeral, she handed out that magazine to the local attendees.

Susumu   This?

Fumiko   . . . I wanted them to understand about this family.

Koharu   What?

Fumiko   About my husband.

Yuji   It's none of their business.

Susumu   Fumiko, you do things like that and our taxi business gets harassed all the more.

Fumiko   But my parents said that reading that article helped them understand the troubles that Dai suffered. The company staff said the same.

Daiki *slams the table as hard as he can.*

Fumiko   Oh no.

Sonoko   Cut it out.

Fumiko   I didn't mean to go around talking about my mother-in-law just for kicks.

Koharu   Um.

Daiki (*filling in the divorce papers*)   It-it's not just that. You went around t-t-telling people that I st-st-ststst-stuttered and had a crooked f-finger.

Fumiko   That was . . .

Daiki   You were b-b-boasting that you'd heal them!

Fumiko *falls silent.*

Daiki (*laughs*)   If it were so s-simple, both would have healed long ago. O-on top of that, you are shaming M-miyo, our daughter, in public. Bring on the s-seal.

Susumu   Huh?

Daiki   The seal.

He completes the form and presses **Susumu** *to pass him the seal that is nearby.*

Maki *having caught wind of the commotion, is looking in from the front entrance.*

Susumu   Oh, but . . .

Daiki *stamps the form with all his might and thrusts the divorce papers at* **Fumiko**.

Susumu *and* **Daiki** *speak almost in unison.*

Susumu   I'm afraid self-inking stamps are not considered legal . . .

Daiki   There you are!

Koharu   Dai. Don't do that.

Daiki   There you are!

Fumiko   You don't like a devoted wife, right? (*She crushes the form in her hand.*) No one knows how I feel. Right?

Daiki   You . . . (*Tries to get it back.*)

Fumiko   Is it wrong to believe that I'm needed? Yeah that's it. You can't forgive anyone. (*Tearing up the papers.*) Your father, your mother, or me or yourself.

Daiki   Fumiko! (*He tries to take the form away from her.*)

Fumiko   You're so closed in, small-minded, hateful, and just so negative!

Daiki *slaps* **Fumiko** *on the cheek.*

Koharu   Daiki!

Daiki   Aaaaargh.

He howls and turns violent. He throws and kicks things. **Doshita** *and* **Yuji** *hurriedly intervene.*

Susumu   Stop, stop. Dai, let's calm down.

Daiki   Aaargh . . .

Koharu   Daiki! You—Do you realize what you are doing?

Daiki *is silent.*

Koharu   Doing what you did. You, like this. You are just . . .

Daiki   Like D-Dad?

Koharu   Yes!

Daiki   So what! If I'm like Dad, would you k-kill me, Mom?

Koharu   Daiki!

Daiki   Mom, you're a-amazing. Are you gonna kill your g-good-for-nothing son? You are a-always so amazing. Me and the rest of us are always going in the wrong direction.

Koharu *is dumbfounded. She turns her back to* **Daiki**, *goes into the nap room, and closes the curtain.*

Doshita   Ms. Koharu.

Susumu   Auntie.

Sonoko   Really . . . (*Hits* **Daiki**.) Why this? Why do you blame Mom? You're wrong. Her solution was right.

Yuji   . . . Big sis, you oversimplify.

Daiki   She's st-stupid.

Sonoko   Is that wrong? I was happy he disappeared . . . I wanted to kill him.

Maki (*interrupts*)   Sono.

Yuji   . . . But there's a price we've had to pay.

Sonoko   Come on, let it go. She's back. Let it go!

Doshita   Ms. Koharu, Ms. Koharu, are you all right?

Susumu   It's better to leave her alone.

Doshita   But she may get desperate and . . .

Sonoko   Uh?

Doshita   She may feel hounded and . . .

Yoshinaga   . . . jump from the hay?

Doshita   . . . (*Worried.*) Ms. Koharu.

Susumu   Auntie!

He runs to the nap room and opens the curtain. Revealed is **Koharu** *sitting on a chair reading a porn mag. Silence.*

Yuji   . . . What the hell are you reading?!

Koharu   A porn mag.

Fumiko   Uh?

Continuing to read the porn mag, **Koharu** *strides out into the office.*

Susumu   . . . (*Somehow he feels overwhelmed.*) What? Uh, what is this?

Koharu   This is a porn mag. In the middle of my second son's late but first adolescent rebellion, behind my crying daughter and daughter-in-law, soon after Yumi's mother-in-law's funeral, Mom was reading porn her son hid under the bunk-beds.

Susumu   What's more, it looks ancient.

Koharu   It's Yu's porn.

Yuji   Hey, cut that out!

Koharu   How about it, Dai? Is Mom so amazing? Ignoring your pain, leaving you all for fifteen years, Mom is reading the porn mag Yuji hid in 9th grade.

Yuji   Stop repeating that.

Koharu   I'm asking you if Mom is really amazing.

Daiki *is silent.*

Yoshinaga (*as if answering the question*)   She is not amazing?

Koharu   Of course!

Silence . . . **Doshita**'s *cell phone vibrates.* **Koharu** *goes back to her porn mag.*

Susumu   . . . A phone call?

Doshita   Oh, excuse me. It's from my son . . . Excuse me while I . . .

Hanging his head in embarrassment, **Doshita** *exits to answer it. An irritated* **Utagawa** *shows his face.*

Utagawa   Hey, what's going on?

Susumu   Nothing.

Utagawa   Isn't anyone coming?

Susumu   I am, I am.

Yuji   I'm coming, too.

Susumu, **Maki**, *and* **Yuji** *exit.* **Fumiko** *collects the torn pieces of the divorce papers and unsteadily heads for the house.* **Koharu** *enthusiastically reads the porn mag.*

Daiki *attempts to leave the office.*

Sonoko   Why don't you chase after her? Just for once

Daiki *says nothing.*

Sonoko   She's walking really slowly.

Fumiko *walks very slowly in silence.*

Sonoko   Very soon, she will look back at you with puppy eyes full of contrition.

Fumiko *looks back with puppy eyes.* **Daiki** *says nothing.*

Sonoko   Fumiko was happy as she thought that there was something she could do. I can understand that.

Daiki *says nothing.*

Sonoko   You married out of love, right?

Koharu (*reading the porn mag*)   That's right. That's right.

Sonoko   Mom, (*Pushing the porn away.*) It's distracting.

Koharu, *sensitive to* **Sonoko***'s wishes, shifts the angle of the magazine and continues to read. Blackout.*

Scene Six: That Night

6.1 The Car Park

Doshita *on the phone comes walking by.*

Doshita   I understand. Well, then . . .

Ending the phone call, he goes off walking with drooping shoulders.

6.2 At the Inamaru Taxi Office

The same day at midnight. A lively countdown from ten can be heard. The voices belong to **Sonoko**, **Yumi**, *and* **Yoshinaga**. **Yumi** *covers her eyes with her hands.*

Yoshinaga *holds a hand mirror and has his eyes closed tight. When the countdown reaches zero,* **Sonoko** *whips off the haircutting cape from* **Yoshinaga***'s head, neck, and shoulders. He now has a shaved head.*

Yoshinaga   Woweeee—

Yumi *and* **Sonoko** *burst out in laughter. Hearing the voices,* **Susumu** *shows his face at the entrance and laughs out loud.*

Yoshinaga   A bonze head!

Sonoko   I'm sorry. So very sorry.

Yoshinaga   Ah-hah! (*Checks his hair in the mirror.*)

Yumi   You look like a sentimental ballad singer.

Yoshinaga   All gone.

Sonoko   Sorry. I didn't go to a hairdressing school.

Yoshinaga   It's over the top—

He walks around excitedly. Hearing the noise, **Yuji**, **Maki**, *and* **Utagawa** *look in from the entrance and laugh out loud.* **Yoshinaga** *is the center of the whirlpool of laughter.*

Daiki *and* **Fumiko** *also open the front door of the house, look out, laugh, and go back inside.*

Sonoko   Yoshi, Yoshi, wait.

Yoshinaga   You're a hairdresser, right?

Sonoko   No, I'm not.

Yumi   My stomach, my stomach is hurting.

Yuji (*looking at* **Yoshinaga**)   He's crying, you know.

Sonoko   What? You're kidding.

Maki   He's really crying!

Yoshinaga   It's the night the cow stomped on me—!

Utagawa   What does that mean?

Susumu (*laughing out loud*)   Yo, Auntie, Auntie, take a look, take a look.

Susumu *opens the nap room curtain to find* **Koharu** *still reading the same porn mag. The others turn sour.*

Yuji   How long is she gonna read that thing!

Maki (*whispering*)   What time is it now?

Susumu (*whispering*)   She doesn't know how to back out.

Utagawa (*whispering*)   Is there so much to read in porn?

Sonoko   Yoshi—I'll brush off the loose hair. Come over here.

Yoshinaga   Oh, bother.

Sonoko *and* **Yoshinaga** *go out to the patio. The others scatter, too.* **Utagawa** *approaches* **Yumi**.

Yumi   I'm glad I came over here.

Utagawa   Are you feeling better?

Yumi   Yes, yes.

Yumi   Umm. Ah, that was so funny . . . (*She wipes her tears.*)

Utagawa   Is it something to cry over?

Yumi   Um . . . Hehehe.

Utagawa *strokes* **Yumi**'s *head.*

Yumi   Hehe. Oh really, I don't know, but it's funny.

Koharu *says nothing.*

Utagawa   It's not funny.

Yumi   Have to get back.

Utagawa (*to the others outside*)   Is it OK to finish up now?

Maki   No problem. (*Comes back.*) It's time to clean up.

She goes into the washroom.

Utagawa   Why don't you stay for a bit?

Yumi (*shakes her head*)   Tsugumi is waiting.

Utagawa   I'll drive you home.

Yumi   . . . Do you realize that the neighborhood rumor mill is grinding away over you?

Utagawa   A boy toy?

Yumi   Hehe.

Utagawa   Let them talk.

Yumi   Are you OK with that?

Utagawa   I'm hardly a boy toy.

Yumi   . . . Thanks.

Utagawa   Let's go then.

Yumi   Koharu, I'll be pushing on then.

Koharu   Are you leaving already?

Yumi   Well, you're into your "reading."

Koharu   Oh . . . (*Throws the mag onto the table.*)

Yumi   It's OK. I'm coming tomorrow anyway.

Koharu   You can come back to work when you've regained your peace of mind.

Yumi   No, without my mother-in-law, there's nothing to do.

Koharu   . . . Then, let's have tea together.

Yumi   Yes, let's. I have lots to gripe over. The relatives are really a nasty bunch.

Utagawa   Ready to go.

Yumi   Yes, yes. Then, see you tomorrow.

Sonoko   See you tomorrow.

Maki   Take it easy now. Take care.

Yumi   Thank you.

Koharu   Yumi.

Yumi   Um?

Koharu   . . . It's not your fault, Yumi.

Yumi   . . . I thought I'd feel much better when she died.

Koharu   Um.

Yumi   I hated her.

Koharu (*beat*)   Um.

Yumi   'Night.

Utagawa   Good night—

Yumi *and* **Utagawa** *walk together.* **Maki** *looks out from the washroom to say goodbye.*

Yumi   What about supper?

Utagawa   I'm hungry.

Yumi   Would you like to come over for a meal?

Utagawa   Eek! Tsugumi doesn't like me, you know.

●Susumu   Thanks for everything.

As **Koharu** *heads for the washroom, she smiles at* **Maki**, *who has come out.* **Maki** *now sits on a dining chair and rests. She casually picks up* **Koharu**'s *porn mag and gazes at it.*

Sonoko   Oh, are you beginning to like it? (*Brushing away the cut-off hair.*)

Yoshinaga (*looking at himself in the mirror*)   This is . . . a transition period.

Sonoko   Huh?

Yoshinaga   For me.

Sonoko   Sometimes you use a difficult word. Where are you from?

Yoshinaga   I am Japanese!

Sonoko (*laughing*)   Do you cry in a transition period?

Yoshinaga   Um.

Sonoko   Like when the cow stomped on you?

Yoshinaga   Right. The cow fell asleep, so I was stomped on all night.

Sonoko   Um.

Yoshinaga   I waited for the night to end.

Sonoko   Uh-huh.

Yoshinaga   While I waited . . . I thought that when the cow moved off, I would start.

Sonoko   Oh really, and what happened?

Yoshinaga   Then, I came here.

Sonoko   Uh? So this happened recently.

Yoshinaga   Umm.

Sonoko   Your transition period.

Unnoticed, **Yuji** *has returned, and he doesn't see* **Maki** *reading the porn mag with enthusiasm.*

Yuji   Hi, thanks.

Maki   Hi, thank you—(*Taken by surprise, she tosses the mag into the nap room.*)

Yuji *falls silent.*

Sonoko   Hi, thanks for everything.

Yuji   Where is Doshita?

Maki (*tilting her head*)   He's gone off somewhere.

Sonoko   I recalled my vocational school days and felt happy.

Yoshinaga   Hey, come on, cut off more.

Sonoko   There's nothing left to cut.

Yoshinaga   Become a hairdresser! (*Goes into the house.*)

Sonoko *doesn't answer.*

Maki (*looking at* **Yoshinaga**)   You're looking good, you're looking good.

Yoshinaga   How are the taxis?

Maki   After we replaced the punctured tires with the spare ones, we were able to revive half of them.

Yoshinaga   My head feels so good.

Maki   Are you listening?

Yoshinaga *goes outside.* **Maki** *also tries to go outside.* **Sonoko** *is cleaning up the cut-off hair when* **Daiki** *comes out. After him, follows* **Fumiko**, *looking around. She hangs on to* **Sonoko** *and talks to her in a low voice.*

Sonoko   Have you calmed down?

Fumiko   Yes. (*Heads back.*) I'll go ahead and rest.

Daiki   Um.

Yuji   Aren't you going home?

Maki   I'll clean the garage a little more.

●**Yoshinaga**   I feel so refreshed!

Susumu   Be quiet. (*Showing his face.*) I'm going now. Tomorrow, work will start early.

Maki   Um.

Susumu (*getting his own belongings*)   Where's the key?

Yuji   I'll take care of lock-up.

Susumu   Don't turn off the lights. They stay on to prevent mischief. (*Looking around.*) Is Auntie Koharu OK?

Yuji *nods.*

Susumu   Get along together, alright? Oh, I didn't mean you two.

Maki   I know that.

Susumu   Good night—

He goes home.

Maki   How about you?

Yuji   What should I do? I'm not sleepy.

Maki   We could go on the drive we talked about before?

Yuji   Now? Uh, you have the stamina for it?

Maki   Do you know what my job is?

Yoshinaga (*showing his face*)   I'll go.

Maki   This doesn't concern you. So what do you want to do?

She goes outside. **Koharu** *comes back from the washroom and exchanges glances with* **Yuji***.*

Yuji   I won't go today.

Maki   . . . Um.

She goes outside. **Yuji** *and* **Koharu** *sit side by side.* **Sonoko** *and* **Daiki** *also enter the office.* **Koharu** *serves tea to her children.*

Koharu   Where's Fumiko?

Daiki   . . . Um.

Koharu   Aha.

Yuji   Huh? You understood just from his "um"?

Koharu   Not really.

Daiki   It's O-O-O-OK. OK.

Sonoko *pokes* **Daiki**.

Daiki   Sorry . . . s-sorry.

Koharu   It's all right.

Yuji   Have you finished with the porn mag?

Koharu   . . . I've read it before.

Sonoko   Aha—

Yuji   Come on, just quit it.

At the entrance, **Hinako** *shows up. She makes eye contact with the others and bows lightly.*

Hinako (*to the other side of the entrance*)   It's still open, you know.

Tomokuni *enters dragging a drunken* **Doshita**.

Koharu   Oh, Mr. Doshita.

Sonoko   What's happened?

Tomokuni   Excuse us for coming by so late. Could you take care of this man?

Sonoko   Huh?

Doshita   Hey you, don't bring me here. (*He wacks* **Tomokuni**.)

Tomokuni   Yeowch, that's because you won't tell me your address. He's a bit, uh drunk. I mean, when I met him, he was already drunk.

Doshita (*slurring his words*)   Haha, excuse me for bothering you during your work hours.

Koharu   Are you alright?

Sonoko   You quit drinking before, and now this . . .

Tomokuni   He's unmanageable.

Doshita   No, I'm not, stupid.

Koharu   Something up?

Hinako   Come on—Let's go.

Tomokuni   He's had some trouble with his son.

Doshita   Hey, shut the fuck up, you asshole.

Koharu   Did something happen to his son?

Tomokuni   Oh, no, no.

Doshita   Wrong, wrong, wrong, hehe . . . (*Falls asleep.*)

Tomokuni   Nothing happened to his son, if anything . . .

Hinako   . . . the dad was the mug being milked.

Koharu   What?

Tomokuni   With big bro's cash, his kid went around buying bikes and drugs.

Koharu   He said it was for college entrance, didn't he?

Tomokuni   Well, it's not an unusual story, is it? Freeloading kids around the world all think the same shit.

Hinako   Tomo, you've said that kind of thing before, right?

Tomokuni   The ex-wife noticed their son was spending money wildly, so she checked his cell phone, and called his dad.

Koharu   Is that so . . .

Tomokuni   It's a pity. He quit drinking and worked his butt off.

Doshita   Shithead.

Hinako   I love this!

Sonoko (*to* **Yuji**)   Should we give him some water?

Koharu   Mr. Doshita, here's some water.

Hinako   But you know, isn't this dude in the wrong to begin with?

Doshita   No, I don't want it, don't want it. (*The water he refuses spills out of the glass.*)

Hinako   For starters, you were an alcoholic. Then during your prison sentence, you abandoned your family.

Yuji   What?

Tomokuni   I said don't blab.

Hinako   Huh, Tomo, *you* told me that.

Doshita   Yeah—all my fucking fault, asshole.

Hinako (*sarcastically*)   Don't pretend to be the victim. If I were your daughter, I'd squeeze you dry.

Tomokuni   Cut it out.

Hinako   Come on, let's go. I'm tired of all this.

Tomokuni   Excuse me, please let him sleep here for a while. I don't know where he lives.

Koharu   Uh-huh.

Doshita   I'm OK, I'm OK.

Tomokuni   You'd better rest, you know . . .

Doshita Shut it, you asshole. (*Hits* **Tomokuni***.*)

Tomokuni Ow . . .

Doshita Never mind. I'm leaving. I'm getting out of here, getting out of here.

He tries to stand up. But losing his balance, he knocks over a chair nearby. **Koharu** *and* **Daiki** *instinctively go to help, while* **Sonoko** *backs off frightened.*

Koharu Mr. Doshita. You can't move, can you?

Sonoko Wow. Somehow this feels so familiar.

Daiki (*to* **Sonoko**) Y-you can go to bed, Sono.

Hinako Let's go, Tomo! . . .

Tomokuni I know. . . I'm very sorry. Big bro, see you.

Doshita Yeah go, get lost.

Tomokuni *and* **Hinako** *make to leave.*

Yuji No, take him with you.

Tomokuni It's only till he recovers.

Yuji We are closing now.

Tomokuni Well, it'll only be a short time.

Yuji It's an imposition.

Tomokuni He's a shithead employee at your fucking taxi company, ain't he?

Koharu Yu, it's not a problem. Please leave, OK. Please leave.

Tomokuni Really . . . (*Starts to go.*) How low are you going to fall?

Doshita Whaddaya say? (*Goes to grab him.*) Hey, whaddaya say, you asshole.

Tomokuni (*fearfully*) I'm sorry. I'm sorry.

Koharu Mr. Doshita . . .

Daiki (*takes* **Koharu***'s hand*) Y-you don't have to help.

Hinako (*trying to pull* **Doshita** *away*) Let go will ya.

Doshita Yeah, all my fault for falling.

Tomokuni Excuse me, I didn't mean . . .

Doshita I didn't fall because I wanted to, fuckface.

Koharu Mr. Doshita . . . (*Facilitates* **Hinako***'s escape, and tries to stop him herself.*)

Doshita Shurrup and get outa my way.

Doshita *pushes* **Koharu** *aside in a large sweeping movement. In fact, his hand hits her and, giving a small cry of pain, she lands on her rear end. The next moment,* **Yuji** *jumps out to where* **Doshita** *is and kicks him hard.* **Doshita** *'s legs collapse from under him and he falls down.* **Yuji** *then showers him with more kicks.*

Yuji Who the fuck are you?

Koharu Yuji, stop it.

Yuji Think you can lay hands on me, you bastard?

Hinako (*afraid*) We're going, OK . . . we are going!

She as good as drags **Tomokuni** *outside with her. Resisting,* **Doshita** *gets up, and ends up clinging to* **Yuji**.

Yuji You're in deep shit and it's all your own fucking fault, right?

Doshita Oh, oh, oh. (*Hangs on to him.*)

Yuji (*trying to rip* **Doshita** *off himself*) It's all your own fault. You fucking destroyed everything.

Daiki (*stopping* **Yuji**) Yuji!

Doshita Ohhh . . .

Yuji It's your fault!

Daiki Hey, he's not our dad.

Yuji *falls silent.*

Doshita (*still clinging on to* **Yuji**) I was, I was, I was so happy that night. What was that night about, eh? What was that night? What was it about? What was that night about?

Koharu (*beat*) It was just one night.

Doshita That night . . .

Koharu It was a special night for you, but for others, it was nothing.

Doshita *is silent.*

Koharu But if it was special to you, isn't that enough?

Doshita (*beat*) Yes . . .

Releasing his hold, **Doshita** *lets* **Yuji** *free.*

6.3 Parking Lot

Having finished her work, **Maki** *is carrying a dirty backpack and walking along.*

Yoshinaga *comes by.*

Yoshinaga It's mine, right?

Maki   This? It was in the garage.

Yoshinaga   It's mine.

Maki   What, you left it in the garage all this time?

Yoshinaga   Are you going for a drive?

Maki   Not any more.

Yoshinaga   Take me on one.

Maki   I'll charge you.

Yoshinaga   That's OK.

Maki   Huh? Are you going somewhere?

Yoshinaga   Yep.

Maki   Tonight?

Yoshinaga   It's my transition period.

Maki   What?

Yoshinaga (*beat*)   I can become your ghost.

6.4 At the Inamaru Taxi Office

Koharu *puts a blanket over the sleeping* **Doshita**. *By them is* **Sonoko**. *In the patio,* **Daiki** *and* **Yuji** *are sitting on chairs. They are having difficulty trying to light cigarettes.*

Yuji   Ah, there's that airship again.

Daiki   H'n? Nnn—(*He cannot light the cigarette.*)

Yuji (*lighting it for him*)   Quit smoking, why don't you?

Sonoko   Should we carry him somewhere more comfortable?

Koharu   Let's wait a little longer till he is in a deep sleep. A drunk can become very heavy.

Yuji   Why does it fly at night?

Daiki *shakes his head in puzzlement.*

Yuji   Do you like night views?

Koharu (*to* **Yuji** *and others*)   Look, please don't fire him, OK?

Daiki   Mm, it's unmanned, isn't it? The a-airship?

Yuji   Is it?

Koharu   He can't hear me.

Sonoko (*approaching* **Yuji** *and others*)   She said not to fire him.

Yuji   Who? Ohh.

Koharu   He's a good man.

Yuji   You are kind.

Koharu (*cannot hear*)   What?

Sonoko   He said, "You are kind."

Koharu   Tell him, "I am kind."

Sonoko   I can't be bothered.

Koharu *laughs.*

Yuji   People are on the airship.

Daiki   No, they aren't.

Koharu   Am I kind? . . .

Sonoko *goes out to the patio.* **Koharu** *looks at* **Doshita**. *He turns over softly in his sleep.*

Sonoko   What are you looking at?

Yuji   The airship.

Sonoko   Oh, where, where?

Daiki *points at his own finger.*

Koharu (*looking at* **Doshita**, *and speaking to her children*)   Was I kind to Dad, too?

Sonoko (*she cannot hear* **Koharu**)   Where?

Daiki   Other there.

Yuji   It's gone deeper into the dark.

Sonoko   I mean, with that finger, I can't tell where you're pointing at.

Daiki   Huh? Oh yeah. (*Looks at his crooked finger and laughs.*)

Yuji   Hahaha.

The siblings laugh. **Koharu** *approaches them.*

Koharu   What are you laughing about?

Sonoko (*pointing at* **Daiki**'s *finger*)   This.

Koharu   Huh?

Daiki   W-where do you think it's pointing?

Yuji and Sonoko   Hahaha.

Drawn in by the trio's laughter, **Koharu** *laughs, too. But then she suddenly breaks into tears and cries out loud.*

Koharu   Aaaahn waaahn . . .

She collapses on the spot. She howls loudly like a wounded beast. The siblings watch her in consternation, but eventually go to her side.

6.5 Inside a Taxi

Slamming the door shut, **Maki**, *still in her work wear, sits in the driver's position. In the back seat is* **Yoshinaga**.

Maki   Yes, sir, where to?

Yoshinaga   West.

Maki   Huh?

Yoshinaga   Or east.

Maki   Be serious, wontcha.

Yoshinaga   In that case . . . till the night ends.

Maki *tightens her shoulders and starts the engine.* **Yoshinaga** *hangs out of the window, and raises his voice, "Yo-hooooooo." The taxi begins to move toward the morning.*

The End.

Notes

1. Tsugumi is the daughter of Yumi and her deceased husband. They live with Tsugumi's granny.
2. Hwasa is a popular woman vocalist and rapper from South Korea.
3. Monaka wafers are bean jam filled wafers.
4. From "Jidai (Those days)" (2001) by Miyuki Nakajima.
5. The pun in the original line is on the pivot word "*kumo*," which can mean both spider and cloud.
6. Evening/night shift workers often say "Good morning." when they start work regardless of the actual time.
7. Ababa is a popular expression on social media. It makes light fun of a reader who doesn't get the joke or meaning of a write-in.

Isn't Anyone Alive?

Shiro Maeda

Introduction to the Playwright and the Play

Youichi Uchida (*cultural journalist*)

Translated by Miwa Monden

In his work, Shiro Maeda is well known for imposing an awkward touch onto the simple and ordinary life of people. Considered one of his masterpieces, *Isn't Anyone Alive?* premiered in 2007 and won the prestigious Kunio Kishida Drama Award. Gakuryu Ishii filmed a movie version of the work five years later. The prevailing view is that this absurd theatre piece effectively presents not death itself, but how people die. Maeda is also acclaimed as an award-winning novelist and TV scenario writer.

In the production staged at the small theatre, there were no major stage sets, only props. Places such as a university's break room and the café near the university are located apart, but still share the same physical space on stage, regardless of how this affects the consistency of the time and place. This technique is found and identified in the theatre logic articulated by Oriza Hirata, director and playwright of an earlier generation, in his book *For Contemporary Colloquial Theatre Theory* (1995). The importance of the consistency of time, place, and storyline that is found in French classic theatre is also fundamental to modern theatre in Japan, but breaking this rule has become a big trend in contemporary theatre.

In this play, no major situations arise. Even though catastrophe looms, the cause is not a subject to be mentioned. Instead, events that imminently await the characters are discussed in detail. The idea that the things happening around you immediately become your "world" itself is a kind of trend in contemporary theatre in Japan. The playwright is quite well known for making this point, especially through his extraordinary ability to depict conversations among characters.

There are no big dramas. There is a story of a man who expects to get married at the same time as an ex-girlfriend has found out that she is pregnant with his child. It is followed by a discussion among university seniors who are friends of the bride and debate about what they would perform at her wedding reception. Meanwhile a strange mood settles over the group as they talk about the news of the train accidents and rumors of a secret virus introduced by some students who research urban legends. Then, for unknown reasons, characters seize up and crumple to the floor one by one, and all eventually die except one. At the end, seventeen bodies are strewn all over and occupy the stage.

It would be possible to seek out allegorical meaning in this theatre production, but it would also be true that there is no such thing. The playwright created this work when he was thirty years old. I can imagine he was trying to figure out the texture of how to portray death through theatre when it has become so diluted in our modern society. In modern Japan, it is common to end life at the hospital alone, without the companionship of family, and it is rare to grasp and articulate the feeling of the moment of death. However, to live life without knowing real death leads us to lose our awareness of the reality of life. This sense of inadequacy, in relation to feeling the reality of death, is dominant throughout the play.

Maeda's outstanding short lines and articulation lack the texture of life that is vivid and lurid. Rhythmical pitch is one element of this absurd theatre piece, and the void foreshadows catastrophe. It is exactly the forefeeling of catastrophe which confirms this play as distinguished, and in fact the Japanese people were later going to be inundated by invisible frightfulness such as radioactive substances leaked out by the nuclear power plant meltdown incidents or the new coronavirus.

Playwright Biography

Shiro Maeda

Playwright, director, novelist, film director, screenwriter, and actor.

Born in 1977, he founded the theatre company GOTANNDADAN in 1997 while he was a university student. He won the 52nd Kishida Kunio Drama Award for *Isn't Anyone Alive?* (2007). In the 2009 Festival Tokyo, this piece was presented along with *Are We Alive?* which he also wrote and directed. While *Isn't Anyone Alive?* begins with people who die one by one until the end, *Are We Alive?* begins with a scene where all of the people are spread out dead on the stage and become alive one after another in a reversed timeline of events.

He and his theatre companies have been invited by esteemed and prestigious theatres and festivals worldwide in Belgium, France, Switzerland, Hungary, Luxembourg, and Singapore. His texts have been translated into French, Spanish, English, and Korean, performed in productions in the UK, New York, and South Korea.

As a novelist, he won the 22nd Mishima Yukio Prize for *The Mermen of Summer Water* (2009) and was nominated for the 137th Akutagawa Prize for *The Great Life Adventure* (2007) and again for the 158th Akutagawa Prize for *Triple Bind* (2017). He also won the 46th Galaxy Award for Excellence for his teleplay for the NHK drama *Shopping* (2009) and the Mukouda Kuniko Award for his script for the NHK drama *Seven Minutes on Foot* (2015).

In 2013, he wrote and directed the film *The Extreme Sukiyaki* and won the 8th TAMA Film Award for Best Emerging Director. His film *Kako: My Sullen Past* (2016) was invited to be included in the 19th Shanghai International Film Festival. He is one of the most acclaimed contemporary artists in Japan.

Isn't Anyone Alive?

Shiro Maeda

Translated by Miwa Monden

Characters

Nana, *university senior; researches urban legends.*

Match, *university senior; researches urban legends; Nana's boyfriend.*

Katsuo, *university senior; helps Nana write her graduation thesis; he has a crush on Nana and is an acquaintance of Miki; he works part time at Keisuke's Café.*

Eiko, *university senior; prepares for the performance at Ryoko's wedding reception; she has repeated her senior year at the university; she has a crush on Andre.*

Enari, *university senior; prepares for the performance at Ryoko's wedding reception.*

Andre, *university junior; prepares for the performance at Ryoko's wedding reception.*

Shoji, *university freshman; a member of the pop group Toho Kenbun Rock.*

Yoneda, **Katsufumi**, *Ryoko's fiancé; had a past relationship with Kaori.*

Ryoko, *the same grade (age) as Eiko; engaged to Katsufumi.*

Kaori, *Katsufumi's ex-girlfriend; she is pregnant with Katsufumi's child.*

Maki, *office administrator working at the university hospital; Koichi is her stepfather.*

Koichi, *Maki's stepfather; recently released from prison.*

Miki, *patient admitted by the university hospital; acquainted with Katsuo.*

Naito, *doctor at the university hospital; has feelings for Maki.*

Keisuke, *waiter at a café.*

Sachie, *Katsuo's mother.*

Sakana Hakase, *expert in fish; Yama San's friend.*

Yama San, *has gastrointestinal disorder; Sakana Hakase's friend.*

Several different locations co-exist on the stage at the same time. As the story progresses, their boundaries gradually start to dissolve, to the point where they become a united scene at the end.

Lights fade in.

△*A break room space at the university.*

Nana *is sitting and is listening to music with headphones.*

△*A café near the university.*

Ryoko *and* **Yoneda** *are seated in chairs.* **Kaori** *is also seated in a chair across from them. They all are silent. There is a menu and three glasses of water on the table in front of them.*

△*A break room space at the university.*

Koichi *enters and approaches* **Nana**.

Koichi　Er, excuse me.

Nana *takes off her headphones.*

Nana　Yes?

Koichi　Ah, where is the university hospital?

Nana　Oh, that building is nearby. Go down this street and you'll see it in the open area.

Koichi　OK, do you mean the street that you go by when you come from the station?

Nana　Yes, I do.

Koichi　I just came from the street.

Nana　Oh, you are in the university area right now. You'll have to take a right at the open area to get to the hospital. If you go right from there, it is actually left after that, you'll see the hospital entrance on your left.

Koichi　Oh, I see.

Nana　Yes.

Koichi *tries to leave and stops.*

Koichi　Well, thank you.

Nana *bows.*

Koichi *exits.*

△*A café near the university.*

Ryoko *gulps the glass of water.*

Ryoko　Could you please explain?

Yoneda   . . .

Ryoko   . . .

Yoneda   I'm sorry.

Ryoko   No, it is not your fault, Katsufumi.

Yoneda   . . .

Kaori   It's because he is sloppy.

Ryoko   But you didn't cheat on me, did you?

Yoneda   No . . . well, I didn't.

Silence.

Ryoko   Well, could you tell me your name again?

Kaori   Shijima.

Ryoko   Pardon?

Kaori   It is S-H-I-J-I-M-A. My name is Kaori Shijima.

Ryoko   That's an unusual name.

Kaori   Well.

Ryoko   What would you like to do, Kaori?

Kaori   Well, ah.

Keisuke *observes* **Kaori**, **Ryoko**, *and* **Yoneda** *while holding a tray. He approaches their table.*

Keisuke   Forgive me for interrupting, but may I please take your order?

Ryoko   Ah, well, we need a minute. I am leaving.

Keisuke   Huh?

Ryoko   I'll talk to my mom about this. You two should discuss it, too, otherwise we're getting nowhere.

Kaori   . . .

Ryoko   You got that, Katsufumi?

Yoneda   Yeah. Got it.

Ryoko *takes a cell phone out of her bag and exits.*

Kaori   What are you going to do?

Yoneda   What should I do?

Kaori   Come on.

Keisuke   What would you like to order?

Yoneda   Ah, yes.

Kaori   A cup of plain drip coffee, please.

Keisuke   Just one cup of plain drip coffee?

Kaori *looks at* **Yoneda** *as* **Keisuke** *asks him if he would also like to have a cup of coffee.*

Yoneda   What is this brown sugar parfait like?

Kaori   Who could eat a fancy brown sugar parfait at a time like this?

Yoneda   No, I won't. I was just asking how brown sugar is used in the parfait.

Kaori   Don't even ask.

Yoneda   Well, then, does this caramel green tea latte have some ice cream in it?

Keisuke   No, but I can add some in.

Yoneda   Good. Please put that in.

Kaori   Are you seriously ordering an over-the-top drink like that?

Yoneda   Why not? I am thirsty.

Kaori   Just a glass of oolong tea will do then.

Keisuke   Well, would you like to order a cup of plain drip coffee and a caramel green tea latte with ice cream on top?

Kaori   Ah, then may I change to a black sesame soy milk latte?

Keisuke   Yes. A black sesame soy milk latte it is.

Kaori   Yes.

Keisuke   Is that all?

Kaori   Yes.

Keisuke *exits.*

Yoneda   Do you normally drink black sesame soy milk latte?

Kaori   Is there a problem with that?

Yoneda   That's food.

Kaori   No, it isn't. It is a latte.

Yoneda   But they pour it over stuff.

Kaori   Are you saying that you eat some black sesame seeds and soy milk over a bowl of rice?

Yoneda   . . . No. Never.

Kaori   Then it's not food.

Yoneda   Yeah, but it'll probably taste like a sesame dish.

Kaori   It's popular now to have that kind of drink.

Yoneda   Yuck.

Kaori   Yuck what? What are you going to do?

Yoneda   . . . What am I going to do? What do you think I should do?

Kaori   I'm going to keep my baby.

Yoneda   Why?

Kaori   I don't want to get an abortion.

Yoneda   . . . I see.

Kaori   So, what are you going to do?

Yoneda   . . . What kind of options do I have?

Kaori   What?

Yoneda   What options are there?

Kaori   You . . .

Yoneda   . . .?

Kaori   Break up with her and marry me. Or, marry her and pay me the child support. Or, break up with everyone and just pay me the child support. Just FYI, I don't intend to marry you at all.

Yoneda   Oh, really. Don't I have an option to not give you any financial support?

Kaori   No, you don't.

Yoneda   No?

Kaori   Of course not. That's the law. You will get arrested if you don't.

Yoneda   Really. So I have another option to get arrested for not paying you.

Kaori   It's not even an option. You can't put it on the list.

Yoneda   Of course I wouldn't choose that, but we would have to consider all of the options. We should put it there just in case.

Kaori   What case? Are you an idiot?

Yoneda   No, I'm not.

Kaori   . . .

Yoneda   What do you think I should do?

Kaori   I don't know. You decide what to do.

Yoneda   Can I decide?

Kaori Who else is going to decide?

Yoneda We can talk about taking a vote.

Kaori Do you think we can vote on the matter like this?

Yoneda Of course not.

Kaori Hey, if you get married with that girl, Ryoko, you'll probably end up being in a big mess. So don't even be evasive.

Yoneda Do you really think so?

Kaori Yeah. Of course. You know what, whether you go like this, or that, you don't have much of a choice.

Yoneda Is that so?

He holds his head in his hands and starts thinking. He wiggles his head.

Kaori ...

Kaori I'll go and talk to Ryoko.

Yoneda Should I come with you?

Kaori If we're all leaving, why don't we all just stay here instead?

Yoneda Should we do that?

Kaori ...

Kaori *exits.*

△ *The break room space at the university.*

Nana *is reading a magazine.*

Enari *and* **Eiko** *enter.*

Eiko *is scrolling through her cell phone.*

Nana *looks at* **Enari** *and takes her headphones off.*

Enari *points at the magazine that* **Nana** *is reading. The magazine is not something college girls would likely read.*

Enari That's something weird you are reading.

Nana Yeah. It focuses on urban legends.

Enari Ah, you're reading it because of the urban legends.

Nana That's right.

Eiko *looks up from the screen of the cell phone.*

Eiko What about?

Nana What?

Eiko   Is an urban legend like a rumor?

Nana   Yeah, when a magazine features horror stories, you can also find some urban legends there.

Eiko   Oh.

Nana   You have no interest in urban legends, do you?

Eiko   No.

Enari   Were there any urban legends? Let me see.

He takes the magazine from **Nana**.

Nana   Yes, there are some.

Eiko *looks at the news on her cell phone.*

Eiko   Look. It seems like it's happened again.

Nana   . . . What?

Eiko   I don't know. The train service is suspended right now.

Nana   Do you mean the one metro line came to a halt this morning?

Eiko   No. It's the JR[1] this time.

Nana   What? Really? Where did it happen?

Eiko   At Sakamuke.

Nana   We are close. Is that somehow related to the metro thing this morning?

Eiko   It doesn't say.   **Enari**   Hey, did anyone die in the metro?[2]

Eiko   No one died, did they?

Enari   Is that in an email?

Eiko   No, it's on the internet.   **Enari**   Can you get the internet on your phone?

Eiko   Of course you can.

Enari   I thought I could, but I've never understood how. Do you know how to do anything besides send e-mails and use the camera? I don't really know about the camera.

Nana   Yeah. So, what does it say?

Eiko   The driver fainted or something while operating the train and it seems like a terrible mess.

Nana   Gee. That's scary.

Enari   Is that something, like you know, a terrorist attack?

Eiko   A terrorist attack? In Sakamuke?

Enari   I don't know.   **Nana**   Is the metro line still suspended?

Eiko   I don't know. It could have resumed by now.

Enari   Do you commute here by metro?

He becomes disinterested in the subject and looks at the magazine.

Nana   Yeah, I can also take the JR if I walk from the nearest JR station back home. But you said that the JR has also suspended its operations.

Eiko   You can stay at my place if you can't go home.

Nana   Thanks, but I can stay at Masahiko's place.

Eiko   Phew.   **Enari**   Hey, this is boring, isn't it?

Enari *closes the magazine.*

Nana   What do you expect?

Enari   Nothing.

Nana   But here's the article about the university hospital.

Enari   Seriously? Where?

Enari *opens the magazine again.*

Nana   Of course they left out details, though.

She takes a look at the magazine with **Enari**. **Eiko** *also pokes in.*

Eiko   What about? What is it?

Nana   What?

Eiko   What details did they leave out?

Nana   You're not interested, are you?

Eiko   No.

Nana   It's a long story.

Eiko   Make it short. I have to run an errand.

Enari   What is it? A guy?

Nana   No way.

Eiko   Why do you deny it?

Nana   I did it for you.

Eiko   Thank you.

Enari   So what is it?

Eiko   The performance for Ryoko's wedding reception.

Nana   The performance for Ryoko's wedding reception?   **Enari**   Yeah.

Eiko   Enari, you're also coming.

Enari   I know.

Eiko   Andre is also invited.

Nana   Ah.

Eiko   Nana, you're not invited, are you?

Nana   Well, I'm not that close to Ryoko, you know.

Eiko   You could say that.

Nana   I have to finish my graduation thesis anyway.

Enari   We still have a lot of time.

Nana   We don't really have a lot of time left, do we?

Enari   Oh, I'll have to get started soon.

Eiko   You can still make it.

Enari   How can I trust the person who flunked out before?

Nana *points to the article in the magazine.*

Nana   Hey, look.

Enari   What?

Nana   This one here.

Eiko   What? A scary story?

Nana   Do you remember what I told you about the university hospital?

Eiko   What? I don't remember.

Nana   I told you when you came to sleep over.

Eiko   Came where?

Nana   To my place.

Eiko   When?

Nana   Not so long ago. It was during summer vacation or something.

Eiko   Was it? Ah, is that related to human experiments happening in their basement or something??

Nana   Yup, yup.

Eiko   What about it?

Nana   That's what I found in this magazine.

Eiko Cool.

Nana I didn't make it up. It's just an urban legend.

Eiko What is an urban legend? You told me once, but I didn't get it.

Enari Then there'll be no use explaining it one more time.

Nana Like, you know, you've heard of the Slit Mouth Woman,[3] haven't you?

Eiko Yes, like, woman who has a slit mouth.

Nana . . . well, yes.

Eiko So?

Nana That's an urban legend.

Eiko It's totally bogus.

Nana That's different.

Eiko I don't understand how it's different,

Nana You see, studying an urban legend sheds light on human nature.

Eiko Like what?

Nana I don't know . . . What is it that humans fear? Well, I mean, the hospital in the article could be the university hospital right here.

Eiko That's not true.

Nana We don't know for sure.   **Enari** Hey, look, I saw the guy.

Nana Who?

Enari The pop star.

Nana Huh?

Eiko When?

Enari A while ago, near the library.   **Nana** Who?

Enari I told you he's a freshman here.

Nana Ah. So he goes to classes?

Enari Of course he does.   **Eiko** I'm jealous.

Nana Are you really?

Eiko Hey, is he cool?

Enari Well, maybe he looks better on TV.

Andre enters.

Enari greets **Andre**.

Nana *and* **Eiko** *notice* **Andre**.

Nana   Do they usually say that a person looks better in real life?

Enari   You tell me.

Andre   What are you guys talking about?

Nana   Well, well.

Andre   Hey, there is big news going around. Did you guys hear about it already?

Eiko   What about?

Enari   Do you mean the accident?

Andre   Yes. Did you hear about it?

Enari   No, but Eiko saw the headlines about it on her cell phone.

Andre   Well, it's a really big deal. I checked it out on the internet at the library and it said many people died.

Eiko   Really? On what line did people die?

Andre   JR.

Nana   Seriously?

Andre   I heard that the driver dozed off or something while the train was moving.

Nana   Is it possible to have another accident so soon after the one that happened this morning?

Andre   Yeah.

Nana   The driver must have been completely out of it.

Enari   I know there is a disease when you randomly doze off.

Nana   Yeah, there is.

Andre   I look forward to the broadcast news today.

Enari   But is there any chance that someone we know is involved in those accidents?

Andre *sits*.

Nana   I hope not.   **Eiko**   Did you rent the CD?

Andre   About the CD, I contacted the organizers.

Enari   Who are the organizers?

Andre   A friend of the groom and Ryoko's friend from her hometown.

Enari   That explains it.

Andre   What?

Enari   Well, they are not really helping us.

Andre   Yeah, so, they are not really helpful. Or rather it's hard to get a hold of them.

△*A café near the university.*

Kaori *returns.*

Yoneda *looks at* **Kaori**.

Kaori *shakes her head. She sits down with her arms crossed.*

△*A break room space at the university.*

Eiko   What's wrong?

Andre   Well, I was told to give the CD in advance and let the person from the wedding venue know about the music we would use.

Eiko   What do you mean?

Andre   I mean we can't play the CD.

Eiko   Really?

Enari   Sure, we can.

Andre   I totally agree, but I don't want to be awkward with them by pushing them to use it.

Enari   Ah . . . but that doesn't sound right.

Andre   Well, yeah, but we really can't do so.

Enari   But . . . we should be able to play CDs, shouldn't we?

Andre   So I would assume that we would have to submit an application or something in advance.

Enari   It can't be true.

Eiko   What should we do then? Sing a cappella?

Andre   Yeah, so, we have to come up with something else.

Enari   We don't have enough time left to get something together.

Andre   So let's see what we can do about it today.

Enari   No. I can't keep my spirits up.

Andre   That's not our fault.

Enari   What do we do then?

Nana   I think a cappella isn't quite convincing.

Enari   Huh, what else do you think we can do?

Nana   How about a dance performance?

Enari   No way!

Eiko   What else can we do?

Enari   Are you going to dance?

Eiko   Yes, I think that is the only option.

Enari   No, there has to be another option. Let's think.

Eiko   Well, can we do anything else besides singing and dancing?

△*A café near the university. Conversation occurs simultaneously.*

Kaori *looks in the direction of the inside café.*

Keisuke *enters with two drinks. One of them looks black.*

Keisuke   There you go.

He puts the drinks on the table.

Is there anything else that you need?

Kaori   No.

Keisuke *puts the bill and exits.*

Keisuke   Enjoy.

Yoneda   It looks black.

Kaori   None of your business.

The two have their drinks.

△*A break room space at the university. The conversation there almost overlaps with the conversation at the café.*

Andre   . . . Like Manzai?[4]

Eiko   Huh?

Enari   . . .

Eiko   Isn't it too challenging for us?

Nana *answers her cell phone.*

Nana   Yes . . . Ah-huh . . . Huh, already here . . . Where are you now? . . . Really? . . . OK. Hey, did you bring a tape recorder? . . . Hello? Hello? Hey, hello? Do you hear me? Hello?

Andre   . . .

Enari   A dance performance wouldn't be any easier.

Andre   Probably. Do you want to quit?

Enari   If we can.

Andre   Let's not do this.

Eiko   Is that Match?

Nana   Yeah. Katsuo is also on the way.

Enari   Hey, we can bring our own radio-cassette player, can't we?

Andre Ah, yes, we can. How's the sound quality?

Enari It's less difficult than singing a cappella or something.

Andre Yeah, you are right, but . . .

Eiko OK, then.

Andre Well, like I, well, my sister recently got married. You know, you sometimes see some kind of performances there, right?

Eiko I guess so. It's common to have some.

Andre Like . . .

He holds back laughing.

Enari What is it?

Andre Well, I took my girlfriend with me there, and saw a cute little boy, like this tall. She kept saying how adorable and cute he is and all that. He has red cheeks and is really cute. So I go, like, "He is going to burst out crying if I slap his head so hard now."

He can't hold back and bursts out laughing.

Well, so I said to her, that he is going to cry out loud if I slap his head. I said that to her . . .

He is laughing.

What do you think about that?

Enari Huh? Ah . . . you took your girlfriend with you to your sister's wedding.

Andre Ah, yes, I did.

Silence.

Eiko Well, shall we go practice?

Enari Did you book a room?

Eiko and **Enari** *stand up and get ready.*

Andre Yeah, I did.

Enari What's the room number?

Andre It is either 203 or 204. The smaller room in tower D.

Enari That's 203.

Nana Are you going?

Eiko Yes, I am.

Nana   See you later.

Eiko   Aren't you coming?

Nana   I have a meeting to attend.

Enari   A meeting?

Nana   Yeah, we have something really interesting going on right now.

Andre   What about? A meeting?

Eiko   This girl belongs to the urban legends research group.

Andre   Oh. What is the urban legends research group? Is Match a member of the group?

Nana   Yeah.

Andre   Like that? Like research on urban legends?

Nana   Right.

Andre   They call them urban legends, but many of them aren't urban at all, are they?

Nana   What?

Andre   Many of them are like "that's not even urban" kind of things, aren't they?

Nana   . . .

Eiko   Come on.

Andre   Yes.

Nana   See you.

Andre   Can we stop at Seikyo on the way?   **Enari**   Until what time?

Eiko   Yes. What for?   **Nana**   I was planning to stay for an hour or so. I may stay longer because the train isn't running right now.

Andre   Some bread. I am peckish.   **Eiko**   See ya.

Enari   Good luck.

Nana   Thanks.

Nana   See you. Are you coming to the school tomorrow?

Eiko   Yes, yes.

Enari   I might give you a call later.

Nana   OK, OK.

Eiko, **Andre**, *and* **Enari** *exit.*

△*A café near the university.*

Ryoko *enters.*

Yoneda *concentrates on the drink. He voraciously eats the ice cream on the top of his drink.*

Yoneda Can I have a taste?

Kaori Huh?

Yoneda Please.

Kaori All right, but let me taste yours.

Yoneda OK, but don't touch my ice cream.

Kaori Why? They're supposed to go together.

She eats the ice cream off the top of **Yoneda** *'s drink.*

Yoneda Hey, stop.

Kaori *notices* **Ryoko** *and gives a sign to* **Yoneda**.

Yoneda *put the spoon on the table.*

Ryoko *looks at* **Yoneda**.

Ryoko You two seem cozy together.

Yoneda Not really.

Ryoko What are you going to do? Did you make up your mind?

Yoneda Not yet.

Ryoko Can you take it seriously?

Yoneda I am taking it seriously.

Ryoko You two are having frivolous drinks like that and you're not taking it seriously. Please get down to business and think.

She becomes overwhelmed.

Yoneda . . . You are so right, aren't you?

Ryoko Why are you asking? I'm damn right, that's for sure.

Yoneda Oh, OK.

Ryoko I can raise her baby with you, you know.

Yoneda Oh, great.

Kaori Hold on. Hold on. Where is that idea coming from?

Ryoko You don't like it? That's what you want me to do, isn't it?

Kaori No, no no. Not at all. I can raise the baby by myself. If you pay me child support, go ahead and get married or do anything you want.

Ryoko   But Katsufumi is responsible for half of it.

Kaori   . . . What half?

Ryoko   The baby.

Kaori   Huh?

Yoneda   . . . I think I want to be able to play and spend some time with my baby.

Kaori   . . . Are you an idiot?

Yoneda   No, I am not. Why?

Kaori   I don't understand what that's supposed to mean. You want me to get an abortion, don't you?

Yoneda   . . . But that's a form of murder, isn't it?

Kaori   That's right.

Yoneda   That's too cruel.

Kaori   Wait, that's what you told me to do, isn't it?

Yoneda   Yeah, I said so, but I was out of my mind.

Kaori   Don't you ever say something like that when you're out of your mind.

Kaori *raises her voice.*

Keisuke *comes and checks to see if they are all right. He leaves.*

Yoneda   That is, you are so right, aren't you?

Kaori   Why are you asking? I said I am right. I think you're a fool after all, aren't you?

Yoneda   No, I'm not a fool. Don't make a fool out of me.

Kaori   . . .

Yoneda   What will make us all happy? That's what we have to think about, isn't it?

Ryoko   That's right.

Kaori   You said that's right? That's exactly what he wasn't thinking. That's why it turned out this way.

Ryoko   Don't just blame Katsufumi for the responsibility. Apparently, you weren't careful either. That's why it happened. Or can you get pregnant alone?

Kaori   . . . No.

Ryoko   You are also responsible for what happened.

Kaori   . . .

Ryoko   Well, please calm down and let's talk.

Kaori . . . Well, it's simple. I want to raise my baby alone. I just want some financial support from him.

Ryoko Do you think he is able to support you financially?

Kaori . . .

Yoneda . . .

Ryoko It will probably end up coming out of my pocket instead.

Kaori . . . That's inevitable. Don't marry him if you don't want to.

Ryoko . . .

Yoneda As a father, instead of providing financial support, I want to teach my kid how tough life is and all the things he can't learn at school—

Kaori Shut up.

Yoneda . . . Yes.

Silence.

Kaori Do you have a minute?

Ryoko Why?

Kaori Can we talk alone?

Yoneda You just did, didn't you?

Kaori Yes, but she was on the phone.

Ryoko What is it? We can talk right here.

Kaori Well, it's him who makes things complicated.

Yoneda I can keep my mouth shut except on the occasion that I need to say something

Kaori That's exactly what makes things complicated.

Yoneda . . . I can see that.

Kaori Let's get out of here.

*She tries to take **Ryoko**'s hand.*

Ryoko Please get off of me.

Kaori Huh?

Ryoko I know the way out.

Kaori Of course.

Ryoko I am leaving, Katsufumi.

Yoneda Oh, yes, OK.

Kaori *and* **Ryoko** *start to exit.*

Ryoko   Where are we going?

Kaori   Somewhere near here.

Yoneda *starts eating some ice cream.*

△*A break room space at the university. As* **Kaori** *and* **Ryoko** *start to exit, the next line overlaps with their conversation.*

Match *and* **Katsuo** *enter.* **Match** *is fiddling with his cell phone.*

Nana *bows.*

Match   Hey.

Nana   You arrived quicker than I thought.

Match   Yeah, I did.

He sits.

Katsuo   What time is it?

He grabs the cell phone from **Match**.

Katsuo   Thanks.

Match   What happened to your phone?

Katsuo   I left it at home. They disconnected it.

Match   Pay the bill.

△*A room inside the university hospital.*

Maki *enters. She turns the fluorescent light on to start checking some documents.*

△*A break room space at the university.*

Katsuo   Uh, yeah.   **Nana**   What is it?

Katsuo   Well, it's a . . .

Nana   Are you visiting anyone at the hospital?

Katsuo   Yes.   **Match**   Who is it?

Katsuo   Someone I know has been admitted.

Match   Where?

Nana   It turned out to be our university hospital.

Match   Really?

Katsuo   Well, ah, it's a bit of a serious situation.

Match   Why?

Katsuo   It seems that she won't be long, and I really don't know what to say to her.

Nana   I would assume so.

Match   It's a girl?

Katsuo   Yeah, so.

Match   Really?

Nana *stands up.*

Nana   Excuse me. I'm going to a bathroom.

Match   I'll come too.

Nana *and* **Match** *start to exit.*

Katsuo   Ah, do you want to talk here?

Nana *and* **Match** *stop.*

Nana   I can come to the meeting space.

Match   Maybe it's not so convenient.

Katsuo   Why?

Match   Because Oribe and others will be there.

Katsuo   Who?

Match   It's Nana's . . . ah, ex.

Katsuo   Oh. Ah.

Nana   I'll be fine.

Match   I know but—

Silence.

Nana   Well, then, I have to go to the bathroom.

Katsuo   OK, OK. Go.

Match   I'll go too.

Katsuo   Well, then I'll go too.

Match   You just did.

Katsuo   You don't have to remind me of that.

Match   I just remember things like that. I can't help it.

Nana *takes some paper out of her bag.*

Nana   Would you mind taking a look, Katsuo?

Katsuo   What is it?

Nana   My resume.

Katsuo   Oh, thanks.

Nana *and* **Match** *start to exit. Audience can still hear their conversation after they leave.*

Match   Did you put the cactus inside?

Nana   What?

Match (*voice*)   It is going to rain today.

Nana (*voice*)   Oh really?

Match (*voice*)   I asked you to put it inside from the balcony.

Nana (*voice*)   I forgot.

Match (*voice*)   It'll get wet.

Nana (*voice*)   It'll be fine. It can also rain in the desert.

Match (*voice*)   It doesn't rain in the desert, that's why it's always full of sand.

Nana (*voice*)   Is that right?

Match (*voice*)   Don't you know that? That cactus should stay away from the rain.

Katsuo *sits down to take a look at* **Nana**'*s resume.*

△*At a street by the café. As* **Match** *and* **Nana** *start to exit, the next scene overlaps with their conversation.*

Kaori *and* **Ryoko** *enter across the stage.*

Ryoko   What are you up to, Kaori?

Kaori   What?

Ryoko   What would you like to do about Katsufumi?

Kaori   Ah, nothing. I already told you.

Ryoko   Why are you going to keep the baby then?

Kaori   It's none of your business.

Ryoko   Yes, it is.

Kaori   Hummm.

Ryoko   You know, the baby is also Katsufumi's.

Kaori   I know, but we didn't exactly plan this.

Ryoko   Why are you keeping it then?

Kaori   Because I feel bad.

Ryoko   About what?

Kaori   The baby.

Ryoko   Hmmm. If you say so, I won't say anything more.

Kaori   But I don't have enough money or a sustainable job to raise this baby.

Ryoko   I guess that'll be tough then.

Yama san *and* **Sakana Hakase** *enter, passing by* **Kaori** *and* **Ryoko**.

Yama san *doesn't feel well.*

Sakana Hakase *takes care of* **Yama san**.

Kaori   . . .

Ryoko   Where are we heading to?

Kaori   Ah, I don't know.

Ryoko   Are we just walking aimlessly?   **Yama** . . .

Kaori   I just thought it'd better to   **Sakana**   Do you want some water?
talk while we walk.

Ryoko   Let's sit down somewhere to talk.   **Yama**   No thanks.

Kaori   Well, then let's go to a park   **Sakana**   Did you think I was
or somewhere.   shocked?

Kaori *and* **Ryoko** *exit.*

Yama   I think so.

Sakana   Maybe you should have gone and talked to the police.

Yama   I know but it would be too complicated.

Sakana   But then you wouldn't get paid out of the insurance.

Yama   We wouldn't. A lot of people died, and they should pay to the victims' family anyway. We just happened to be there and became sick. They wouldn't pay us for that.

Sakana   Right.

Yama   I feel that the blood is draining out of my head.

Sakana   Oh, blood draining out of your head doesn't sound good.

The two walk.

Sakana   That's why we should go to the hospital.

Yama   Yeah.

Sakana   We are almost there. Hang in there.

Yama   Hakase . . .

Sakana   Hmm?

Yama   I'm sorry. You came all the way to see me.

Sakana   No problem. I like being with you anyway. Besides, it wasn't your fault. Who could predict that the train would have an accident?

Yama   I appreciate that.

Sakana   Hey, stop.

Yama san *grins.*

Sakana   Please.

The two exit.

△*A room inside the university hospital. As* **Sakana Hakase** *and* **Yama san** *exit, the next scene overlaps with their departure.*

Koichi *enters.*

Maki *notices him.*

Koichi   . . .

Maki   . . .

Koichi   Hey, it's been a long time.

Maki   . . .

Koichi   Do you work here?

Maki   Yeah.

Koichi   I see.

Maki   How did you find me?

Koichi   I asked Kawashima.

Maki   Why? I told you to leave me alone.

Koichi   Yes, you did.

Maki   Why are you here?

Koichi   I came to see you.

Maki   You just did. So that's already done.

Koichi   Yes, ah, I mean, I wanted to talk to you about our future . . .

Naito *enters. He notices* **Koichi**.

Naito   . . . Hey, I can come back.

Maki   No problem. He's just leaving.

Naito   Ah, yeah.

Naito *wonders if he should stay as* **Maki** *has indicated.* **Koichi** *talks to him.*

Koichi . . . Hi.

Naito . . . Ah . . .

Naito *looks at* **Maki**.

Maki Well, this is my stepfather.

Naito Your father? Oh, hey, ah, I'm Naito.

Koichi Hello. Nice to meet you.

Maki Aren't you leaving?

Koichi Ah, yeah.

Maki Goodbye.

Koichi What time are you going to finish? I'll wait outside.

Maki You don't have to wait for me.

Koichi I know, but . . .

Maki Please leave.

Koichi Well, but.

Maki I'll be in touch.

Koichi OK, then. Be careful.

Maki Regarding what? Related to what?

Koichi *exits.*

Maki I am sorry.

Naito No, not at all.

Maki . . .

Silence.

Naito It's totally chaotic in the surgery ward.

Maki Ah.

Naito They're all gone, helping out.

Maki Why did it happen?

Naito They don't know yet. Kawauchi told me that the driver fainted all of a sudden.

Maki Was it his heart?

Naito I guess. I heard he's still young.

Maki   Oh.

Naito   Our hospital is safely located far away from the station, but the hospital in Sakamuke where Kitajima works must be in chaos.

Maki   I would assume so.

Silence.

Naito   You don't look like your father.

Maki   Ah, he is my stepfather.

Naito   Oh, ah, yes.

Maki   . . .

Naito   So he has been released?

Maki   I guess so.

Naito   Are you going to live together again?

Maki   I don't think that's going to happen anymore. He's like that, you know.

Naito   But isn't he your only father you've got?

Maki   . . . Well, ah, it's like that but, you know . . .

Naito   Well . . . you can talk to me.

Maki   Yes. Thank you.

Naito   . . . Yeah, do you need my email address just in case?

He gestures as if typing on a keyboard.

Maki   I'm fine.

Naito   You know, a computer is more convenient than a cell phone for reading longer messages.

He gestures as if typing on a keyboard.

Maki   Yeah . . . Well, did you come here for any particular reason?

Naito   What?

Maki   Did someone call me?

Naito   Oh, yes, they need some extra helping hands because there are only a few people left here.

Maki   Ah, of course.

She sorts out the documents.

I'll come right after I finish this.

Naito   Thanks.

Maki   Sure.

Naito   . . . Maki.

He takes a cassette tape out of the pocket of his white medical coat and brings it as high as his chest, before putting it back.

Maki   . . .

Naito   . . . Ah, this can wait.

Maki   What?

Naito   See you later.

Maki   . . .

Naito *exits.*

Maki *thinks of something and continues to take care of the documents.*

△*A café near the university.*

Sachie *enters.*

Sachie   Hello.

Keisuke *enters.*

Keisuke   Hello. Oh, hi.

Sachie   Hi. Is Katsuo here?

Keisuke   Well, he's not working a shift today.

Sachie   Is that so?

Keisuke   . . .?

Sachie   Well, you know, I heard about the accident and I just wanted to make sure he's OK. I tried to call him, but I couldn't reach him.

Keisuke   The line may be busy due to those accidents.

Sachie   You're right.

Keisuke   Well, he could be in school.

Sachie   . . . Yes, of course . . .

Silence.

Keisuke   Would you like something to drink?

Sachie   No, thank you. I am fine.

She tries to exit.

Ah, well, thank you always.

Keisuke   Oh? No, it's no problem. If I find him, I'll tell him to call you.

Sachie   I appreciate it.

Keisuke   No problem.

Sachie *bows to* **Keisuke** *once again and exits.*

Keisuke *tries to go inside the café.*

Yoneda   Excuse me.

Keisuke   . . . Yes?

Yoneda   How does the brown sugar work with this brown sugar parfait?

Keisuke   Excuse me?

Yoneda   Do you just use brown sugar instead of regular sugar?

Keisuke   No. You can enjoy both a brown sugar syrup on top and brown sugar jelly at the bottom.

Yoneda   . . . Excuse me?

Keisuke   What? Would you like one?

Yoneda   No, thank you.

Keisuke   . . .

Keisuke *exits.*

A room inside the university hospital. The very next scene overlaps the interaction between **Keisuke** *and* **Yoneda**.

Miki *enters.*

Miki   . . .

Maki   Hi, Miki.

Miki   . . .

Maki   Did you see Dr. Naito over there?

Miki   No, I didn't.

Maki   Oh. What's wrong?

Miki   Can you come with me, Maki?

Maki   Yeah, what happened?

Miki   I think I lost my mom.

Maki   What?

Miki   It seems my mom is dead.

She exits.

Maki   What? Hey!

She exits in order to follow **Miki**.

△*A break room space at the university.*

Katsuo *checks his fat around his waist.*

Match *returns.*

Katsuo   Where is Nana?

Match   She was talking to some students. She should be here in a minute.

Katsuo   Do you guys live together?

Match   What? No, we don't.

Katsuo   Oh.

Match   Hey, Katsuo. Do you always address Nana so casually, without an honorific?

Katsuo   Huh?

Match   Well, it's not a big deal, but I was wondering if you usually do.

Katsuo   I think I do, but I don't really remember.

Match   You don't really remember?

Katsuo   I don't call her by name that much anyway.

Match   Yeah, right.

Silence.

Katsuo   Well, I'm usually so friendly that I don't use an honorific with most people.

Match   Oh.

Katsuo   I was already comfortable enough to call you Match from the beginning.

Match   Match is my nickname.

Katsuo   Yeah, you're right.

Match   No, no, I mean, I don't mind it at all.

Katsuo   Yeah, I know I know.

Silence.

Match   So, did you try the elevator at the university hospital?

Katsuo   I did, but you can't use it. I hit the button, but it never came. So maybe you can only use it at 2 am, just like the urban legend says.

Match   So, it's not just a rumor?

Katsuo   I don't know, I felt something strange. I have talked to some patients in the smoking area at the university hospital, and they all seemed to know the rumor about the elevator and the third basement.

Nana *enters eating sukonbu.*[5]

Katsuo *greets* **Nana** *with direct eye contact.*

Match   Oh, is it really?

Katsuo   Yeah, they have nothing else to do, you know. They just sleep most of the time.

He looks intently at **Nana**.

Nana   Hey, did you talk to someone involved?

Katsuo   What?

Nana   Doctors or like administrators, nurses.

Katsuo   Oh, yes, maybe not that one who was directly involved, but I talked to his friend.

Nana *eats sukonbu.*

Nana   Is he a doctor? Do you want some sukonbu?

Katsuo   No, he isn't. He is not a doctor, I don't know, something besides a doctor or a nurse, like an administrator.

Nana   Like an administrator?

Katsuo   Yeah, I'm not really sure, but someone who gives you support or assistance for your day-to-day issues.

Shoji *passes by.*

Nana *stares at* **Shoji**.

Katsuo *stops talking as* **Nana** *takes her eyes off of him.*

Shoji *looks* **Nana** *in the eye and exits swiftly.*

Katsuo   Do you know him?

Nana   No, I don't. That guy . . . that's him, isn't he?

Match   Who?

Nana   The pop star.

Katsuo   Ah, something something Kenbun Rock?

Match   Hmm? Kenbun Rock? What's that?

Nana   Ah, you know something like a pop group.

Match   Really? Is that him?

He stands up and looks at **Shoji** *from back.*

Nana   You know they said a pop star entered our school.

Match   Ah, but . . .   **Nana**   Hey, did he know something?

Katsuo   He?

Nana   The guy at the hospital.

Katsuo   Ah, no. He snubbed me.

Match   Maybe he was trying to hide something.

Nana   I mean, people with his title don't know anything. Only a few people know the truth. They pick a good patient and send him over to the basement.

Match   What's a good patient?

Nana   I don't know, someone appropriate for the human experiment happening in the basement.

Katsuo   So you believe that rumor?

Nana   The most believable and legendary story says that some Americans are conducting some experiments in the basement on some kind of virus for military purposes. Since they are not able to do it in the U.S., they opted for a rural hospital in Japan, in its basement or somewhere.

Match *exaggerates his body gestures and makes a face saying, "It can't be."* **Nana** *is fervently trying to convince him.*

Match   That's bizarre.

Nana   I know but that sounds much more realistic than aliens or zombies, doesn't it?

Match   Does it? I don't see any difference.

Nana   So do you believe that aliens and zombies exist?

Match   No, I don't. What if they're doing human experiments to find the secret to eternal life, and the failures turned out to be like zombies.

Nana   Why do they have to become zombies? And if they do, isn't it kind of a success? They go on forever.

Match   That's why I don't believe it. I am just saying there are some rumors.

Katsuo   I think that they just want to nail it down to find out the truth.

Match   That's right.

Nana   You just love zombies. That's why.

Match   I guess you can say that.   **Katsuo**   You guess?

Nana   Are zombies related to voodooism?

She starts coughing.

Match   Well, I say it doesn't have to be zombies. Are you all right?

Nana *gestures him "I am fine."*

Match   So something must most likely be in the basement.

Katsuo   Do you think there's something there?

Match   I think there's something.

Nana   I agree, but . . .

She coughs.

Match   Are you all right?

Nana   It's sukonbu. Just sukonbu.

Match   You're silly.

Nana   So, what I mean is that, if there is anything, there must absolutely be something in the hospital that . . .

She holds her coughs.

Match   What?

Nana   Something that's financially lucrative for the hospital or something like that, I think.

Katsuo   They may be hiding some money down there to avoid paying taxes.

Match   So typical.

Katsuo   We'll become part of an urban legend if we find it.

Nana   We'll just be in the newspaper instead.

She coughs intensely.

Katsuo   Hey.

Match   Are you really all right?

Nana *coughs and raises her hands to tell them she's all right. She steps away from them.*

Match   The vinegar powder or something must have gone down the wrong pipe.

Katsuo   Ah, the flavor powder?

Nana *bends her body. She is almost sitting down.*

Match   Are you sure you are OK?

Nana *looks at* **Match** *and waves her hand coughing with a half smile.*

Katsuo   It must've really hit her.

Nana *smiles and coughs at the same time, repeating gestures indicating that this is not funny.*

Match *and* **Katsuo** *smile.*

Nana *keeps coughing with a smile.*

Nana   This is not funny.

Match   Huh? What?

Match *and* **Katsuo** *are beginning to worry but still have slight smile on their faces.*

Nana *finally falls down.*

Match   Hey!

Katsuo   Oh!

Match *and* **Katsuo** *are bewildered and frozen, but also consider approaching her.*

Nana *crawls to come closer to* **Match** *and* **Katsuo**.

Match   Hey, Nana, are you OK?

Nana   Oh . . . Ogami.

Match   Ogami? What? Nana?

Nana   Oga . . . Ogami.

She reaches her hand to grab something in the air and dies. She crumples out of **Match** *'s arms.*

Silence.

Match   Nana? Hey! Come on. Nana!

Match *looks at* **Katsuo**.

Katsuo   . . .

Match   Nana, hey, don't play with me. Nana?

Silence.

Match *takes* **Nana** *'s hand and releases it. Her arm drops to the ground.*

Match   No . . . This is wrong. Woah! Ah . . . Ah . . .

He backs away from **Nana** *inch by inch, finally turning and running away to exit.*

Katsuo   . . . What? . . . Ah . . . Ah . . . Match? Hey, Nana? Woah!

Match   Ah!

Katsuo *becomes himself again and exits to follow* **Match**.

Katsuo   Match! Match! Hey! Wait up! Whoa!

Nana *'s body still remains on the stage.*

△*A café near the university. The very next scene overlaps with* **Match** *and* **Katsuo** *'s screaming.*

Yoneda *cramps as he holds the glass. He wonders why. Then his whole arm starts to cramp.*

Yoneda   Hmm?

He tries to stand up and walk, but he is not able to control his own body. He falls down.

Keisuke *hears the sound of* **Yoneda** *falling down and comes in.*

Keisuke   Hey, are you all right?

Yoneda   Huh?

His body twitches and writhes.

Keisuke   Is something wrong?

Yoneda   Ah, I just don't know what. Huh?

Keisuke   . . .

Yoneda   Oh.

He tries to raise himself but his body keeps cramping. He can't stand up.

Keisuke   . . .

Yoneda *can't raise himself up and struggles on the ground. He moves wildly and squirms around on the floor.*

Keisuke   Hey! What?

Yoneda *becomes rigid.*

Yoneda   Huh?

He dies.

Keisuke   Oh, no! Oh, my god. What should I do? What? Anybody? Anybody please!

Silence.

Keisuke *checks* **Yoneda**'s *pulse, tries to bring some water to his mouth, and so on. He paces inside the café and calls someone. Eventually, he exits.*

Yoneda's *body remains on the stage.*

△*Classroom #203 in tower D. The very next line overlaps with* **Keisuke**'s *voice.*

Andre, **Eiko**, *and* **Enari** *enter.* **Andre** *is eating some bread.*

Andre   Does anybody have an idea?

Eiko   For the beginning . . . what should we do . . . I think dancing is one idea.

Andre   Isn't it too risky to try?

Eiko   No, no, we should definitely do it. You know the music, don't you?

Andre   Yes. I know the music.

Eiko   The audience will be bored without it.

Andre   Yeah, but.

He chews and shoves some more bread in his mouth.

Do we need to challenge?

Eiko   But it's for Ryoko's big day.

Andre   I know.

Eiko   I want to do something as a friend. I want to do everything I can do for her.

Andre   So you dance?

Eiko   Anything else?

Andre   Of course.

Eiko   Like what?

Enari   Is it possible that there might not be enough space to dance?

Eiko   . . .

Andre   Ah, you are right.

Eiko   I think there would be enough space for dance.

Enari   If not?

Eiko   We don't have to dance if there isn't.

Enari   Why? Do you want to dance?

Eiko   No, I don't.

Enari   . . . Huh?

Eiko   I don't want to but sometimes we have no choice.

Enari   . . .

Eiko   I am so grateful for Ryoko because she and I started school at the same time together, and she graduated before me, and she is going to get married before I will, but I still feel a friendship with her. I don't know about you guys though.

Enari   Well, she took care of me in many ways.

Andre   Me too.

Eiko   See? Let's dance then.

Enari   Hum, ah, yes . . . well, are you going to choreograph, Eiko?

Eiko   Yes, I can do that.

Enari   You think you can.

Eiko   No problem.

Enari   Ah . . .

Enari   We don't do the white makeup, do we?

Eiko   Huh? What?

Enari   I mean, you danced or did some kind of performance at the student auditorium before with the white makeup.

Eiko   Yes, I remember that.

Enari   We are not going to do something like that, aren't we?

Eiko   Oh, do you want to do something like that?

Enari   No, no. Things like that would be . . . a bit . . . you know.

Andre   That would go way too state-of-the-art.

Eiko   I know. You think something "pop" is better.

Enari   Right. Wearing something like a kimono and taking off layer by layer is . . .

Eiko   It's not easy. It takes a lot of practice because you have to think about how much you show.

Enari   Yeah, so maybe it's better to do something ordinary. I think it's better to avoid something like you did.

Eiko   . . . Yeah, yeah. Of course, I won't do anything like that. Let's see. Go right over there.

Andre   I'm still eating some bread.

Eiko   Finish it. We don't have enough time.

Andre   . . .

Andre *is forced to finish eating.*

He and **Enari** *stand in front of* **Eiko***.*

Eiko   Ready?

Enari   For what?

Eiko   Let's go!

Enari   What?

Eiko   Say "Go!" to sing along and dance.

Enari   All right, but we can't dance.

Andre   I can't dance.

Eiko   So, just copy me.

Enari   Yeah.

Eiko   Ready?

Silence.

Sing!

Enari   I can't.

Andre   No.

Enari   Isn't it hard to sing without music? I am not used to listening to French pop.

Eiko   Sure, you can.

Andre   You sing it alone, Eiko.

Eiko   I don't want to.

Enari   I only know the refrain, but I don't know the rest.

Eiko   Well, then just repeat it a thousand times.

Enari   Does it mean anything?

Eiko   Yes, it does. Here we go.

She moves like an orchestra conductor.

Enari *and* **Andre** *try to catch the rhythm.*

Andre   Say when? When do we start?

Eiko *does it for them to see.*

Eiko   When.

Enari   I don't get it.

Eiko *moves like an orchestra conductor.*

Eiko   When!

Enari   Huh? Hmm?

Eiko   . . . When!

Enari   You should sing.

Eiko   What? Are you blaming me?

Enari   Yes.

Eiko   . . . Sing when I say "go."

Enari   OK.

Andre   Hold it. Let me check the lyrics.

He takes his notebook out of his bag and opens the page where he wrote the lyrics.

Eiko   Get ready.

Andre *rushes back to his position.*

Eiko *moves like an orchestra conductor.*

Eiko   Go!

Eiko, **Andre**, *and* **Enari** *start singing softly and tentatively.*

All Three

    Ryoko and Katsufumi live happily ever after. Just married.

Eiko *starts to do box steps.* **Andre** *and* **Enari** *follow her.*

The three of them don't look happy at all.

Eiko   Go!

She starts clapping her hands. **Andre** *and* **Enari** *follow her.*

Eiko

    Ryoko and Katsufumi, live happily ever after and forever.

She turns around.

Enari   What was that?

Eiko

    Live happily ever after.

She turns around.

    And forever.

Andre   Good. What are you going to do with the wire if you have a microphone in your hand?

He demonstrates as if wire becomes tangled around his body after the spin.

Eiko   . . .

Eiko *places the microphone on the imaginary microphone stand and then turns around.*

Eiko

    Live happily ever after and forever.

She picks up the microphone from the imaginary stand.

Silence.

Let's try this!

Hit it! Ryoko and . . .

All Three

    Ryoko and Katsufumi, live happily ever after. Just married.

All three, put their microphones on the stands and turn around.

Eiko   Enari, you're slow. Andre, that was one of the best tries. Let's do that one more time.

All Three

Ryoko and Katsufumi, live happily ever after and forever.

Enari *turns. Then whirls and falls down.*

Eiko Hey, Enari. That's enough. Get up.

Enari . . .

Enari *looks like she is struggling.*

Andre How about putting our hands up with the turn?

Eiko How?

Andre *demonstrates to* **Eiko**.

Andre Here, this

Live happily ever after and forever.

We can be cool a bit, you know.

Eiko That is way too cool, isn't it? This music is French. So I want to have a feeling of ennui.

Andre I know, but does the wedding have to have a feeling of "ennui" at all?

Andre *looks at* **Enari**.

Enari . . .

Eiko Look. How about moving your hand like this?

She turns around and puts her hand up with an air of ennui.

Andre Wow, how did you do it?

Eiko Like this. Make it smooth around here a little bit.

She does that again.

Andre Ah, that really gives it a sense of "ennui."

He copies the way **Eiko** *puts her hand up.*

Enari *wraps her arms around herself and curls up.*

Eiko . . . Are you OK?

Enari Hun? Yes. Maybe it's been a while since I danced so much.

He breathes a heavy sigh.

Eiko Are you all right?

Enari Yeah, I'm all right.

Eiko . . .

Andre

Live happily ever after.

He turns around and raises his arm up.

Eiko   That's a bit too fast.

Andre   What?

Eiko   Too fast to end.

Andre   See this.

   Live happily ever after.

He turns around and raises his arm up.

Enari *goes into convulsions.*

Eiko   Come on.

Enari   . . .

Andre   . . .

Eiko   Enari, what's wrong with you?

Enari   . . .

Enari *unintentionally puts her hand to her mouth as if she is eating something.*

Andre   Do you want to eat something? Do you want a piece of bread?

Eiko *and* **Andre** *half smile.*

Enari   No thanks. No.

She doubles over. She is embarrassed about her condition and smiles sheepishly.

Eiko   Hey, are you really OK, Enari?

Andre   What are you doing? Watch out. Be careful. Are you hungry?

Enari   No, I ah hine (am fine). Jus hine.

She forces herself to smile.

She doubles over further.

Eiko   What? Hey!

Enari   Yeahhh, don't . . . wo-wo-worry abou me.

Eiko   Huh?

Enari   Don worr . . .

Eiko   I do worry.

Andre   You'd better eat something.

Enari *can't hold herself together.*

Enari   Call a doctor.

Andre   What?

Enari   A hoctor, hoctor.

Eiko *tries to hold* **Enari** *to stop her from cramping.*

Eiko   What? A doctor? Do you really want me to call a doctor?

Andre   Huh?

Eiko   Oh, no. We need one now.

Andre   Huh? Ah, yes.

Eiko   . . .

Enari   I can't breathe. I can't. Hey. Oh . . .

Her body twitches severely and becomes rigid. Then her body goes limp all of a sudden and dies.

Silence.

Eiko   Enari?

Andre   Ugh . . . Ah . . .

Silence.

Eiko *comes close to* **Enari** *and shakes her body. She examines her face. She releases her hands after realizing the fact that she is really dead.*

Andre *looks at* **Eiko.**

Eiko   Oh, no. Oh, what? Oh, shit! Oh no.

Andre *can't move as if he is overcome by a sleep-like kind of paralysis. He can't help staring at* **Enari.** **Andre** *begins to breathe heavily.*

Eiko   . . .

Andre *breathes heavily. He is struggling to breathe.*

Andre   . . .

He looks at **Eiko** *with a facial expression of "This is strange. What is going on?"*

Andre   . . .

Eiko   Hey, what's wrong? Are you hyperventilating?

Andre   Ka . . . Ka . . .

He sounds like something has gotten stuck in his throat.

. . . I can't breathe.

Eiko   . . .

Andre   I can't breathe . . . Help.

Eiko   Oh . . . oh.

Andre   Help me.

Eiko   . . .

Andre   . . .

He suffers as he scratches his body and glares at **Eiko** *with his eyes wide open. He crumples down and dies.*

Andre   . . .

Eiko   Andre? Andre . . . Andre . . . Ugh! Ah! Whaaa . . . Ah . . .

She lurches, dragging herself along and exits.

Enari *and* **Andre***'s bodies remain on the stage.*

△*A hallway inside the hospital. The next scene overlaps with* **Eiko's** *voice.*

Maki *and* **Miki** *enter.*

Maki   You stay here.

Miki   What's going on?

Maki   I don't know.

Miki   Why are people dying? A medical incident or something?

Maki   I don't know.

Miki   That must be it. Doctors are never serious about doing their jobs.

Maki   I really don't know anything.

Miki   Calm down, Maki.

Maki   . . .

Maki *puts her head in her hands to think.*

Miki   Oh, hey. Hey. Hey!

Maki   Shut up.

Miki   Hey, are we all going to die?

Maki   I don't know. That's absurd.

Miki   Where are you going?

Maki   I'm going to the medical office.

Miki   What about me?

Maki   Stay around here. I'll be right back.

Miki   Ah, I want to come with you.

Maki   . . .

Maki *exits.*

Miki *remains alone. She also exits after a while.*

△*A café near the university. Next scene starts after* **Maki** *exits.*

Kaori *and* **Ryoko** *enter.*

Kaori *and* **Ryoko** *notice* **Katsufumi***'s body on the floor and realize that he is dead.*

Ryoko . . . Katsufumi? Katsufumi!

Ryoko *clings to* **Yoneda***'s body crying.*

Kaori *puts her palms over her face.*

Ryoko Wake up, Katsufumi! Stay alive!

She tries to resuscitate him, pushing hard on his belly.

Kaori Stop that. He's already dead.

Ryoko He can't be dead. He is dead, but . . . Wake up! Come alive!

Yoneda *doesn't come back.* **Ryoko** *keeps pushing on the soft area of his belly hard.*

Ryoko . . .

Ryoko *crumples crying on* **Yoneda***'s body.*

Kaori What's happening? What's all this?

Ryoko *lies next to* **Yoneda**.

Kaori What are you doing?

Ryoko I'll die next to him.

Kaori Huh?

Ryoko Farewell.

Kaori Hey, why are you dying?

Ryoko Why?

Kaori Yes, why? What are you dying for?

Ryoko I don't know. We're all going to die, no?

Kaori Huh?

Ryoko All of the people in this town will die soon, no?

Kaori . . . Why?

Ryoko Because we saw them dying.

Kaori But you're still alive.

Ryoko It won't be long.

Kaori Hey, you don't know anything about him. He is dead already. It's no use dying next to his body right there.

Ryoko   I don't know about him well, but I love him.

Kaori   How come you say you love him without knowing him.

Ryoko   I love him because I don't know him well.

Kaori   What? Ah, well, you should fight somehow to stay alive.

Ryoko   That's not necessary. Please leave.

Kaori   . . . Ah.

She stares at **Ryoko** *for a while. She realizes that there is nothing she can do. She exits.*

△*An alley inside the campus. Next scene starts after the conversation between* **Ryoko** *and* **Kaori***.*

Match *enters with his hands and knees.*

Katsuo *enters after some time and falls down over* **Match***.*

Katsuo   We should call a doctor.

Match   She was dead.

Katsuo   Why did you run?

Match   Because . . . you ran too.

Katsuo   Because I didn't want to be alone with her. I can't be alone with her.

Match   . . .

Katsuo   Nana. . .

He crouches down.

Katsuo   Ugh . . . Nana . . . Nana . . .

He starts crying. He crouches down and hits the ground.

Match *stands up and stares at him blankly. He grabs* **Katsuo** *and flips him over.*

Katsuo *looks at* **Match** *confused.*

Katsuo   . . .

Katsuo *resumes crying harder.*

Match   Nana is my girlfriend.

Katsuo   Nanaaaa. . . .

Match   You don't deserve to be crying.

He pounces on **Katsuo***.*

Katsuo   Why not?

Match   You should cry less than I do.

He and **Katsuo** *scuffle.* **Katsuo** *holds* **Match** *down as he is the stronger one. It looks almost like they are in a sexual position.* **Katsuo** *is on top of* **Match**.

As **Match** *is being held down by* **Katsuo***, he becomes exhausted. He starts sobbing.*

Katsuo *realizes* **Match** *is sobbing. He caresses* **Match***'s hair.*

Match *pulls* **Katsuo** *towards him and sobs on his chest.*

Katsuo *puts his hand on* **Match***'s head and caresses it. He calms down and cools off observing the way* **Match** *sobs.*

Match   Nana . . .

Katsuo   . . .

Match   Why? How come?

Katsuo   Ah, did Nana have any chronic disease?

Match   I don't know.

Katsuo   Did she have any heart trouble?

Match   I don't know.

Katsuo   . . .

Match   Nana was murdered.

Katsuo   . . . Why?

Match   I don't know. But people like her wouldn't die so easily.

Katsuo   . . .

Match   She may be alive. I didn't know if she was really dead.

Katsuo   . . . Do you want to find that out?

Match   . . .

Katsuo   Something is strange. There was a series of train accidents. There must be something going on. Maybe a war. I don't know.

Match   A war?

Katsuo   . . . I don't know. It could be some kind of virus.

Match   Do you mean the human testing done by the American military in the basement of the hospital? Like Nana said?

Katsuo   I don't know . . . She could be a victim.

Match   That's ridiculous. She must have been sick.

△*A café near the university.*

Keisuke *returns and is surprised to find another body. He sits on a chair thinking for a while then exits to go into the back of the café.*

△*An alley inside the campus.*

Katsuo   Can people die just like that? The sukonbu must have been poisoned.

Match   Do you think it was poisoned? Why?

Katsuo   Where did she buy it? The co-op store?

Match   I don't know.

Katsuo   How about us?

Match   What?

Katsuo   If she was murdered, are we next?

Match   Hey, we don't know if she was killed.

Katsuo   You just said so.

Match   I did, but.

Katsuo   What should we do?

Match   How do I know?

Katsuo   What are we supposed to do?

Match   . . .

Katsuo   I am leaving.

He moves away from **Match** *and stands up.*

Match   Huh?

Katsuo   I am going home.

Match   You can't leave.

Katsuo   Why not?

Match   What are you going to do at home?

Katsuo   I am scared of staying here. I'll go talk to my mom.

Match   What about Nana?

Katsuo   I'll call the police.

Match   That's it. Yes.

He takes out of his phone and dials.

Should I dial 1-1-0 in a case like this?

Katsuo   I think so.

Match   What should I say?

Katsuo   I don't know. I guess they'll talk and ask you questions.

Match   What are they going to ask me? I stole a bicycle and got caught once. You call the police.

Katsuo   You'll be fine.

Match   You call them. You're older than I am, and your grades are better than mine.

Katsuo   No, they aren't. You have more credits than I do.

Match   But my grades are mostly Cs. You're smarter than I am. You wear glasses.

Katsuo   These are glasses for being farsighted.

Match   Whatever.

He passes the cell phone to **Katsuo**.

Katsuo *refuses.*

Match *put the phone in front of* **Katsuo**.

Katsuo   Hey!

Match   It is ringing. The police will pick it up.

Katsuo   No. What am I supposed to say?

Match   I don't know. Say, "My friend is in trouble."

Katsuo *picks up the cell phone.*

Katsuo   Hey, you. This is your cell phone. You talk to them. You're one year younger than I am.

Match   . . .

Match *steps away from* **Katsuo**.

Katsuo   Come on. Seriously. Hey.

He puts his ear to the phone and then gives the phone to **Match** *and repeats that gesture again until he finally puts his ear to the phone.*

Match   Did they answer? Did they?

Katsuo   . . .

Katsuo *thrusts the cell phone to* **Match**.

Match   What.

Katsuo   Line is busy.

Match   Huh?

Katsuo   It's just the tone.

Match   . . .

Katsuo   Did you check the number?

Match   . . .

Match *puts the phone to his ear and then checks the call history, etc. He calls 110 again and puts the phone to his ear.*

Match   . . . It's just the dial tone.

Katsuo   Police is 1-1-0.

Match   Yes, I know.

Katsuo   How is the reception?

Match   The reception is fine. What is this? What do we do?

Katsuo   I don't know.

Match   Who else should we call in the situation like this?

Katsuo   Do you have any friends that you can depend on?

Match   . . . Nana. I only have Nana, you know.

Katsuo   There should be more than one.

Match   Do you know someone?

Katsuo   . . . No, I don't. Give it to me.

He calls someone.

Match   Who are you calling?

Katsuo   My home. Oh, my god. Match, Match.

Match   What?

Katsuo   They aren't there. My parents aren't home.

Match   They maybe went out to Marunan[6] or somewhere.

Katsuo   What is Marunan?

Match   You know what? Maybe all lines are occupied.

Katsuo   I see. People are all calling because it's an emergency.

Yama san *and* **Sakana Hakase** *enter.*

Yama san *is debilitated.*

Katsuo *and* **Match** *notice them.*

Yama san *and* **Sakana Hakase** *stop walking.*

Katsuo   Hi.

Sakana   . . .

Sakana Hakase *bows.*

Yama san *seems like he doesn't feel well.*

Yama   Hi.

Katsuo   ...

Yama   ...

Match   Do you know anything about this?

Yama   What thing?

Match   Like what's going on?

Yama   No idea.

Sakana   We walked all the way and—

Katsuo   Yes.

He coughs.

Sakana   There were many people and some of them were dead.

Yama   It was chaos. People were all in panic.

Match   ... Oh. So we are ...

Sakana   Is something happening?

Katsuo   Don't know.

He coughs.

Sakana   ...

Yama   Is he all right?

Match   What?

Yama   He is coughing.

Katsuo *pretends not to cough.*

Match   ...

Katsuo   It's just something attached to my throat. It's dry because I'm thirsty.

Sakana   What thing? What is attached to your throat?

Katsuo   A piece of my skin.

Sakana   ...

Match   How are you?

Yama   I saw the accident on the train this morning, and I've felt sick ever since.

Match   Really?

Yama   Why would I lie?

Silence.

Katsuo *coughs.*

Match　. . . Katsuo?

Katsuo　What?

He tries to stifle the cough. He coughs with his mouth closed.

Match　That cough . . .

Katsuo　No, this is different.

He coughs. He slumps down. He can't stop coughing.

Match *intentionally keeps his distance from* **Katsuo**.

Katsuo　Ma . . . tch . . .

Match *pretends he doesn't hear anything.*

Match　. . .

Yama　He called your name.

Match　. . .

Katsuo　This is it.

Match　Katsuo.

Sakana　Yama san, let's get out of here.

Yama　Yes.

Match　Wait.

He stops **Yama san** *and* **Sakana Hakase**.

Katsuo　Mat . . . ch . . . Match . . . Hold me.

Match　Huh?

Katsuo *coughs.*

Katsuo　I can't breathe. Hold me now.

Match　What?

Yama　Hug him.

Match　. . .

Katsuo　Match . . .

He wriggles. He looks like he is suffering.

Match　Are you contagious?

Katsuo　. . .

Sakana Is he sick?

Match I don't know, but there's a rumor.

Sakana A rumor?   **Katsuo** Match . . . Matchiii . . .

Katsuo *dies.*

Match The rumor says that they are cultivating some kind of virus for military purposes in the basement of the hospital.

Sakana Huh? Is that the cause of all this?

Match I don't really know. That's the urban legend. I mean the rumor.

Yama san *realized that* **Katsuo** *is dead. He points to him.*

Yama . . . Your friend . . .

Match Huh? Oh, Katsuo.

He stares at **Katsuo***'s body from a distance. He covers his face with his hands. It happened all of a sudden and he's not very close to* **Katsuo***. He's stunned but he's not very sad. Because he cares about what people think about him, he forces himself to look like he is mourning, but he is not very successful.*

Sakana Do you think it's the virus? If it is the virus, we must be in danger.

Match I don't know.

Yama If so, what should we do? What are we supposed to do?

Match . . .

Sakana What should I do?

Match You should just try not to die.

Sakana How?

Match . . . I have no idea.

Sakana We should go to the hospital to seek out a cure.

Match I agree. They can give us something like an antidote. What do you call it? It's at the hospital where you can get it.

Sakana Ah. What do you think?

Yama . . . I have nowhere else to go.

Match I'll go because I don't have anything else to do.

Yama OK, I'll go too.

Match Let's go.

Yama Yes.

Match I'm Kondo.

Yama   Masahiko?

Match   Ah, yeah. Well.

Yama   I'm Yamamoto. He's Sakana Hakase.

Sakana   Hi.

Match   . . . Hello.

Silence.

OK, then.

Match *exits.*

Shall we?

Yama *and* **Sakana** *follow* **Match** *towards the exit.*

They pray for **Katsuo**'s *body and exit.*

△*A café near the university.*

Miki *enters tired. She drinks the leftovers of a drink. She looks at the bodies of* **Yoneda** *and* **Ryoko**.

Ryoko   Who are you?

Miki *jumps up.*

Ryoko   What are you doing?

Miki   Taking a walk.

Ryoko   How is it outside? Any updates?

Miki   Since when?

Ryoko   Are people still dying?

Miki   Yes, they are.

Ryoko   Are you wandering around?

Miki   Yeah, I got a little thirsty and so.

Ryoko   I'm scared. Could you stay with me?

Miki   Huh?

Ryoko   I think I'm going to die soon. I can't see things well.

Miki   What?

Ryoko   I've become blind.

Miki   Why?

Ryoko   I don't know. It's scary.

Miki   I am sorry to hear that.

Ryoko   I am terrified.

Miki   Who is this person next to you?

Ryoko   My husband.

Miki   . . . Oh.

Ryoko   Would you stay with me and watch me die?

Miki   No.

Ryoko   Why?

Miki   Well, how long is it going to take?

Ryoko   I don't know, but it will be soon. Please. I am scared to die alone.

Miki   . . . Well . . .

Ryoko   Please.

She gropes to reach **Miki** *and holds onto her leg.*

Miki *tries to pluck her hand away.*

She tries to get **Ryoko** *away from her hand but* **Ryoko** *grabs it to pull towards her.*

Ryoko   Thank you.

She pulls **Miki** *close to her.*

Ryoko   I am in a horrible situation right now, but I feel content, even a bit happ—

Miki *puts her hands on* **Ryoko***'s neck.*

Ryoko   Huh? What?

Miki *finally strangles* **Ryoko** *with both of her hands.*

Ryoko   Hey!

Keisuke *enters. He gives them a look of shock. He exits.*

Miki *is strangling* **Ryoko***'s neck.* **Ryoko** *fights back, thrashing her legs.*

Keisuke *suddenly grabs something nearby and intends to stop* **Miki** *with it, but he doesn't go further than imagining it.* **Miki** *glares at him. He can't do anything.*

Ryoko *stops fighting back. She dies.*

Miki *falls down, breathing hard. She realizes that something is attached to her hand.*

Miki   Ugh! Gross! Something's stuck on my hand.

She wipes her hand off with **Ryoko***'s clothes and sniffs it.*

Keisuke   Did you kill her?

Miki   . . Didn't you see?

Keisuke   Did you do it?

Miki   Yeah.

Keisuke   Why?

Miki   Because she was already starting to die. She also looked in pain.

Keisuke   . . . What? What's going on?

Miki   Do you work here?

Keisuke   . . . Who are you?

Miki   I came from the hospital.

Keisuke   . . .

Miki   Can I use the bathroom?

Keisuke   Yes. In the back.

Miki *is disturbed by whatever is on her hand and exits to the back of the café.*

Keisuke *sits down helplessly right there.*

Ryoko *'s body remains on the stage.*

△*On a street.*

Sachie *enters. She looks around. She feels lonely and calls her son's name.*

Sachie   Katsuo! Katsuo!

She exits.

△*A break room space at the university.*

Eiko *enters. She is scrolling her cell phone. She looks around.*

Eiko   . . .

She finds **Nana** *'s body.*

Eiko   Nana . . . whoa . . . er . . . whoa . . .

She flops down and starts crying.

Shoji *enters. His hand is on his butt trying to hold something.*

Shoji   . . .

Eiko *cries and stares at* **Shoji***.*

Shoji *can't ignore* **Eiko** *as she is staring at him.*

Shoji   Are you all right?

Eiko   . . . Nana is dead. Enari is dead too. Also Andre.

Shoji What? Ah, I see. I am so sorry.

Eiko . . . Ahhh, I am scared.

Shoji Yes.

Eiko I am very scared.

Shoji Calm down. What happened?

Eiko They died while they were dancing.

Shoji Dance? Why did they dance?

Eiko Huh? Hmm? Because sometimes we have no choice but to dance.

Shoji Oh, I see. Hmm?

Eiko The phone line has been busy. It's like the night we have fireworks. I can't get through to anyone. Where did you come from?

Shoji What?

Eiko Where did you come from? How was the station?

Shoji I don't know. I was in school all day.

Eiko *stares at* **Shoji***.*

Eiko Are you Shoji?

Shoji . . .

Eiko Are you Shoji of the Toho Kenbun Rock?

Shoji Er, yes.

Eiko *slowly picks her cell phone and puts it close to* **Shoji***'s face. She takes a photo.*

Silence.

Eiko *stares at the phone and starts sobbing.*

Eiko Uhhh, I can't thank you. Ah . . . just my luck—right place wrong time.

She cries.

Shoji Oh, I am sorry.

Eiko Ah . . . Woo . . .

Shoji . . .

Eiko *starts struggling holding her belly with her hands.*

Eiko No, no.

Shoji What's wrong?

Eiko I'm dying.

Shoji   What?

Eiko   I think I am dying.

Shoji   Oh, hang in there! Hold on!

Eiko   I can't breathe.

Shoji   Yes.

Eiko *stares at* **Shoji**.

Eiko   Mom?

Shoji   Huh? No, I'm not.

Eiko   I'm so sorry, Mom.

Shoji   Huh?

Eiko   I'm sorry I didn't know that.

Shoji   Hmm?

Koichi *enters*.

Eiko   I just didn't know.

Shoji   What? What is it you didn't know?

Eiko   Woo, woo.

Koichi *observes* **Shoji**.

Eiko   Forgive me, Mom.   **Koichi**   Er, I, may I go?

Shoji   Ah, can . . . can you just hold on a second?

Eiko *says the next line when* **Shoji** *looks at* **Koichi**.

Eiko   Mom!

Shoji   Yes?

Koichi   Oh, she is . . .

Shoji   Er, yeah.

Eiko   . . .

Shoji *pretends to be her mother.*

Shoji   It's OK. OK. I am sorry.

Eiko   Do you forgive me then?

Shoji   Of course. I'm always on your side.

Eiko   . . .

Eiko *stares peacefully at* **Shoji**.

Eiko Wh . . .

Shoji Wh?

Eiko Who . . .

She glares using all the power that she has left.

Who the hell are you?

She dies.

Shoji . . .

Shoji *looks at* **Koichi** *and grins.*

Koichi Er, do you know her?

Shoji Er, well, I am, I have been on TV. So . . . er, I am Shoji from the Toho Kenbun Rock.

Koichi Oh, yeah. KENBUN "ROKU."

Shoji Yes.

Koichi I, er, I've had some duties and haven't been able to watch TV.

Shoji Oh, you are a businessman. Have you been busy?

Koichi Ah, well, I'm actually not.

Shoji Oh.

Koichi I'm looking for my daughter.

Shoji Ah.

Koichi What are you doing?

Shoji Well, I don't know what's going on at all. So I was wandering around the hospital and here.

Koichi Ah, I totally understand.

Shoji Yes.

Koichi Er, bye.

He starts walking.

Shoji Er, wait. Do we leave this person like this?

Koichi Huh? What?

Shoji Don't we need to get this body cremated?

Koichi Well, er, it's an emergency situation. So I think it's fine. See you then.

Shoji Oh, hey.

Koichi Yes?

Shoji   Ah, I mean, I . . . er . . .

Koichi   What?

Shoji   Well, er, something has come out of my backside.

He whispers.

Koichi   Huh? Your what?

Shoji   Er, something is coming out of my ass.

Koichi   Huh? Go to the bathroom.

Shoji   No, no, I mean a part of my insides is coming out.

Koichi   What?

Shoji   Take a look.

Koichi   I don't want to.

Shoji   It's right here.

He sticks his hip out and pulls down the back of his pants to show him.

Koichi   I said no.

Shoji   Ah! Ah!

He freezes looking up.

Ah.

Koichi   What happened?

Shoji   Yes, I think I am about to die. Would you mind staying with me while I die?

Koichi   You know I am in a hurry.

Shoji   It's soon. So soon.

Koichi   Really soon?

Shoji   Yes.

Koichi   . . . Oh, please hurry. I am really in a hurry.

Shoji   Why are you so rushed?

Koichi   My daughter must be around here somewhere. I want to see her.

Shoji   What are you going to do after that?

Koichi   I am not sure about afterward. I just want to see her.

Shoji   Do you want to see your daughter?

Koichi   Of course, I do.

Shoji   Maybe she would rather see her boyfriend instead.

Koichi   Huh? . . . Well, I, I'm her step . . . stepfather.

Shoji   Oh. I think it doesn't matter.

Koichi   Her real father died early, and I got married then. I became her father after that. Are you dead yet? If so, I am sorry I have to go.

Shoji   Wait, wait, wait, wait. It will be soon.

Koichi   Er, hey, this could be . . . well, maybe good I think.

Shoji   Yes.

Koichi   You look like you're recovering.

Shoji   Oh, no. I am totally fading.

Koichi   Oh, then I have to go.

Shoji   Uh.

Koichi   Hey, wait. I am going, but you can follow me. And if you want to, you can er . . . pass away on the way. I wouldn't mind it at all. Please go and I can watch you die.

Shoji   Ah, but it is too hard for me to walk.

Koichi   Hey, you know you may be a bit selfish.

Shoji   Huh? But I'll die soon.

Koichi   I understand. Don't get me wrong. What I'm saying is that I don't know when I'm going to die. So the time I have left until I die . . . or my life . . . maybe "life" is too dramatic a word, but I think I am not exaggerating—

Shoji   Well, but you still look fine.

Koichi   No, no. I totally have a stomachache. I think a headache has just started.

Shoji   You're lying.

Koichi   But I'm sorry I don't have time for you. So you're welcome to follow me. Or follow me and do it when it's convenient for you. Or you could just do it right now and take care of yourself.

Shoji   Oh, no. Not fair. You wait.

Koichi   . . . I'm really sorry. I'm so sorry. I have things to do.

Shoji   Wait, wait. Look. Almost. Just wait.

Koichi   Take care then.

He exits.

Shoji   Ah, wait. Oh.

He concentrates.

Oh, no. I can't. Wait up.

He follows **Koichi** *to exit.*

△*A café near the university.*

Miki *enters. Her hands are wet.*

Miki   Do you have something to dry them with?

Keisuke *looks around but can't find anything suitable. He pulls his apron towards her.*

Miki *goes close to* **Keisuke**, *and wipes her hands on his apron.*

Keisuke   . . . Well . . . you are tough.

Miki   No, I am not.

Keisuke   . . .

Miki   Goodbye then.

Keisuke   Are you going somewhere?

Miki   Yeah.

Keisuke   Where to? It's the same everywhere. People are dying.

Miki   I am going to the sea.

Keisuke   What?

Miki   To the sea.

Keisuke   Why?

Miki   I don't know.

Keisuke   People are all dying.

Miki   . . . Yeah.

Keisuke   We might die soon too.

Miki   But it's natural. We will all die for sure.

Keisuke   Yeah but . . . we didn't do anything.

Miki   No matter what you did or you didn't do, everybody is going to die sometime.

Silence.

Keisuke   What are you going to do at the sea?

Miki   Nothing in particular . . . I just want to see it. Bye.

She tries to leave.

Keisuke   Hey, can I come with you?

Miki   . . . No, you can't.

Keisuke   Why not?

Miki   I would rather be alone.

Keisuke   Why? It's better to be with someone in a situation like this.

Miki   I prefer to be alone.

Keisuke   Ah, why?

Miki   That's how I feel.

Keisuke   Well, then, I am following you at a distance.

Miki   How much?

Keisuke   What?

Miki   How far are you going to be away from me?

Keisuke   How far do you need to feel alone?

Miki   . . . 100 meters.

Keisuke *calculates the distance in his head.*

Keisuke   That's way too far.

Miki   Then 50 meters.

Keisuke   I want to be a bit closer.

Miki   But I wouldn't feel alone if you are closer than that.

Keisuke   I know you want to be alone, but I am the kind of person who doesn't want to be alone. So I don't want to be alone now. OK?

Miki   . . .

Keisuke   So let's be at a win-win distance that makes us even somewhere between alone and not alone. How about that?

Miki   How far do you mean?

Keisuke   I don't know.

Miki *moves close to* **Keisuke.**

Miki   How about here?

Keisuke   Ah, I don't feel alone.

Miki   Really?

Keisuke   But if you say so, I might feel alone.

Miki   Then.

Miki *moves close to* **Keisuke***.*

Miki   How about here?

Keisuke   I don't feel alone from this distance.

Miki   Fine. This is about the distance from you.

Keisuke   Deal.

Miki *starts walking.*

Keisuke   Where are you heading?

Miki   I said, to the sea.

Keisuke   It's far.

Miki   I know.

Keisuke   We should cut across the university.

Miki   Yeah, I know.

Miki *and* **Keisuke** *exit.*

△*An alley inside the campus.*

Sachie *enters. She finds* **Katsuo***'s body and runs to him.*

Sachie   Katsuo, Katsuooooo, My boy. Oh, ayyy, Katuoooo!

She performs CPR on **Katsuo***. She slaps his face and such.*

Sachie   Katsuo, why? Oh, why?

She gives up and hunches next to **Katsuo***'s body.*

△*At a street leading to the university hospital.*

Match*,* **Sakana Hakase***, and* **Yama san** *enter.*

Match   That's why they call you Sakana Hakase.

Sakana   Ah, yeah.

Yama   He doesn't really want anybody to call him Hakase except those who are very close to him.

Sakana   Not really.

Yama   . . .

Sakana   "Not really" means that some people who are not so close to me still call me by that name. I certainly don't mean that all people who call me by that name are not close.

Yama   Who do you mean by that?

Sakana   What?

Yama   Who calls you Hakase, even though they're not so close to you?

Sakana   Er . . . well, Muraki, and . . .

Yama   Who? Who is Muraki?

Sakana   A friend from the school.

Yama   Which school?

Sakana   Er, university.

Yama   Oh.

Sakana   Ah . . . but we are not that close at all.

Yama   How did you meet him?

Sakana   We were members of the same extracurricular club.

Yama   What club?

Sakana   Ah, fishing club.

Yama   Huh. I didn't know that.

Sakana   Didn't I tell you before?

Yama   Oh, my blood is draining out of my head.

Match   Are you all right?

Yama   Fine, thank you.

Yama san *looks at* **Sakana Hakase**.

Sakana   Ah, are you OK?

Yama   You don't mean it. I don't need just empty words.

Sakana   I mean it.

Match   Would you like to try your head down?

Yama   I see. I can elevate my feet above my head so that the blood will return to my head.

Match   Yeah.

Yama san *looks at* **Sakana Hakase**.

Sakana   . . .

Yama san *lies down and puts his feet up high. Legs are not stable because he doesn't have enough muscle strength to hold them.*

Match *helps* **Yama san** *to hold his feet.*

Yama   Thank you.

Sakana Hakase *takes a turn with* **Match**.

Yama   . . .

Sakana   Are you OK?

Yama   Yes. Match is taking care of me and making me feel better.

Sakana   . . . I handled some fish today, and I thought you hated that smell.

Yama   It's not just today that you smell fishy.

Sakana   Yes, you are right.

Match   . . .

Naito *enters agitated.*

Naito   Are you all right?

Naito *runs to* **Yama san**.

Naito   You guys do something. Your friend is fighting right now.

Match   . . . Ah.

Sakana Hakase *is surprised while holding* **Yama san** *'s feet.*

Naito *rips off* **Yama san** *'s clothes and bares his chest.*

Yama   Ugh!

Naito   I know. I know. Hang in there.

He attaches his ear to **Yama san** *'s chest.*

Yama san *tries to refuse him.*

Sakana Hakase *tries to do something by holding* **Yama san** *'s legs.*

Match *rudely pulls* **Naito** *away from* **Yama san**. **Naito** *is stunned and looks at* **Match**.

Silence.

Naito   I'm a doctor.

Silence.

Match   Oh, you are. That's why.

Naito   This is an emergency.

Match   Ah, well, this . . . this situation or things now are caused by something like a virus? And that made things like this?

Naito   . . . Ah, I don't know that.

Silence.

I mean, I need to perform a checkup to offer a diagnosis. Otherwise, I wouldn't know that cause.

Match   Yes.

Naito   How long has he been like this?

Sakana   What? He's been like this for quite a long time.

Naito   . . .

Naito *looks at* **Yama san**. **Yama san** *covers up his chest.*

Match   Ah, what hospital do you work at? Do you work for this university hospital?

Naito   Yes. Are you a student at KU?

Match   Yes, I am.

Naito   Oh yeah? I am also from the KU. Are you from the MD program?

Match   Not me.

Naito   Oh.

Yama   Am I sick?

Naito   What?

Yama   Am I sick?

Naito   I don't know.

Yama   I feel the blood draining from my head.

Naito   You might be dehydrated.

Yama   No, I don't think that I am.

Naito   Did you have breakfast?

Yama   I did.

Naito   You aren't sick. You have digestive disorder.

Yama   If I don't eat breakfast, am I sick?

Naito   I don't think so.

Yama   . . .

Sakana   My heart starts pounding when I try to talk to people. I can't carry on conversations.

Naito   That's just your personality.

Sakana   Ah, I thought so.

Silence.

Naito   I am an ENT doctor.

Sakana   Ah, so you know a lot about ears and noses.

Silence.

Match   Do you know what?

Naito   What?

Match   The university hospital only has two floors in the basement.

Naito   Ah . . . rumor has it that we have a third floor in the basement.

Match   Yes.

Naito   I know there's a rumor.

Match   Is that the rumor?

Naito   I've been around for a long time, but I've never been to the third floor in the basement.

Match   So they have one?

Naito   I think so.

Match   I heard that the American military cultivated some kind of virus there.

Naito   American military?

Match   I don't know, but the rumor or an urban legend says as much.

Naito   Oh, I've never heard that. I only heard that they revived the hospital director three times using the eternal life compound that they experimented with in the basement.

Match   What?

Naito   The rumor is that the eternal life cure brought him back to life three times.

Yama san's *back arches upward.*

Sakana Hakase *is still holding* **Yama san**'s *legs.*

Sakana   . . .?   **Match**   Is that true?

Yama   . . .   **Naito**   It can't be true.

Yama san *jumps with his back.*

Sakana   Yama san?

Yama   I can't stop this. Hakase, I can't.

Sakana   Yama san.

Sakana Hakase *tries to hold down* **Yama san**.

Yama san *springs up.*

Yama   Woah!

Sakana   Yama saaaaan.

Sakana Hakase *wraps* **Yama san**'s *body to stop him from moving.*

Sakana   Yama san.

Yama   Hakase . . . I . . . I . . .

Sakana   Yama san?

Yama   . . .

Yama san *drops his head.*

Sakana   Yama san? Yama san? Yama saaaaaaaan!

Sakana Hakase *remembers memories of* **Yama san** *in his head and becomes overwhelmed. He adjusts his breathing to cry out loud.*

Yama san *comes back alive all of a sudden.*

Yama   Whoa!

Yama san *breathes heavily.*

Yama   Huh?

Sakana   Ah . . .

Yama   I feel better.

Sakana   . . . Oh, really.

Naito   Ack! Ugh!

Match   What?

Naito *begins to suffer with his hands on his chest.*

Match   Hey, look at him.

Naito   Oooh! Wahhh! Ack!

He glares at **Match** *and comes close to him.*

Naito   . . . You guys . . . please . . . give this to her.

He takes out a cassette tape out of his bag.

Match   What? What?

Naito   Give this to Ms. Maki Endo for me.

Match   What?

Naito   This . . . to Maki Endo.

Match   Ah, I can't. I can't.

Naito   Please. If you stay here, she'll pass by. Please.

Match   What?

Naito *writhes intensely.*

Naito   . . . Stay alive!

He dies. His body remains still there.

Match   . . .

Yama   I think I would pretend that I didn't hear anything.

Match   I would too.

Sakana   Ah, I think he asked us to give that to Maki Endo.

Silence.

Yama   Well, then, Hakase you stay here and give that to her.

Sakana   What?

Match   We don't even know if Endo is still alive.

Sakana   You have a point.

Yama   I don't agree.

Sakana   I don't either, but this is his last word.

Yama   Right, but we don't know him. We only know he is loud and also a doctor.

Match *takes the cassette tape from* **Naito**'*s hand and puts the tape in front of* **Sakana Hakase**.

Sakana   I don't want to.

Match   But I think it's better for you to have it.

Sakana   What are you going to do now, Match?

Match   I think I want to find out the truth about this matter.

Sakana   Like how?

Match   So I'll go to the hospital to ask the people there a lot of questions. I might find out something then.

Sakana   This person here works for the hospital, but he didn't know anything.

Match   I think because he wasn't popular.

Sakana   . . .

Yama   I think this person probably wasn't popular.

Sakana   Well, then we can meet Endo to find that out. It kills two birds with one stone.

Match Ah, I see what you mean. That's good, but I don't want to spend the rest of my life waiting for the last word of someone I don't even know well.

Sakana . . .

Yama What's on the cassette tape?

Match It's a cassette tape, you know.

Sakana I think he asked Endo to marry him on this tape.

Match Ah.

Yama That would sound about right, I guess. You're quick-witted. That's why they call you Hakase.

Sakana Not really.

Match *looks for something inside his bag.*

Yama What are you doing?

Match Ah, I have a device to play the tape.

Sakana Why?

Match I was supposed to have a meeting today. I tried to record it and will transcribe it for my graduation thesis.

Sakana I see.

Yama What are you graduating from?

Match . . .

Yama What are you graduating from?

Match University.

Yama We are going to die, aren't we?

Match Yes.

Sakana Do you think we are going to die?

Yama I think so.

Sakana What about the fish? I feel sorry if they're going to die as well.

Match I think they're going to be fine.

Sakana How do you know?

Match They've been around long enough on Earth. This virus could only be contagious among humans.

Sakana I see. You're right. I have some hope.

Yama Excuse me for interrupting you guys while you're talking.

Sakana What's wrong, Yama san?

Yama   Well, I think that the time is up.

Sakana   What?

Yama   Yeah, maybe.

Sakana   You almost died a while ago and have just been revived.

Yama   Yeah, to tell you the truth, I have pains all over my belly.

Sakana   Do you think going to the bathroom would help?

Yama   I don't think so.

Sakana   Oh, no.

Yama san *put his hands to his belly and starts struggling.*

Yama   Woooh, whoa!

Sakana   Yama san?

Match   Are you all right?

Yama   No, I'm not all right.

He writhes.

Sakana   Yama san, don't leave me alone, Yama san!

Yama   Sakana Hakase . . . well . . . Toshinori . . . I'm happy to be dying with you by my side.

Yama san *suffers and suffers before he dies, leaving his eyes wide open.*

Sakana   Yama san!

Sakana Hakase *clings to* **Yama san** *and cries.*

Match *goes to* **Sakana Hakase**'*s side and tries to hold him.*

Sakana Hakase *is stunned as he is not sure what* **Match** *is trying to do. Finally understanding his intentions, he intensely resists him. He clings to* **Yama san***.*

Match *is taken aback by* **Sakana Hakase**'*s resistance. As he sees* **Sakana Hakase** *crying, he pretends to hold back his tears. He sits down besides* **Yama san** *and puts his palm over his eyes, trying to slide them closed.*

Match   . . .?

Yama san'*s eyes remain wide open.*

Match *repeats the same move.*

Match   . . .?

Match *tries a few times and looks at* **Sakana Hakase***. He tries again, but* **Yama san** *doesn't close his eyes.*

Sakana   . . .?

Sakana Hakase *notices* **Match**.

Match *repeats the same move deliberately enough for* **Sakana Hakase** *to see.*

Sakana   Are you touching him?

Match   What?

Sakana   Did you touch his eyelids?

Match   Can I touch them?

Sakana   Yes, you should use your hands to close them.

Sakana Hakase *gestures towards himself, asking if he can do that for him.*

Match *accepts* **Sakana Hakase**'s *offer to do it for him.*

Sakana Hakase *pinches* **Yama san**'s *eyelids with his fingers and closes them.*

Yama san's *body remains on the stage.*

Match   Well, I didn't realize how hands-on you have to be.

Sakana   Yeah they won't close unless we actually touch them.

Match   Oh, I see. I thought people would keep doing such involuntary movements after death and close their eyes naturally.

Sakana   Oh.

Match   I'll make sure and die with my eyes closed.

Sakana   Fish don't have eyelids, so their eyes are wide open after they die. You can see proof of this on a sashimi dish at an izakaya restaurant and such.

Match   I knew that.

Sakana   Really?

Maki *enters.*

Maki   . . .

Match   . . . Hello.

Maki   Hi.

Match   Hi.

Maki   Er . . .

Match   Yes?

Maki   Have you been here long?

Match   Long? I am not sure.

Sakana   Maybe five or ten minutes.

Match   I would assume so.

Maki   Have you seen a lady in pajamas?

Match   No, I haven't. Have you?

Sakana   No.

Maki   I see. Did you talk to him?

She is looking at **Naito***'s body.*

Match   Yes, he said he is a doctor.

Maki   Yes.

Match   Do you know him?

Maki   Sort of.

Match   Are you Ms. Ando?

Maki   I'm Endo.

Match   Yes, Endo.

Maki   . . .?

Match   Hakase.

Sakana   Yeah, er, this . . . I think he probably left this for you.

Sakana Hakase *picks up the cassette tape on the ground and gives it to* **Maki***.*

Maki   . . .

Match   You can play it with this if you would like.

He hands over the tape recorder.

Maki   What's this?

Match   I don't know. He just asked us to give it to Endo.

Maki   I have no idea what this could be.

Match *puts the cassette tape in the tape recorder and plays it.*

Naito (*voice*)   Maki, please listen to this.

Naito *speaks followed by the sound of a guitar.* **Naito** *starts to sing but it's not a kind of love song or anything. Instead, he sings a simple song such as Mayim Mayim.*[7] *But he sings out as loud as he can.*

People there are embarrassed by the noise, but they all feel sorry about stopping the tape in the middle. They endure the discomfort and listen to **Naito***'s song.*

Match   . . .

Sakana   . . .

Maki   . . . Ah, really, I didn't ask him to do this.

Match What did he mean by this?

Sakana It's too late to find out.

Maki . . .

Match *put his hands to his chest.*

Match Whoa!

Sakana Match?

Match Ugh.

Maki . . .

Match I can't breathe.

He falls down. He starts to writhe in agony.

Sakana Are you all right? OK? Hold on.

Match I didn't want to die listening to the song of a guy I don't even know.

Sakana Match.

Match Mom. Mom. I wanted to eat your warm cre—

He dies. His body remains on the stage.

Sakana Match, what do you mean by "warm cre—"? Match!

Silence.

Sakana Hakase *is stumped and looks at* **Maki***.*

Maki *looks like she wants to say something, but* **Naito** *is still singing loud on the tape.* **Maki** *stops the player.*

Maki . . .

Sakana . . .

Maki I think he meant "cream stew."

Sakana . . . Who wants to eat thick food like cream stew when you are dying? I assumed people would probably want to eat something more watery.

Maki . . .

Koichi *enters. He becomes emotional and runs to* **Maki***.*

Koichi Maki, Maki.

He tries to hug **Maki***.*

Maki *somewhat refuses.*

Koichi *thinks it can't be true, and tries again to hug her.*

Maki *apparently refuses.*

Koichi *realizes and gives up trying to hug her.*

Silence.

Sakana   Do you know him?

Maki   Yeah.

Koichi   Is he your boyfriend?

Maki   No, he isn't.

Koichi   Hi.

Sakana   Hello.

Koichi   Maki, you're safe now. I'll . . . you'll protect me, I mean . . . Let's get out of this town.

Maki   What?

Koichi   Let's get out of here.

Maki   You don't know, do you?

Koichi   What is it?

Maki   It's not only happening in here.

Koichi   Huh?

Maki   Everywhere in the world is like this.

Koichi   How come?

Maki   Who knows. People just die one after another before doing some research to find out the cause.

Koichi   Why?

Maki   . . .

Sakana   Could be dissemination of a virus.

Maki   What virus?

Sakana   I heard that the American military has cultivated some kind of virus on the third floor of the hospital's basement and it seeped out.

Maki   Isn't it just an urban legend? It can't be true.

Sakana   I don't know.

Maki   When I was a student, I was a member of the urban legend research club. One of the members distributed a bogus theory in order to write her graduation thesis. I was there with her when we made that up. We were there at the café making it up.

Sakana   Oh. Ah, why are they dying like this then?

Maki   I don't know. Neither the TV nor the internet is working.

Sakana   Ah, right.

Koichi   I don't get it.

Maki   Nobody will be able to make it.

Koichi   That wouldn't be true. We're still alive.

Maki   . . .

Koichi   The police or the self-defense force will come to rescue us soon.

Maki   Why not now?

Koichi   They are still making preparations, aren't they?

Maki   Preparations for what?

Koichi   . . . Americans would come and rescue us.

Maki   They're dying as well.

Koichi   How many Americans do you think there are?

Maki   I don't know . . . we all will die.

She sits.

Sakana Hakase *sits.*

Koichi   No way!

He sits.

△*On the street.*

Miki *and* **Keisuke** *are walking.*

Miki *looks tired.*

Keisuke   Are you all right? Do you want to take a break?

Miki   Fine.

Kaori *enters. She puts her hands on her chest.*

Keisuke   . . .

Miki   . . .

Kaori   Hi.

Keisuke   Hello.

Keisuke *and* **Miki** *exit.*

Kaori *drops down and sits.*

She caresses her belly.

Kaori   This is it? Holy shit.

She writhes in agony and dies. Her body remains on the stage.

△*At a street leading to the university hospital.*

Sakana   Is it better to think about the last words and such?

Maki   What?

Sakana   I've seen several people pass away, and they all said something like their last words, then died.

Maki   Ah.

Koichi   I already have one.

Sakana   Now?

Koichi   Yes.

Maki   What is it?

Koichi   No, I'll wait to say it until the very last moment.

Maki   If you die last, none of us will be able to hear it.

Koichi   If I die last, I'll tell it to the person who is second to last.

Maki   Don't do that.

Koichi   What else can I do?

Sakana   What would you say?

Koichi   What?

Sakana   I want to be inspired.

Koichi   But if I say it, you'll know what I would say.

He looks at **Maki**.

Maki   Don't say anything about me.

Koichi   . . .

Sakana   I would say something related to fish.

Maki   Do you like fish?

Sakana   I love them.

Koichi   To eat?

Sakana   I like eating them, but they are more like friends.

Maki   Do you eat your friends then?

Sakana   Oh, that's not what I meant. Or maybe I meant it. I have mixed emotions and it's very difficult to explain.

Maki   No wonder.

Sakana   I'm sorry.

Koichi *feels a twitch in his stomach.*

Koichi   Would you excuse me?

Maki   What?

Koichi   Can I have a moment?

He feels something serious in his stomach.

Maki   What's wrong?

Koichi   I think the time has come.

Maki   What?

Koichi   Sorry. This must be it.

Maki   Oh, no. Don't.

Koichi   I can't help it.

Maki   . . .

Koichi   I'm sorry, may I die alone with her?

Sakana Hakase *doesn't realize* **Koichi** *means him.*

Koichi   Hey. Hey.

Sakana   What? What?

Koichi   Er, pardon me, we're almost like a family, aren't we?

Sakana   Yes, we are.

Koichi   No, I mean, we are.

He points to himself and **Maki**.

Sakana   She doesn't look like you.

Koichi   Er, I want to die with just the two of us.

Sakana   Are you asking me to go somewhere?

Koichi   Yes. Yes. Hurry.

He starts struggling.

Sakana   What if I die while I'm alone?

Koichi   . . . You're not my family.

Maki   Don't say anything selfish. I don't want you to book in for a one-on-one experience in dying with me!

Koichi   . . . OK, then . . . Maki, I was bad. I was a bad father.

Maki   What? What?

Koichi   Maki, I've been a bad father.

Maki   Yeah. You have. So?

Koichi   . . . I am . . . I'm a bad father . . .

He dies. His body remains.

Maki   Hey . . . Come on . . . Dad . . .

She weeps.

Sakana   Maybe his final phrase was too long for him to say the whole thing.

Maki   I only know he was a bad father.

Sakana   Maybe he wanted to carry on and say something to the contrary.

Maki   . . .

Sakana   Could it have been "I'm a bad father *but* . . ." He should have made it short because he was dying. It's impossible to say so many words in such a time. It has to be concise.

Maki   . . .

Sakana   Would you go out with me?

Maki   Huh?

Sakana   Please.

Maki   No, I am sorry.

Sakana   Ah, fine.

Silence.

The Earth would be more beautiful if all humans became extinct.

Shoji *enters. He seems to be dying.*

Shoji   Ah, er, that's him.

Maki   Hmm?

Shoji   Him.

Maki   Do you know my dad?

Shoji   Ah, sort of.

He falls down.

Sakana   Are you all right?

Shoji   Ah, well, er . . .

Sakana Huh?

Shoji I have some stuff coming out of my butt.

Sakana Huh?

Shoji Could you be with me when I die? It will be soon.

Sakana . . .

Maki No problem.

Shoji Thank you. Here we go.

He reaches his hand. **Sakana Hakase** *takes his hand.*

Shoji Ah.

Sakana Stay focused.

Shoji Yes.

Sakana Hakase *and* **Maki** *stare at* **Shoji**.

Shoji Don't look at me like that. I am embarrassed.

Maki Yes.

Sakana Hakase *and* **Maki** *take their eyes off of* **Shoji**.

Shoji Well, I should be used to people looking at me.

Maki What?

Shoji Well, that's my occupation to be seen and I'm used to it.

Maki What do you do?

Shoji I mean, er, part of my job is to be watched.

Maki What job would that be?

Shoji I'll give you a hint. This may be too easy to guess.

Sakana Hakase *starts to cramp in pain.*

Sakana Please stay focused.

Shoji What?

Maki Hey.

Sakana I think my time is almost up. Can you please hurry?

Maki Oh no, that's going to make me the last one.

Sakana I'll try to live as long as I can. I'll stay alive. I'll extend my life.

Shoji Hey, should I stay focused?

Sakana Yes, please.

Shoji *breathes similar to the Lamaze breathing method, inhaling and exhaling like hee, hee, hoo.*

Maki   I don't want to be alone.   **Sakana**   How is it? How is it?

Shoji   It's right here coming. It's coming. Ah, may I?

Maki   What?

Shoji   May I?

Maki   May I what?

Shoji   Ready.

He starts to suffer in agony.

Thank you . . . world.

He dies. His body remains.

Sakana   Oh, that, I was going to say that too.

Maki   Too bad.

Sakana   Ah, well, excuse me. May I die?

Maki   Uh, can't you hold it?

Sakana   No.

Maki   . . . OK . . . Go.

Sakana   Thank you. Excuse me. Ah, could you hold my hand?

Maki   . . .

She holds **Sakana Hakase***'s hand.*

Sakana Hakase *focuses on the touch of* **Maki***'s hand.*

Sakana   Hmm? Well, I think I feel better now.

Maki   Ugh!

She starts to suffer.

Sakana   What?

Maki   Gah, urgggghhh.

Sakana   Hey, Endo.

Maki   . . . Arggggh.

Sakana   Please go out with me, Endo.

Maki   No, I don't want to. It hurts. I can't breathe . . .

Sakana   Please go out with me. With me.

Maki   No. Ahhggg.

Sakana   Endo! Endo! Stay with me. Hang on. Please! Oh no!

Maki *dies. Her body remains.*

Sakana   Ugh!

He shouts out for a while. He tries to kiss **Maki**'s *body.*

Sakana   . . .

He stops.

Whoa! Ahhhhh.

He looks around.

Anybody? Is there anybody here? Yama saaaan! Yama saaaan! Yamamoto saaaaan!

He comes close to **Yama san**'s *body.*

Sakana   Come back! Yama san! Come back!

He shakes **Yama san**'s *body. He has a pounding headache.*

Sakana   Oh, no. Why?

He holds his head.

Why now? It hurts so much. Ah.

He falls down.

. . . Woooo. Th . . . Thank you . . . world.

He uttered his last words too concisely and still has some time left. He considers for a while.

Fish.

He dies. His body remains there on the stage.

△*On a street.*

There are bodies all over the stage.

Miki *and* **Keisuke** *enter.*

Miki   It's quiet.

Keisuke   Yes, it is.

Miki   Have you seen the ocean?

Keisuke   Yes.

Miki   Me too.

Keisuke   Do you like it?

Miki　I don't know if I like it enough to say so. But I think I do.

Keisuke　Where did you go?

Miki　What?

Keisuke　Which beach?

Miki　Atami.

Keisuke　Oh, Atami it is.

Miki *sits down tired.*

Keisuke *sits down a bit away from* **Miki**.

Miki　I went there with my family once before I became sick. I became sick soon after and I didn't die. I feel it would be soon, and then people started to die one after another.

Keisuke　...

Miki　If they all die, I don't feel lonely.

Keisuke　Oh, yeah?

Miki　Because if I die, it will be the same as the world becoming extinct. So if the world died and I remained, it would mean the same thing.

Keisuke　I don't know how the world could still be the world without people, but I hope some remain after I die.

Miki　Is that right?

Keisuke　I don't know.

Miki　Are we at the beach yet?

Keisuke　No, we haven't walked that far yet.

Miki　... Why are you following?

Keisuke　... I don't want to be alone.

Miki　... I don't get it.

Keisuke　Ah, yeah.

Sachie *notices* **Keisuke** *and raises her head up.*

Miki　...

Keisuke　Oh.

Miki　Do you know her?

Keisuke　Ah, yes.

Sachie *crawls to* **Keisuke**. *She seems to smile.*

Keisuke ...

Keisuke *slides his feet backward to stay away from* **Sachie**.

Sachie *catches* **Keisuke** *with both of her hands*.

Sachie   Kill me.

Keisuke *looks away from* **Sachie**.

Sachie *gives up on* **Keisuke** *and looks at* **Miki**. *She comes to* **Miki**.

Miki   ...

Sachie *falls down over* **Miki**.

Miki *strangles* **Sachie**'s *neck as if she is hugging her*.

Sachie *starts to resist.* **Miki** *mounts on* **Sachie**. **Sachie** *moves wildly and squirms*.

Sachie   Agggh. Agh.

She dies. She collapses onto **Miki**'s *foot*.

Miki *leaves* **Sachie**'s *body. She remembers her mother*.

Keisuke   ... Did you kill her?

Miki   Yes.

Keisuke   ... For real, just like that.

Miki   Not really.

Silence.

Keisuke   I don't understand, but ...

Miki *looks like she is suffering*.

Keisuke   Hey.

Miki   ... I can't breathe ...

Keisuke   ...

Miki   Please ... Help me.

Keisuke   ...

Miki *struggles. She appears to be in pain, but also in a comedic way*.

Keisuke   ...

Miki *sighs a long gravelly breath. She dies*.

Silence.

Keisuke *looks around. There are seventeen dead bodies scattered around him. Those bodies are dressed in clothes of various colors and have died in different postures*.

Keisuke *remains with a slight smirk on his face. He feels somewhat invigorated by the situation that he's in.*

There is a sound like huge raindrops falling on a tin roof. That's the sound of the world's birds falling on the ground. It's also the sound of all the creatures beginning to die.

Keisuke *crouches timidly but holds a slight smirk on his face.*

Neither **Keisuke** *nor the audience knows what this sound is.*

Lights off.

The sound remains.

Ends.

Notes

1. **JR**   Japan Railways Group, which consists of seven regional groups such as JR East. They became a network of non-government-owned private railway companies in 1987 and the JR is considered the biggest and most widespread train system in Japan.
2. **Metro**   In this production, it is a subway system operated in a fictional city.
3. **Slit Mouth Woman**   Appeared in urban legends and folklore in the late 1970s all across Japan. The popular legend says that a young lady wearing a mask that covers the whole lower part of her face asks potential victims if she is pretty. If they respond "no," she will kill them with her weapon such as a pair of scissors. If they say "yes," she will reveal her mouth, a slit from ear to ear, and repeats the question about whether she is still attractive. This legend became a social phenomenon among elementary school and junior high school students throughout Japan.
4. **Manzai**   It is usually a comedy duo performed by two comedians. One performer plays the role of a straight man (*tsukkomi*) who gives a line or prompt to the other performer called funny man (*boke*) to make a joke. They trade jokes which most of the time revolve around mutual misunderstandings, double-talk, puns, and other verbal gags.
5. **Sukonbu**   Dried vinegar powdered kelp sheets which are a kind of snack. The kelp is cut in small pieces and is coated in vinegar powder on both sides. The particular kind used during the theatre production at the 2009 Festival Tokyo is called "Miyako Konbu" (Miyako = city, Konbu = kelp), produced by Kyoto-based Nakano Bussan Co. Ltd,. since 1912.
6. **Marunan**   A fictional local supermarket where people would go quite frequently in everyday life.
7. **Mayim Mayim**   It is an Israeli song widely known throughout Japan since the 1950s, while folk dancing or at bonfires. Mayim means "water" in Hebrew and the song was originally developed by pioneers as they did celebratory dances around water sources that they had discovered in the otherwise drought-ridden land.

The Sun (2016)

Tomohiro Maekawa

Introduction to the Playwright and the Play

Three Wild Cards for Creation

Kumiko Ohori (*editor*)

Translated by Nozomi Abe

If I were to describe three wild cards for creation that the playwright/director Tomohiro Maekawa possesses, it would be "science fiction," "Buddhist thoughts," and "theatre company."

He was born in 1974 in Kashiwazaki city in Niigata. And it was 1996, when he came to Tokyo, that he first encountered the world of theatre, which was probably a little late compared to others. Before that, he dropped out of high school in the beginning of his second year. He started a part-time job as a cook. He would travel a lot whenever he had saved up enough money for that. It was during this period that, through his older brother's influence, he became interested in literature. This led him to take the University Entrance Qualification Examination and eventually he started a BA in Philosophy at Toyo University.

As a boy, he loved the ghosts and *yokai*-monsters in Shigeru Mizuki's manga. In his adolescence, during his travels, he would visit or stay overnight in temples and enjoy conversations with the priests. Then he started reading extensively and became fascinated by Buddhism and its teachings. He became especially interested in the principles of Zen and while he was a university student he traveled around the island of Shikoku as a pilgrim. What he likes and is interested in are consistent and they are strongly connected to the highly unique plays that he creates.

The first card that I mentioned in the beginning, "science fiction and occult (which occasionally includes elements of horror)," is the prime example of his originality. The background of this play, *The Sun* (premiered in 2011), posits the situation of our near future, following the effects of bioterrorism. Also, *Strolling Invader* (premiered in 2005) is set on an Earth invaded by aliens. In *The Obelisk of the Beast* (premiered in 2013), which was derived from the series *Life in the Library* (a collection of short pieces), the world is suffering from "huge Obelisks from the sky that enchant people with the feeling of euphoria and cloud their ability to think and act."

What he depicts in those stories is not panicked people suffering from those histories or spectacles of the situations. It is the process of how people, amid such difficulties, face those issues in their family or society and rethink their values, ultimately making his works even more interesting. The extraordinary setting with ideas from a few leaps of imagination makes the extant standard or concept of values disappear. This way, we get a chance to reconsider how we interact with people and the world, guided by a brand-new set of rules. I believe that this is the greatest enchantment of Maekawa's works.

What adds more to such enchantment is the "Buddhist thoughts" that are scattered throughout the dialogues and that also form the spine of his works. Most of his characters do not fight against the issues or enemies by throwing themselves into facing them. They accept their ordeals at once, admit their own weakness and limits, and then make as much of an effort as they can. There is the spirit of resignation or generosity.

Of course, there are struggles and suffering in the process. However, it feels that the sort of knowledge that we should acquire, as those who are living in the twenty-first century and who have realized that progress and development do not last forever, is reflected in the flexibility of those characters who accept those hardships and overcome them rather than grabbing victory by defeating them. The spirit of resignation and generosity is the philosophy behind three of his works: *To Mr. Gegege* (2018) where there is intercommunion between the humans in a childless city from the near future and the *yokai*-monsters in an abandoned rural area suffering from depopulation; *Time for Lost Children—Talking Room 2020* (2020) where families whose children were mysteriously spirited away decide to take a step towards the future; and *The Sun* where the Curio and the Nox are trying to coexist.

Maekawa often sets those incidents and phenomena in an imaginary town called Konrin, which literally means "gold ring." In Buddhism, the world is supported by three rings: Kon-rin (gold ring), Sui-rin (water ring), and Fu-rin (wind ring). And I suppose the name of the city came from this Kon-rin. It is used in several works and they are sometimes connected. As a result, it adds a tremendous amount of possibility for creation (and imagination), and it is also highly stylish.

Maekawa is a successful playwright in his works with both public and private theatres. Also, some of his works have been made into films. But what is supporting all of this is the third card, Ikiume, his theatre company. The company includes five male actors, Maekawa himself, and a production team. It is not a big company, but we can find a distinct core in the world of his works which, on the surface, look vastly different. Actors are given polar-opposite roles from their previous roles and often receive the opportunity to act as non-humans. It seems like the spirit of resignation and generosity is the philosophy that forms the basis of the company as well. And of course, what leads all this is Maekawa's magic as a director who establishes trust between his actors as well as other actors from other companies and creative members. He inspires them to use their true abilities, which naturally contribute to his plays.

His SF works are highly entertaining, his carefully articulated dialogues show a great power of "storytelling," and they are supported by the flexible thoughts and spirits based on Buddhism. I truly hope to have more opportunities to see Maekawa's works that seek out a stream of light in humanity and the world by fusing those three core elements.

Playwright Biography

Tomohiro Maekawa

In 2003, Tomohiro Maekawa founded the performance group Ikiume (buried alive) where he worked as a playwright and director. He has written and produced SF, occult, and horror such as *Strolling Invader*, *The Sun*, *Holy Land X*, *Mathematical Domino*, and *The Obelisk of the Beast*. He has focused on the relations between humans and invisible forces as well as the depiction of human psychology from the perspective of the shadow world. He has also written plays for other companies including *The Sun 2068* (directed by Yukio Ninagawa) and *From a Dark Place* (directed by Eriko Ogawa), and wrote and directed Super Kabuki *Sculpting the Sky* (starring Ennosuke Ichikawa) and *Endless* (supervised by Mansai Nomura). He is the winner of the Yomiuri Theatre Award, Kinokuniya Theatre Award, and many others. Two films, *Before We Vanish* and *Foreboding*, both based on *Strolling Invader* and directed by Kiyoshi Kurosawa, were submitted to the Un Certain Regard section of the 70th Cannes International Film Festival and to the Panorama section of the 68th Berlin International Film Festival.

The Sun

Tomohiro Maekawa

2016 version*

Translation by Nozomi Abe

Characters

Yū Ikuta, *daughter of Sōichi, twenty years old.*
Tetsuhiko Okudera, *son of Junko, eighteen years old.*
Fujita Morishige, *a Nox, checkpoint guard, twenty-three years old.*
Sōichi Ikuta, *father of Yū, fifty years old.*
Junko Okudera, *older sister of Katsuya, forty years old.*
Seiji Soga, *a Nox, husband of Reiko, public servant at the District Office, fifty-five years old.*
Reiko Soga, *a Nox, mother of Yū, forty-seven years old.*
Yōji Kaneda, *a Nox, physician, from the same town as Sōichi, friend of Reiko, fifty years old.*
Katsuya Okudera, *younger brother of Junko, disappeared after committing a crime, thirty-seven years old.*
Man, *a Nox who begs for help at the beginning of the play.*

Introduction

At the beginning of the twenty-first century, the world's population decreased drastically due to the spread of viruses caused by global bioterrorism. This caused political and economic disorder and destroyed social infrastructure.

A few years later, it became clear that some who had been infected had recovered miraculously.

They had transformed into beings with much better immune and metabolic systems than ordinary humans.

They maintained young and healthy bodies for considerable periods of time; however, they were vulnerable to ultraviolet light and could not function in sunlight. They insisted that such transformation was proof that they represent a transitional phase of evolution and they began to call themselves "the Nox" (*homo Noxensis*: the ones who live in the night).

Once the way to transform into a Nox was discovered, the numbers started growing and they became the target of general disapproval. However, more and more young people decided to become nocturnal, in part because the ability to transform into a Nox could be lost around the age of thirty. Gradually, the Nox began to rule the political and economic centres, and the population ratio was eventually reversed.

Forty years after the emergence of the Nox, the number of ordinary humans has been reduced to around 30 percent, and in those islands that used to be called Japan, the Nox formed self-ruled independent communities in a peaceful alliance.

While the Nox mainly lived in big cities, ordinary humans were allocated to the island of Shikoku although some stayed in their hometowns and still lived in small villages.

One particular village, in Nagano—Ward eight, once saw the murder of a Nox and was condemned to suffer an economic blockade by the neighbouring Nox communities. There are just over twenty villagers remaining.

Now, as the ten years of social ostracism and sanction are coming to an end, the villagers start communicating with the Nox once more . . .

Scene One

Ten years ago. In a farming village in the mountains, Ward eight of Nagano.

Inside a spacious workplace for agriculture. Early in the morning.

*There is a **Man** lying on the ground. He is only wearing a T-shirt, underwear, and socks. His head is covered with a bag. **Katsuya Okudera** is looking at him.*

*The **Man** is freezing, and he struggles to move. **Katsuya** checks his watch. The **Man** notices that the dawn is about to break and he gets frightened.*

*The sun rises. The sunlight from the window approaches the **Man**.*

As the sunlight reaches his feet, the **Man** *jolts with pain. He gets frightened and confused. He begs for help but* **Katsuya** *does not respond to it. The* **Man** *tries to run away but eventually he gives up. He stops moving as he gets the full sunlight. He is burnt by the sun, and he dies.*

Passage of time.

The same place. **Junko Okudera** *enters.* **Katsuya** *by the body is miles away.* **Junko** *looks at the burnt body.*

Katsuya   Sister . . . Sister, I . . .

Junko   Who is it?

Katsuya   It's him . . .

Junko   Why? You were good friends. Why did you do such a thing . . .? What should we do? What should we do? This is one thing we are never allowed to do.

Passage of time.

The same place. **Sōichi Ikuta** *comes in.* **Sōichi** *and* **Junko** *wrap the body in a blanket and tie a rope around it.* **Katsuya** *is simply observing him. As* **Sōichi** *and* **Junko** *make to drag the body away, we hear* **Yū**'*s voice from a distance.*

Yū   Dad? Daaaad?

Sōichi   Stay there, Yū. Wait at home. I'll be back soon.

Yū   I'll make breakfast for you then!

Sōichi   Great, thanks.

Yū   Okay!

Sōichi *brings the body out.*

Passage of time.

At **Okudera**'*s.* **Junko** *enters into the room where* **Katsuya** *is.*

Katsuya   Who is it?

Junko   The police. They want to talk to you.

Katsuya   No, I don't want to.

Junko   I told them you were not here just now. They said they'll come back at eleven pm. We need to come up with a good story by then.

Katsuya   Oh. An alibi.

Junko   You do the talking, okay?

Katsuya   Sure. Fine. Trust me.

Passage of time.

The same place. **Sōichi** *enters.*

Sōichi   They found the body. It's obvious that it was burnt under the sun. This is going to be in the news. Katsuya, surrender to the police, please.

Katsuya   What?

Sōichi   Otherwise, the whole village will be ruined.

Katsuya   But if I go, they'll kill me.

Sōichi   If you surrender now, they won't. Please.

Katsuya   They're not going to find out.

Sōichi   Even then, the whole village will be accused. Our villagers are rioting there. They will ruin us this time.

Katsuya   She said we should hide the body. It wasn't my idea. And you know what? You're an accomplice too.

Sōichi *grabs* **Katsuya**'s *arm and tries to pull him.* **Katsuya** *resists.*

Katsuya   Stop it! No! Let go of me!

He shakes **Sōichi** *off and frees himself.*

Junko   Erm. . . Give us a bit of time. Please.

Sōichi *exits the room.* **Junko** *grabs* **Katsuya**'s *hand.*

Junko   Katsuya, please.

Katsuya   Are you abandoning me?

He exits the room. **Junko** *does not follow him.*

Passage of time.

The same place. **Sōichi** *enters. In a different area,* **Katsuya** *takes his bag and runs away.*

Sōichi   Where's Katsuya? Where has he gone? Junko?

Junko   . . .

Sōichi   The police are outside. The Nox say they will not harm him if he surrenders now.

Junko   He's . . . gone . . .

Sōichi   Did you let him go?

Junko   I'll talk to the police.

Passage of time.

At **Okudera**'s. *Stones are thrown from outside and their windows get smashed. People are roaring outside. They keep throwing stones and their roars get louder and louder. Then, a crackling noise can be heard. The house starts to burn.*

Sōichi   Go! Get out of here! They've set fire to the house!

In the noise and roars, **Sōichi** *and* **Junko** *are surrounded by the flames of fire. Blackout.*

Scene Two

Ten years have passed from Scene One. Night.

In the self-ruled region of the Nox next to Nagano Ward. At the river which functions as the border line with the New Matsumoto city. There is a small hut by the bridge, which is the checkpoint to Ward eight. There is a spacious field in front of the hut.

Junko *and* **Seiji Soga** *are there facing each other.* **Fujita Morishige** *is standing by* **Seiji***.*

Seiji   If there was still such a thing as the law, it would be . . . the statute of limitations. Yes, it is the statute of limitations.

Junko   But why now?

Seiji   It's the wishes of their family. They say there's nothing else they'd wish for. And they're simply exhausted by this whole thing. The feeling of anger can never last too long. Plus, nothing good can come out from clinging to anger, right? We need to move forward. Ten years have passed. Or to be more precise, it took them ten years.

Junko   I'm very sorry.

Seiji   We'll proceed with the paperwork from now on but . . . as of today, the new Matsumoto City and the Ward eight of Nagano will reopen trade.

He hands out an A4 envelope to **Junko***. She checks what is inside.*

Junko   What will it guarantee us?

Seiji   Read it. It's all written in there. Basically, it will be back to what it was ten years ago although the situation has changed drastically for both of us.

Junko   That's right.

Seiji   What's the population now?

Junko   Just enough to do a baseball game.

Seiji   You mean nine? Or eighteen?

Junko   You can't hold a game with just one team.

Seiji   Very true! I see how hard it is. You can't even play baseball that easily. Do you like baseball?

Junko   No.

Seiji   Oh, I love baseball. But I didn't expect the population to be this small. How many did you have before?

Junko   About three hundred.

Seiji   All moved to Shikoku?

Junko   I don't know.

Seiji   I see. The closest settlement from here is about eighty kilometers to the north. The one with about a thousand people just as you enter Niigata. Did you know?

Junko   Yes.

Seiji   A suggestion. As there aren't many left here, I think you should all move there.

Junko   More than half of us are over seventy. They wouldn't move.

Seiji   How can you stand a place like this?

Junko   We like it here.

Seiji   Very well. Understood. As long as there's one person who wants to stay here, we will support you. I mean, why not? Do you have any mains here?

Junko   We only have water.

Seiji   Use electricity, please. Let's go back to civilized life. We'll start sending commodities. Buses will start running from next week. You can enjoy shopping in the city at night.

Junko   Okay.

Seiji   I drove around here a while ago. Actually, I'm surprised to see what ten years of economic blockade can do. I thought things would be better than this even under blockade. Isn't it cruel? Don't you love this village? Well, Ward eight has been infamous. Almost all the Curios who got arrested in Matsumoto were from here. Our crime rate dropped since this place was ruined. If you want a fresh start, make it a good village.

Junko   Yes.

Seiji   Any questions?

Junko   We want to go to the hospital but what about the insurance . . .?

Seiji   Go ask at the Insurance Division at the Ward Office. But remember, it is only open from sunset to one hour prior to the dawn.

Junko   Okay.

Seiji   There aren't many doctors who would examine you guys. But a visiting doctor will start coming here. It's only once a week though.

Junko   Right.

Seiji   I believe your key issue is aging.

Junko   Yes, kind of.

Seiji   It must be hard. What were you going to do though if trades were not recovered? Were you just going to wait and see? I think you should have acted before the statute of limitations. If you really want to reconstruct this village, change your attitude from now on. If you want to become independent, we'll support you in every possible way. But if not, we'll never talk as equals. Believe me, we want to support you. So work hard.

Junko *nods.*

Seiji   Hmm . . . I want you to articulate it. Say "I'll work hard." Okay?

Junko   . . .

Seiji   Now. Say it.

Junko   What?

Seiji   Say "I'll work hard."

Junko   I . . . will work hard.

Seiji   Louder! Don't you want a fresh start? Let your words empower you. Again. I don't want empty promises. I want to see your genuine determination. Go on, say it.

Junko   I'll work hard!

Seiji   Very good. Let's take a photo to commemorate this. (*To* **Morishige**.) Have you got a camera?

Morishige *sets up a camera.*

Seiji   Ms. Okudera. May I take a photo? I want to put it in our local brochure.

Junko   Sure.

Seiji (*to* **Morishige**)   Get it done in one go, okay? I really hate doing this.

Seiji *offers his right hand to* **Junko**.

Junko   What?

Seiji   Shake hands?

Junko   Ah, okay.

Seiji *takes* **Junko's** *hand. He bends his knees a little and gives a big smile to the camera.*

Seiji   Ready.

Morishige   Okay, smile!

The flash goes off. **Seiji** *gets a migraine from the light.*

Seiji   Ouch . . . That hurts . . .

He puts his hands to his temples and turns his head.

Morishige   Is it that bad?

Seiji   It's like eating sorbet with my eyes. By the way, let's do a friendly match.

Junko   Pardon?

Seiji   A baseball match. A night game of course. We have a team.

Junko   Right. (*Gives a forced smile.*)

Seiji   I have to go now. I hope we keep a good relationship. Please send us the list of villagers. Oh, and he'll be here from tomorrow at night.

Morishige   I'm Morishige. Nice to meet you.

Seiji   Bye then.

Seiji *and* **Morishige** *exit.*

Junko   Who said we play baseball, idiot.

She takes out her handkerchief and wipes her hands rigorously.

Scene Three

Ward eight in Nagano. Daytime.

In a garden between **Okudera**'s *and* **Ikuta**'s. **Junko**, **Tetsuhiko Okudera**, *and* **Yū** *are present.*

Tetsuhiko   Does this mean I can go to school?

Junko   School? I'm not sure about that. It might take some time. But we can go there and buy textbooks.

Tetsuhiko   Forget about textbooks. I just want to go to school.

Junko   You do realize that school is a place to study?

Yū   Junko, do you really have to stay here? I think you've done enough. You can regain freedom yourself now.

Junko   Freedom . . .

Yū   You have done your duty. There is no reason you should stay here.

Sōichi   Where would you go?

Yū   To Shikoku.

Sōichi   That nonsense again.

Yū   I heard that there is a great town in Shikoku, which is not inferior to cities of the Nox. They say they even have big hospitals and universities. I heard that they also have a power plant and now they're completely independent.

Sōichi   Said who?

Yū   People.

Sōichi   People? Are they real people? They just want to confine us to Shikoku, that's all.

Yū   I want to go to Shikoku.

Sōichi   Do you even know how far it is? It's very far. We're fine here. I'm sure folks will come back.

Yū   Dad, are you stupid or what? They'll never come back.

Sōichi   That's also fine by me. We can officially keep the fields and orchards as ours. Fruits will sell well. The Nox love them. They're insects.

Junko   Don't speak like that.

Sōichi (*laughs*)   I'm just saying.

Junko   Yū, there is a reason for me to stay here. (*Also to* **Tetsuhiko** *who is reading the documents.*) Tetsuhiko, listen to me. The lottery will be revived first time in ten years.

Tetsuhiko   What? Does that mean we can become Nox?

Sōichi   It's once a year. One percent of those under thirty will win the right to become nocturnal. Normally, it's one in one hundred. But you know what? There are only five who are under thirty in this village. And we have two of them here.

Tetsuhiko   What? Then that means . . .

Sōichi (*laughs*)   A big chance.

Junko   It was good that we stayed here.

Tetsuhiko (*laughs*)   Really? Wow. That's amazing!

Junko   It's like a reward for you for being so patient these ten years.

Yū   I'm not sure if I want to be nocturnal.

Sōichi   We will see them more often. And infection means death for us.

Yū   We can live independently.

Sōichi   That's impossible.

Yū   Shikoku is doing well.

Sōichi   It's not that easy. I'll enter you in the lottery.

Yū   Hey.

Sōichi   If you win the right, you can get vaccinated. In the worst-case scenario, if you get infected, as long as you have the antibody you can still become nocturnal. You can avoid death.

Junko   Most of big towns have already turned nocturnal and life is easier that way. (*Pointing at the document* **Tetsuhiko** *is reading.*) Have a good read.

Tetsuhiko This is kind of difficult.

Junko Don't argue, read it.

Sōichi Help him, Yū.

Junko Sorry.

Yū It's fine. (*Gets the document from* **Tetsuhiko**.)

Junko Read it well.

Tetsuhiko Okay, okay.

Junko That needs to be circulated. Keep it clean.

Yū Okay.

She takes the document from **Tetsuhiko** *and exits.* **Tetsuhiko** *follows.*

Junko Yū's mother is over there, right?

Sōichi Yes, I think so.

Junko What are you going to do?

Sōichi About what?

Junko You know what I mean.

Sōichi What are you going to do from now on, Junko?

Junko I don't know. Freedom? That's not realistic when the village is still like this. (*Laughs.*) Did he say ten years have passed? No wonder Tetsuhiko is not a baby anymore.

Sōichi I think you can free yourself.

Junko Same for you, Sōichi. You can move to somewhere nicer.

Sōichi No. I won't move . . .

Junko *exits and* **Sōichi** *remains on the stage.*

Night falls. **Morishige** *comes to the hut next to the checkpoint to prepare for his post.*

Scene Four

In front of the checkpoint. Night. **Morishige** *is standing with a stick.* **Yōji Kaneda** *enters via a bridge.*

Kaneda Good morning.

Morishige Good morning sir, you are . . .?

Kaneda I'm the visiting doctor of Nagano Ward eight.

Morishige You must be Dr. Yōji Kaneda.

Kaneda   That's right.

Morishige   Welcome. Please come through.

Kaneda   I have come through already.

Morishige   Is it a Cista?

Kaneda   You can tell? Just by listening to the engine?

Morishige   A great car with a complete darkroom. Have you tried driving during day?

Kaneda   Yes. But if the main camera gets broken, then that car suddenly turns into a coffin. Driving with the burning sun for three hours, the temperature inside the car was over fifty degrees. If I were a Curio, I would have died six times. They should recall this really.

Morishige   This happened to someone you know?

Kaneda   I am talking about myself. Get back to work. Good day.

Morishige   Sunrise today is at five thirty-one.

Kaneda   That's right.

Kaneda *walks a little and finds* **Sōichi**. **Morishige** *remains on stage but he is in a different part of the village.*

Sōichi *and* **Kaneda** *are surprised to find each other.*

Sōichi   Kaneda?

Kaneda   Sōichi Ikuta?

He makes to hug **Sōichi** *who keeps his distance from him.*

Kaneda   You look . . . exhausted.

Sōichi   I look my age.

Kaneda   I see, this is aging then. You look like a totally different person. Look at that beard.

Sōichi   I've always had it.

Kaneda   That's right. I wrote to you seven years ago but you never replied. I thought this village was erased, scratched from the map after that incident. But anyway, I'm so happy to see you.

Again, **Kaneda** *makes to hug* **Sōichi** *who jumps away.*

As he talks, **Kaneda** *puts on a mask and gloves.*

Kaneda   You must be wondering why I'm here. Well, I am your visiting doctor. I volunteered. I wanted to help my own hometown and I thought there might be someone I know still living here. Then I found you, my best friend. The one I wanted to see the most. I wanted to ask you, "How are you?" but seeing you so exhausted . . . I mean, you look completely exhausted . . .

Sōichi   Shut up.

Kaneda   But let me say this anyway, "How are you?"

He offers his hand for a handshake.

Now we can.

As **Sōichi** *takes a small step towards him,* **Kaneda** *pulls him with force and hugs him.* **Sōichi** *pushes him away quickly and keeps a distance.*

Kaneda   It's not infectious, you know.

Sōichi   I'm not young any more. Infection means death.

Kaneda (*dusting himself down*)   You worry about virus but you're full of germs.

Sōichi   Shut up. Why are you here?

Kaneda   I just told you. Buy some new clothes. How long have you been wearing that? It was like hugging a rag. Are you poor? I suppose so. Why did you stay in such a place? I know you're clever. Why did you waste ten years in such a place? Actually, why is a village like this when you're here? Since I found you, I cannot stop wondering that. I am a bit disappointed. I'm sure there is a reason that I cannot even imagine. I'm not blaming you. But this place is still my hometown.

Sōichi   Please go. We will ask them to send us a different doctor.

Kaneda   Why? I am genuinely worried for you.

Sōichi   Are you here to make fun of us?

Kaneda   No. Why do you say that?

Sōichi   Kaneda, you look the same, surprisingly so. And you look like a completely different person.

Kaneda   I see. Yes. I suppose it was a wrong approach. Let me fix it. Okay. What made you uncomfortable? It's fine. Forget it. I just came to say hello. Do you know Junko Okudera?

Sōichi   I told you to leave.

Kaneda   I'm here as your visiting doctor. I don't care what you think of me. Let me do my job. I'm specializing in diurnal humans. No need to worry. I can help this village. I'm interested in aging. You guys are interesting subjects.

Sōichi   You were with us before. Mind your tongue. How dare you!

He exits leaving **Kaneda** *alone.* **Kaneda** *goes into the village.*

Scene Five

In front of the checkpoint. **Morishige** *is sitting on a chair reading a magazine.* **Tetsuhiko** *with a torch approaches him. He stops and observes* **Morishige**.

Morishige *notices* **Tetsuhiko** *and gives him a glance. But then he goes back to reading the magazine.*

Tetsuhiko *approaches him gradually. When* **Morishige** *looks up, he freezes. They repeat the same sequence.*

Morishige   What do you want?

Tetsuhiko   Erm . . .

Morishige   Do you want to go shopping? Have you applied for it? If so, tell me your name. Well, I don't think it is the case as I haven't received a list today. You can't just come here and ask. I can't give a permission. Also, if you go without permission, you'll be in trouble . . . Say something.

Tetsuhiko *puts his hand to his bag and makes to take out something.* **Morishige** *gets alarmed and puts his hand to the stick.*

Morishige   Hey. Don't even think about it. What's inside? Answer me! . . . You can't talk? If you can't talk . . . Or perhaps you can't hear. Then it's useless. Freeze!

Tetsuhiko   I . . . can talk.

Morishige   Okay. Good. If you understand what I say, do what I say. Okay? What's in that bag? Put it on the ground.

Tetsuhiko *takes out something from his bag.*

Morishige   Hey, wait! (**Tetsuhiko** *has a plastic bag with brown leaves in his hands.*) What's that?

Tetsuhiko   Tobacco.

Morishige   Tobacco?

Tetsuhiko   Tobacco.

Morishige   Marijuana?

Tetsuhiko   No. Tasty tobacco.

Morishige   I don't smoke tobacco. Put it away.

Tetsuhiko   What about this then?

He takes out another plastic bag. A similar sort of leaves is inside the bag.

Morishige (*looking at it*)   I said, I don't smoke tobacco.

Tetsuhiko   It's tea.

Morishige   Tea?

Tetsuhiko   Homemade. The finest quality. One hundred percent burgeons, so-called FOP, Flowery Orange Pekoe. Needless to say, pesticide free, organically grown.

Morishige   A bag full of FOP?

Tetsuhiko   Yup. Irresistible?

Morishige   Irresistible.

Tetsuhiko   What do you want to do now?

Morishige   I want to put the kettle on right now.

Tetsuhiko   That's your job?

Morishige   Can that mean . . .?

Tetsuhiko   It's yours.

He throws the bag of tea. **Morishige** *receives it.*

Morishige   Ohh. I can smell the aroma even without opening it.

Tetsuhiko *is observing* **Morishige.** **Morishige** *enjoys the aroma.*

Tetsuhiko   How is it?

Morishige   Heavenly.

Tetsuhiko   Have you got a kettle? Try it.

Morishige   I would love to have it right now but I'm on duty now. I think I should try this at home. Is that okay?

Tetsuhiko   Sure.

Morishige *observes* **Tetsuhiko.**

Morishige   Did you think you could pass through here while I'm distracted by the tea? Don't underestimate me. I wouldn't move even if you were a fully naked woman.

Tetsuhiko   Do I look like a naked woman?

Morishige   No. So you see, I will not move from here. You plan was not successful. Now you may leave.

Tetsuhiko   No, I won't

Morishige   If you want to know how I liked the tea, come back tomorrow for a chat. But let me say one thing. If what you said about this is true, then the verdict is almost set. It's tasty.

Tetsuhiko *is keeping a distance from* **Morishige** *throughout this exchange. As they talk, he gets closer but then he moves away again.*

Morishige   Why don't you go?

Tetsuhiko   You are not going to hit me?

Morishige   Why? Why would I hit you for getting tasty tea?

Tetsuhiko   The previous one did.

Morishige   Why? He didn't like tea?

Tetsuhiko   I think he did.

Morishige   Then why?

Tetsuhiko   He said I was trying to bribe him.

Morishige   Did you ask him to do something in return?

Tetsuhiko   No. He hit me before I said anything.

Morishige   Then that's not bribing. He answered your favor with violence. You did nothing wrong. Having said that, if you start negotiating with me inappropriately to do something for you in return for the tea, then I might hit you.

Tetsuhiko   I'll shut up then.

Morishige   It's probably better for you to leave now before you say something unnecessary. But even then, I have no intention of giving this back to you. It's my policy. Once something's given to me, it's mine. If you insist on getting it back, you will be admitting you made an inappropriate request.

Tetsuhiko   What do you mean, then, by inappropriate request?

Something that would make this bag of tea a bribe. That is, if it was to do with my job. But if it is outside of my sphere, this is not a bribe.

Tetsuhiko   Your sphere?

Morishige   Say, if you asked me to make you laugh in return for the tea, then it would not be a bribe. It is a simply a request.

Tetsuhiko   Make me laugh.

Morishige   No, I won't! It's for me to decide if I respond to the request or not. It's a completely different matter.

Tetsuhiko   Okay . . . Requests are something simple.

Morishige   Go on, try. If I'm going to hit you, I'll warn you in advance. So be quick. Run.

Tetsuhiko   I . . . want to become friends with a Nox.

Morishige   Friends?

Tetsuhiko   That's all.

Morishige   What. Do you want to be friends with me?

Tetsuhiko   That's all. Now, are you going to hit me?

Morishige   No, I won't. That's not what friends do, is it? Okay. Let's be friends.

Tetsuhiko   Really?

Morishige   Sure, of course.

Tetsuhiko   Okay, that's good then.

Morishige   Yeah.

Tetsuhiko   What do you want to do?

Morishige   What? No, I'm on duty now.

Tetsuhiko   You weren't working.

Morishige   Yes, I was.

Tetsuhiko   Reading a magazine is your job?

Morishige   It's fine. My job is to be here.

Tetsuhiko   Can you read in such darkness?

Morishige   Yes, I can.

Tetsuhiko   Do you all have such good eyesight?

Morishige   The Nox are nocturnal.

Tetsuhiko   I see. Is it useful?

Morishige   I don't know. It's just normal for us.

Tetsuhiko   I see.

Morishige   Do you know stars are graded?

Tetsuhiko   No.

Morishige   They are graded by how bright they look. There are ten magnitudes. What Curios can see with naked eyes is from grade one, the brightest one, to grade four. We can see up to grade eight. We're looking up at the sky now. But the stars you see and the stars I see are very different. Sorry to tell you this but my stars are magnificent. The sky is full of brilliant stars.

Tetsuhiko   I see. That must be good.

Morishige   Do you really think so?

Tetsuhiko   But my stars are rather beautiful as well.

Morishige   Well, I was born a Nox and they are the only stars I know. Perhaps this is not something that can ever be compared.

Tetsuhiko   If I become a Nox, do you think I will think that your stars are more beautiful?

Morishige   I don't know. Seeing more doesn't always mean better. Perhaps beauty is not that simple. I mean, you can see colours, right?

Tetsuhiko   You can't?

Morishige   We can. Sort of. But our colours are very different from yours.

Tetsuhiko   Okay.

Morishige   Those turned into a Nox tend to be surprised by it. The spectrum is different.

Tetsuhiko   The spectrum. Aren't you smart?

Morishige   Nope. Unfortunately, I dropped out from school.

Tetsuhiko   Will you tell me more about the Nox and other things you know?

Morishige   Yup. Anything I know.

Tetsuhiko   That'd be great.

Morishige   Why don't we start with this? (*Offers the magazine he was reading.*)

Tetsuhiko   What's that?

Morishige   Come here. Come closer.

Tetsuhiko *hesitates.*

Morishige   It's fine. You don't get infected so easily.

Tetsuhiko   Really?

Morishige   Yes. It's just a rumour that you'll get infected by a handshake.

Tetsuhiko   Is that right?

Morishige   It's the twenty-first century. There. There.

Tetsuhiko *takes the magazine and opens it.*

Tetsuhiko   What? Oh my god. This is porn. I've never seen this.

Morishige (*laughs*)   No, this is just a fashion magazine.

Tetsuhiko   What? Really?

Morishige (*laughs*)   Yes.

Tetsuhiko   Okay then. (*Laughs.*)

Morishige   There are some pages about the city of the Nox.

Tetsuhiko   Okay.

Morishige   I'll bring porn next time.

Tetsuhiko   What? Really?

Morishige (*chuckles*)

Yū *has entered already.*

Yū   What are you doing here?

Tetsuhiko   Erm . . . nothing.

Yū   Go home. It's dangerous.

Tetsuhiko   Yes, okay.

Morishige   It's not dangerous at all.

Yū   Are you going to take responsibility if he gets infected?

Morishige   We were just chatting. He won't get infected.

Yū   Give that back to him.

Tetsuhiko *resists.*

Yū   Give that back.

She grabs the magazine and throws it.

She takes **Tetsuhiko** *home.* **Morishige** *watches them exit. Blackout.*

Scene Six

In New Matsumoto city. In the living room at **Soga**'s. **Reiko Soga** *and* **Kaneda** *are in the room.*

Kaneda   I see. I'm sorry to hear that. How many times did you get pregnant with Seiji?

Reiko   Twice. Twice in three years.

Kaneda   Hmmm. Not a great match, is it?

Reiko   Right? I am deeply disappointed this time.

Kaneda   But you're doing it with other guys in the meantime, right?

Reiko   Of course. I got pregnant from some, too. But the foetuses didn't grow.

Kaneda   Not easy then.

Reiko   Nowadays, in the middle of doing it, I even wonder, "Have we done it before?" That's not good, is it?

Kaneda   That happened to me as well.

Reiko   If he's good at it, maybe it's fine. But it tends to happen with the bad ones. Matching is made based on our records, so maybe it's intentional.

Kaneda   They have our chromosomal information. It must be on purpose.

Reiko   Perhaps I should go to a different company.

Kaneda   By the way, I'm wondering how do you define being "good at it" or "bad at it."

Reiko   It's all about flexibility. Skills should always be improved.

Kaneda   Okay, so when you say "flexibility," does that mean making adjustment to meet someone's taste sort of thing?

Reiko   Anyone with normal insight would have it. We create our own story in a short time. Like writing a play. Without a story, it's just breeding. Oh, but the pleasure we get after playing the story together! And the sense of pride that I am actually contributing to the species of the Nox! I can almost hear a hymn. But after animal-like sex, it's the worst. I keep hearing "Donna Donna."

Kaneda   I see. Inspiring.

Reiko   In this sense, Seiji is very smart at it.

Kaneda   Is he?

Reiko   Very.

Kaneda   Okay . . .

Reiko   He has no issue with his lifestyle. Sometimes he is too serious though.

Kaneda   It's a shame about bad chromosomal match.

Reiko   He's a great partner. We can always adopt a child.

Kaneda   Reiko, why don't you have sex with me?

Reiko   No. That'd be too embarrassing.

Kaneda   Embarrassing? Why?

Reiko   Won't you be?

Kaneda   I might be. A little. But I'll be fine.

Reiko   I won't be fine.

Kaneda   Why?

Reiko   We knew each other when we were Curios. No way. That's disgusting.

Kaneda   Disgusting? I see. I just wanted to hear your honest opinion.

Reiko   How about lunch? There's a nice Italian vegetarian place downstairs. Fancy that?

Kaneda   No, I have eaten. Night comes quickly when you're a visiting doctor.

Reiko   You should have told me. I was waiting for you.

Kaneda   Sorry.

Reiko   And? You wanted to talk about something.

Kaneda   I'm in charge of Nagano Ward eight. I went there the other day and met Sōichi.

Reiko   He's still there?

Kaneda   So is your daughter. I thought I should tell you that.

Thank you. Did you see Yū?

Kaneda   Not yet.

Reiko   How was Sōichi?

Kaneda   He's an old man. I couldn't believe we were the same age.

Reiko   That's what happens to Curios.

Kaneda   I've seen elderly patients, but I haven't seen anyone growing old. It was shocking because I knew him when he was young. It's not hard to imagine. I should have known.

Reiko   Poor Curios. There's this old woman selling vegetables at the basement of the station, a Curio from Yamanashi. Sometimes I think she is rather beautiful. It'd be nice to see Sōichi.

Kaneda   It'll be difficult. He was upset with me. How we look at things are totally different now.

Reiko   Maybe I should pay a visit.

Kaneda   I wouldn't recommend it.

Reiko   Or just go see Yū.

Kaneda   When was the last time you saw her?

Reiko   When she was only three.

Kaneda   They value blood relations very much. You'll cause much trouble if you come into her life again after so many years.

Reiko   I'm not going to tell her that I'm her mother.

Kaneda   What will you do if you look alike?

Reiko   I'll wear glasses.

Kaneda   What if she's wearing glasses as well?

Reiko   Then I'll take off my glasses.

Kaneda   She'll find out.

Reiko   Sunglasses might be better

Kaneda   No. That won't make any difference.

Reiko   I'll come with you next time.

Kaneda   Why don't you understand? You're not coming with me.

Reiko   Then, I'll go by myself.

Kaneda   Do you have any idea what could happen if a Nox woman walked in a Curio region?

Reiko   I'll be assaulted, and you'll suffer from of guilt.

Kaneda   Exactly. Not good for anyone.

Reiko   Please.

Kaneda   Why? You haven't even thought about her until now.

Reiko   But she's right there.

Kaneda   No.

Reiko   Please.

Kaneda   Okay. Then, have sex with me.

Reiko   Isn't it immoral to use sex as a condition here?

Kaneda   Exactly.

Reiko   Shame on you.

Kaneda *covers his face with his hand.*

Reiko   Poor you. You're suffering.

Kaneda   Exactly.

*As **Kaneda** suffers, **Seiji** comes home.*

Reiko   You're back.

Seiji   Hi. (*Pointing to **Kaneda**.*) What happened?

Kaneda   Excuse me. (*Stands up.*)

Seiji   Are you okay?

Kaneda   I'm okay. I just asked your wife to have sex with me and got refused.

Seiji   I see. Sorry to hear that.

Kaneda   I'll go home.

Seiji   Sounds like a good idea.

Kaneda   Seiji, you're truly a skilled man. Inspiring.

Seiji   What do you mean?

Kaneda   Nothing. Goodbye.

Seiji   Kaneda, I should let you know this. I can be jealous. True we're all brothers, but as "Yoji Kaneda" you're also a man. Am I clear?

Kaneda   Crystal.

Seiji   Of course, I understand that it's our duty to create offspring.

Kaneda   That's right.

He exits. **Reiko** *and* **Seiji** *embrace each other.*

Seiji   Together we'll get through this. We're not the only ones.

Reiko   I know.

Seiji   I heard a seventy-two-year-old woman gave birth. The birth rate has been rising over the last few years, and we are beginning to overcome this problem.

Reiko   That's good news.

Seiji   And we have all the time in the world.

Reiko (*smiles*)   At the hospital, they told me that we could also adopt a child.

Seiji   It won't solve the problem, but a life with a child will be great.

Reiko   What do you think about an adoption?

Seiji   I have nothing against it. But, what if we could have our own child?

Reiko   We can give it up for adoption.

Seiji   That's true.

Reiko   Sounds like the Miura's also decided to adopt.

Seiji   Which one is it?

Reiki   A Curio.

Seiji   I thought so. How old?

Reiko   Three.

Seiji   Can a three-year-old be operated on?

Reiko   Depends on the health of the child.

Seiji   Well, better sooner than later to become a Nox.

Reiko   You're right. You know, I had a baby when I was a Curio.

Seiji   You told me once.

Reiko   I heard she's still in Nagano Ward eight. Kaneda just told me.

Seiji   That's just right there.

Reiko   I know.

Seiji   She's still a Curio then. How old?

Reiko   Twenty exactly. I wonder what she is like now.

Seiji   Was it a boy?

Reiko   It's a girl.

Seiji   I wonder if she looks like you.

Reiko *laughs.*

Seiji   Nurture over nature. Plus, she's a Curio.

Reikok   You're right. But because we were talking about adoption, I was thinking perhaps she could be one of the candidates. She's twenty. She must want to become a Nox.

Seiji   It's not like you being hooked up with blood relations. Besides, she's already a grown-up. It really doesn't have to be her.

Reiko   I'm just interested.

Seiji   She's twenty. And she's a Curio . . . I don't think you can find any connection with her. Even if you did, that's just an illusion. You'd put anything to the frame you prepared and be pleased. That's sick.

Reiko   I'm simply interested. It's you who is caught up with blood relations.

Seiji   No. The biggest concern here is her age. And it does not go well with our initial purpose. Let me be honest with you, Perhaps I am caught up with blood relations. So please don't talk about her anymore. I don't want you to go see her.

Reiko   If you say so. Okay.

Seiji   Thank you.

They embrace each other.

Scene Seven

Ward eight of Nagano. Daytime. In the garden of **Okudera** *'s.* **Tetsuhiko** *and* **Yū** *enter. They are in the middle of a conversation.*

Tetsuhiko   I heard that they'd go out to find city jobs.

Yū   Said who?

Tetsuhiko   That old man, Mr. Tokieda. You can't get infected so easily.

Yū   You were still young, so you may not remember, but . . .

Tetsuhiko   Not by much. It's just a rumor that you'll get infected by a handshake. Come on, it's the twenty-first century. You take everything your dad says too seriously. That's why you hate the Nox.

Yū   Your dad died because of them.

Tetsuhiko   I want to become a Nox.

Yū   What are you going to do when you become a Nox?

Tetsuhiko   Live in the city and go to school.

Yū   You can't even read kanji characters.

Tetsuhiko   But I can stay young.

Yū (*laughs*)   Young? You're still a child, You idiot. Why don't you grow up first?

Tetsuhiko   You'll become an old woman soon.

Yū   Shut up.

Tetsuhiko   Your mum became a Nox.

Yū   Shut up now before it's too late.

Tetsuhiko   If you're a Nox, you don't get sick, you're strong, and you have great eyesight. Sounds perfect.

Yū   But you can't be in the sun.

Tetsuhiko   That's the only disadvantage. The era of Curio is over.

Yū   Do you even know what that means?

Teruo   What?

Yū   Curio.

Tetsuhiko   No. Wait, why do they call us Curio?

Yū   Curio comes from "curiosity," antique. It's a negative term they use to make fun of us. That's why you don't see it on the paper.

Tetsuhiko   Really? That sucks.

Yū   You know nothing. Idiot. You know nothing.

Tetsuhiko   What do you know then? I'm an idiot because I'm stuck in this village.

He exits leaving **Yū**. *At night.* **Morishige** *comes to work.*

Scene Eight

In front of the checkpoint. Night. **Morishige** *is getting ready for work.* **Kaneda** *and* **Reiko** *come in.*

Kaneda   Good morning.

Morishige   Good morning. Your visit was not scheduled for today.

Kaneda   Exactly. This is my personal visit.

Morishige   And the lady is . . .?

Kaneda   She's fine.

Morishige   It's my job to check.

Kaneda   Sure. She's kind of . . . sort of . . . my daughter.

Morishige   She isn't then.

Kaneda   You're a good detective. Very good. But being loyal isn't always the best thing. I'm in no position to give orders to you but I believe you're a clever man.

Morishige   ID please.

Kaneda (*to* **Reiko**)   Got ID with you?

Reiko *shows her ID to* **Morishige**.

Reiko   Here.

Morishige   Thank you.

Reiko   It's okay.

Kaneda   Sorry to have troubled you.

Morishige   No problem at all.

Kaneda *and* **Reiko** *walk away from* **Morishige**. **Morishige** *stays on stage but he is in a different part of the village.*

Kaneda *and* **Reiko** *go to see* **Yū**, *who is waiting for them.*

Kaneda   Thank you for coming here.

Yū   Erm . . . It's fine.

Kaneda   Do you know what? We have met before. Your father is an old friend of mine. My name is Kaneda. Do you remember me?

Yū   Erm . . . Sorry.

Kaneda   You were so small. Maybe five? I visited you at New Year's and you insisted on receiving a New Year's card. So, I wrote you one on the spot. Then that card had the winning number. You were so grateful to me. Well, it was a card that was in stock at yours, so you had no reason to thank me. Do you remember?

Yū   Maybe . . . yes.

Kaneda   After that, the situation got worse and I stopped visiting. But now, I am your visiting doctor

Yū   Okay.

Kaneda   How have you been?

Yū   Okay.

Kaneda   You've grown.

Yū   I . . .

She is keeping a distance from **Kaneda**.

Kaneda   Don't you worry. It's just a rumor. It's not that infectious. Plus, you are young and healthy. There's nothing to worry about.

Yū   Okay.

Reiko   You don't talk much, do you?

Yū   What?

Reiko   You barely respond.

Yū   Erm . . . right.

Reiko   Right? Why is that?

Yū   Erm, I suppose it's because we did not have much chance to communicate with you. So we're not used to this kind of thing.

Reiko   There's no need to get used to us. We're the same human beings. But thank you for answering my question. I understand very well now. But we're gifted with words. Not responding enough in words is actually rude.

Kaneda   Don't talk like that. It's only natural. We're not used to each other. I'm sorry. This is . . . my daughter . . . Noriko.

Reiko   I'm Noriko. You could have picked a better name.

Kaneda   She's interested in day people. So I brought her with me. And I remembered about you.

Reiko   Could we have a little chat?

Kaneda   What do you think? If you don't mind.

Yū   I don't mind.

Reiko   Thank you.

Kaneda   Great. It will attract people's attention here. Go talk in the car. I'm going to go talk to your father. Enjoy. (*Makes to leave.*)

Reiko   Oh, Kaneda, give me the car key?

Kaneda   Of course. (*Takes out the key from his pocket.*) There. By the way, don't call your father by his surname, okay? It's a horrible habit.

Reiko   I'm sorry, Dad.

Kaneda   Be careful.

He exits.

Reiko *observes* **Yū**. **Yū** *is uncomfortable.*

Yū   Sunglasses at night?

Reiko   Oh, my vision is too good. (*She takes off the sunglasses.*)

Yū   Isn't it ironical that you're wearing sunglasses when you can't be in the sun?

Reiko   You know? You can have them.

She offers her sunglasses. **Yū** *hesitates but she takes them.*

Reiko   Let's go.

Yū   Let's what here.

Reiko   Why?

Yū   I don't want to go in the car.

Reiko   Are you scared?

Yū   A little.

Reiko   I see. Try them on.

Yū   Sorry?

Reiko   Sunglasses.

Yū   Sure. (*Puts the sunglasses on.*)

Reiko   Oh, they don't suit you at all. (*Laughs.*)

Yū   Ha ha . . . (*Forced laughter.*)

Reiko *gets closer to* **Yū** *and looks at her face.*

Reiko   Your skin is rough. It must be the sun.

She touches **Yū's** *cheek.* **Yū** *tries to push her hand away but* **Reiko** *grabs her hands and looks at them.*

Reiko   And your hands. Scratches take ages to heal.

Yū   Let go of me. (**Reiko's** *hand is too strong to remove.*)

Reiko *lets go of her.*

Yū   Don't look at me as if you're looking at an object. (*She rubs her arm.*)

Reiko   I'm sorry. (*Referring to her arm.*) Are you okay?

Yū   Yes.

Reiko   But, you're so attractive.

Yū   Please. Don't.

Reiko   So very attractive. How do you put it . . .? Healthy? We're the healthier ones that's for sure. But . . . There's no doubt that you're unhealthy. But at closer look, you look healthier. (*Gives a contented smile.*)

Yū   What's funny?

Reiko (*laughs*)   No. I don't know why I'm laughing but it's so funny.

Yū (*sighs*)   Okay . . . Erm, how old are you, Noriko?

Reiko   About the same age as you?

Yū   Tell me, please.

Reiko   I'm twenty-four.

Yū   Okay. And your zodiac?

Reiko   Rabbit. Why . . .?

Yū   Because we can never tell by your looks.

Reiko   Do you think I'm thirty-six? Or forty-eight? Age means nothing for us and we never judge anyone by how they look. What's important is what's in your heart. Having said that, it is good manners to keep your appearance nice and tidy and beautiful.

Yū *starts worrying about what she is wearing.*

Reiko   Have you heard of B&D cafe?

Yū   No.

Reiko   It's pretty famous.

Yū   B&D?

Reiko   Breakfast for us, dinner for you.

Yū   Okay.

Reiko   It's a cafe with a concept of helping us solve misunderstandings between us. There are several in Matsumoto. Why don't you go?

Yū   Do you go there often, Ms. Noriko?

Reiko   No. But you have inspired me to go.

Yū   There are such places then.

Reiko   It's cheaper for day people, so that's good for you, isn't it? Of course, they have a dress code to keep beggars away. Make sure you wear something nice.

Yū   Okay.

Pause.

Reiko   Okay that was good. Thank you.

She offers her hand to shake. **Yū** *shakes the proffered hand.*

Reiko *pulls her in and hugs her. They separate.*

Reiko   Thank you. Please tell him I'm waiting in the car.

Yū   Erm . . . Ms. Noriko . . . Are you my mother?

Reiko   Yup. You could tell? How did you know?

Yū   I don't know.

Reiko   You knew it without knowing? Amazing. That is quite amazing. Bye then.

Reiko *goes back to the car.* **Yū** *is in shock for a while.*

Scene Nine

In front of the checkpoint. **Morishige** *is on duty.*

Morishige *notices* **Tetsuhiko** *and stands up. They exchange exaggerated gestures of salute.*

Tetsuhiko   Good evening, sir!

Morishige   Good evening!

Tetsuhiko   And how was it?

Morishige   Good evening! Well . . .

Tetsuhiko   Well?

Morishige   It was weak.

Tetsuhiko   Steeping time?

Morishige   Three minutes.

Tetsuhiko   But, even three should make it strong enough.

Morishige   It was strangely weak, sir!

Tetsuhiko   Wait a minute. Don't tell me you put it in as it is.

Morishige   What do you mean?

Tetsuhiko   Did you blend it?

Morishige   What? No.

Tetsuhiko   Have you lost your mind? Tips of FOP do not taste of that much. You blend it with OP to create an amazing mellowness. What sort of an idiot drinks it on its own? You disappointed me.

Morishige   No, I won't.

Tetsuhiko   Do you have good Orange Pekoe?

Morishige   No.

Tetsuhiko   I'll bring some tomorrow.

Morishige   Thank you.

Tetsuhiko   It's fine.

Morishige   Are you a tea dealer?

Tetsuhiko   I've been growing nothing but tea since I was ten years old.

Morishige   Wow. That's a real skill.

Tetsuhiko   Well . . . Figure out the blend ratio yourself and find what you like best.

Morishige   Okay. So, then, what's the FOP they sell in stores?

Tetsuhiko   Those are already blended. By the way, the one I gave you yesterday was golden tips. Or to be more precise, it was GFOP, Golden Flowery Orange Pekoe. So if you do it well, you can enjoy the best kind of FTGFOP, Fine Tippy Golden Flowery Orange Pekoe. I'll bring my original blend. The ratio is five, two, two, one, with ninety degrees hot water and the best steeping time is three minutes thirty seconds.

Morishige   Fine Tippy Golden Flowery Orange Pekoe . . . Sounds good. Five, two, two, one, ninety degrees and three minutes thirty seconds. I will make it work next time.

Tetsuhiko   Good memory.

Morishige   Do you think so?

Tetsuhiko   I was going to write it down for you, but I suppose there's no need for that.

Morishige   No. It's all in here. (*Pointing at his head.*) But you surprised me. You have your own tea shop.

Tetsuhiko   Why?

Morishige   Well, isn't that cool? It's a remarkable skill.

Tetsuhiko   You have a fine job yourself.

Morishige   Anyone can do this. But your job is different.

Tetsuhiko   Is that right?

Morishige   Yes. Does your family sell tea?

Tetsuhiko   No, it's just me.

Morishige   I see. But what do you mean "just me"?

Tetsuhiko   There was an abandoned tea plantation, so I took it.

Morishige   What? What? You grow your own tea?

Tetsuhiko   Yup. I'm using elderly people, our neighbours.

Morishige   Really? You mean, you're a CEO?

Tetsuhiko   I'm not a CEO as such.

Morishige   I think you are.

Tetsuhiko   Really?

Morishige   How big is your plantation?

Tetsuhiko   Three hectares.

Morishige   Hectares! What is that?

Tetsuhiko   It's really big.

Morishige   Oh my god. I didn't know I was talking to a CEO. Shit. I'll have to start calling you a CEO.

Tetsuhiko   Then I'll start calling you a checkpoint guard.

Morishige   You know what? Maybe it's not a good idea. Actually, not a good idea to call each other by our titles.

Tetsuhiko   You mean, CEO and checkpoint guard?

Morishige   Stop it . . . How old are you?

Tetsuhiko   What about you?

Morishige   Come on tell me.

Tetsuhiko   I heard that it's impossible to tell how old, when it comes to the Nox. I'll feel bad if you were really old.

Morishige   I'm twenty-three.

Tetsuhiko   I'm eighteen.

Morishige   Younger than me. Just as I thought.

Tetsuhiko   Not that much difference.

Morishige   I think you know a lot more than I do.

Tetsuhiko   No. I haven't even finished primary school.

Morishige   It must be hard being a Curio.

Tetsuhiko   Don't call me Curio.

Morishige   Why?

Tetsuhiko   Don't you know what it means?

Morishige   Diurnal.

Tetsuhiko   No, it's how the Nox call us.

Morishige   Okay.

Tetsuhiko   We never call ourselves Curio. So, stop calling me that.

Morishige   Okay. Okay I got you.

Seiji *enters.* **Morishige** *stiffens up.*

Seiji   Working hard?

Morishige   Apologies, sir.

Seiji   That car over there. Isn't that the visiting doctor's car, right?

Morishige Yes. It's Dr. Kaneda's.

Seiji I believe today is not the day of his scheduled visit.

Morishige He is here for private business.

Seiji Right. I see. Where is he now?

Morishige I don't know. But I think his companion went back to his car.

Seiji His companion?

Morishige A lady.

Seiji Okay.

He stops and thinks for a moment and then turns quickly to the car.

Tetsuhiko Hey. Give it to me now.

Morishige What?

Tetsuhiko That.

Morishige What do you mean?

Tetsuhiko You promised me that you'd bring . . .

Morishige (*laughs*) I have no idea what you're talking about. What is it?

Tetsuhiko That. That! Porn . . .

Morishige *smiles and gives a porn magazine to* **Tetsuhiko**. **Tetsuhiko** *flips through the pages with a smile on his face.*

Morishige (*laughs*) Hey, stop that face. Seriously. (*Laughs.*)

Sōichi *and* **Kaneda** *enter. It appears that* **Sōichi** *is trying to finish the conversation.* **Kaneda** *pursues him.*

Sōichi (*to* **Kaneda**) Shut up, will you? (*To* **Tetsuhiko**.) What are you doing? What did you hide? Give it to me.

Tetsuhiko No. It's not like that. Oh. (**Sōichi** *takes the porn.*)

Sōichi *flips through the pages and then closes it.* **Tetsuhiko** *stands straight.*

Sōichi It's fine.

Tetsuhiko No, it's . . .

Sōichi It's fine. I'm not angry or anything.

Tetsuhiko Really . . .?

Sōichi I was just trying to make sure that you were not bullied or anything.

Tetsuhiko I'll never get bullied. He's a good guy. Totally different from the last guy.

Sōichi That's fine then.

Morishige   Nice to meet you. I'm Morishige.

Sōichi   Hi.

Morishige (*to* **Kaneda**)   Your companion is back in your car.

Kaneda   Okay thank you. Sōichi, please let me say this at least.

Sōichi (*ignores* **Kaneda** *and to* **Morishige**)   Oh by the way, he has entered the lottery. If he wins, please could you help him out?

Morishige   Really?

Tetsuhiko   Yeah, I was going to tell you.

Sōichi   He's rather simple. So, please help him.

Morishige   Sure. I'm sure he'll be fine. Good luck.

Sōichi   It's one in five. He might win.

Morishige   One in five?

Tetsuhiko   One in five.

Morishige   Wow that's unbelievable.

Tetsuhiko   It was worth staying here.

Morishige   But what are you going to do with your tea plantation?

Tetsuhiko   I don't know.

Sōichi   It'll be fine. More folks will come. Someone will take care of it.

Tetsuhiko   Of course, we don't even know yet. If I'll win.

Morishige   One in five? That's amazing!

Tetsuhiko *laughs.*

Seiji *comes back. Everyone notices* **Seiji** *and falls silent.*

Seiji   Hey. Don't forget your duty. Get back to your job.

Morishige   I am sorry, sir.

Seiji (*looking around at everyone*)   Are you popular or what? Eh? Impressive. Excuse me, but can you please try not to talk to him? He's supposed to be on duty.

Tetsuhiko   I'm sorry.

Seiji   Okay.

Sōichi   What's the matter? They were just chatting. This is not an army.

Seiji   Things could get complicated.

Sōichi   Complicated?

Seiji   You know? You know about those things that could get complicated.

Sōichi   You're the ones who always tell us to be friends. Aren't you? They are just being friends. (*To* **Tetsuhiko**.) Right?

Seiji   Still, he should be on duty.

Sōichi (*laughs*)   On duty, eh? You must be bored to death.

Seiji   Please mind your tongue.

Sōichi   You don't have the right to say that. You didn't even say hello.

Seiji   You didn't either.

Sōichi   So childish.

Seiji   Let me tell you one thing, don't judge us by how we look. I may look young but I'm fifty-five. I suppose I'm older than you. Well, age doesn't really matter. But I just hate being judged by how I look. Elderly people tend to do that. Why are you doing that to us? It's not about the appearance. There are many childish adults. So many of them! Age is just a lie. You're an antique because your brain is so old fashioned. That's why you're called Curio. Grow up, please.

Pause.

Kaneda, a word.

He walks to the car. **Kaneda** *follows him.*

Sōichi   You. Don't come here when you don't have to.

He throws the porn to the ground and exits. **Tetsuhiko** *gives a glance to* **Morishige** *but then follows* **Sōichi**.

Morishige *is left alone, disappointed.*

Yū *comes in. Noticing her* **Morishige** *stands straight.* **Yū** *stops.*

Morishige   Hello.

Yū   . . .

Morishige   How may I help you? I mean, you don't need a reason to come here. It's your land. It's not often that I see you around at such a late hour. Well, it's our lunchtime though . . . You're Tetsuhiko's friend, right? Isn't he quite something? He knows everything about tea. A real talent. I respect him. (*As there is no response.*) Sorry. I'll shut up.

Yū   That's the only thing he knows.

Morishige   But perhaps that's a good thing. The best craftsmen and artists are still Curios I mean . . . Sorry.

Yū   Don't apologize.

Morishige   I'm always amazed by your artwork. By your . . . sensibility. I think it's great.

Yū   You don't need to talk like that. What will change when you become a Nox?

Morishige   I wonder . . .

Yū   How old were you when you became a Nox?

Morishige   I was born a Nox. I'm the first generation. So I'm sorry. I don't have an answer to that. Do you hate the Nox? I love you guys.

Yū *turns her back to* **Morishige**. *Blackout.*

Scene Ten

At **Soga**'s. *In their living room.* **Seiji** *and* **Kaneda** *are present.*

Kaneda   These days they say the main specialty of Shikoku is human children. That's not funny.

Seiji   That's awful.

Kaneda   It's because there are people who buy them.

Seiji   Don't talk about it like drugs.

Kaneda   We're the ones making a business out of it.

Seiji   Are you opposed to adoption?

Reiko   No.

Seiji   The Nox birth rate is steadily increasing. There will come a day when we won't need to purchase children anymore.

Kaneda   I really hope so.

Seiji   There was an article that they discovered an effective enzyme against ultraviolet rays. There's no problem that can't be solved.

Kaneda   We're not that perfect.

Seiji   I know. But that doesn't mean we need to go crying on our pillows.

Kaneda   No. I'm sorry. Perhaps I became nostalgic seeing an old friend.

Seiji (*laughs*)   You know, Kaneda, maybe we've grown old.

Kaneda   What do you mean?

Seiji   I see. But our body is still young. But what about here? Are our brain cells still healthy?

Kaneda   Of course. Our brain is part of our body.

Seiji   I wonder if my mind has become inflexible.

Kaneda (*laughs*)   You're fine as long as you're worried about it.

Seiji   I'm asking if that's the case from a medical standpoint.

Kaneda   There is no aging. Flexible or inflexible is a matter of personality.

Seiji   How old were you when you became a Nox?

Kaneda   I was twenty-seven.

Seiji   Was there a change in your consciousness? What did it feel like?

Kaneda   It felt like I was cleansed. Like something got exorcised. Yes.

Seiji   Is that a matter of the body? Was it the effect of your brain refreshing?

Kaneda   If the body changes, the spirit will change. It's same as when you feel unmotivated when you're tired.

Seiji   I was fifteen. When I woke up, everything looked different. The scenery, people, everything. I was fastidious as a young man and I was fighting against various issues, anger and desire. I could be free from those things. I thought it was amazing. I thought we can control everything if we are rational by birth. I could face uncontrollable emotions in a calm manner. I thought I could conquer my uncontrollable self.

Kaneda   Like being some sort of god?

Seiji   I don't think giving up immature ideals makes you an adult. I thought I could face them in a form that's different from simple anger. I'm not afraid of defeat or solitude. With strong heart and body, I was ready to venture into the gloomy forest. You might have felt differently but you know what I mean?

Kaneda   What are you trying to say?

Seiji   I can't control my prejudice against Curios.

Kaneda   You're not the only one.

Kaneda *and* **Seiji** *remain on stage.*

Scene Eleven

In front of the checkpoint. Night. **Morishige** *is on duty.*

Tetsuhiko *enters.* **Morishige** *welcomes* **Tetsuhiko** *who looks somewhat uncomfortable.*

Morishige   Long time.

Tetsuhiko   Yeah, long time.

Morishige   How are you?

Tetsuhiko   Good, good.

Morishige   You're up early.

Tetsuhiko   It's kind of hard getting out at night.

Morishige   I see.

Tetsuhiko   They're like all over me. Pain in the neck.

Morishige   I know. Pain in the neck.

Tetsuhiko   Indeed.

Morishige   Last time, you couldn't get porn . . .

Tetsuhiko   Right?

Morishige   You're obsessed.

Tetsuhiko (*laughs*)   Have you got it?

Morishige   What are you talking about?

Tetsuhiko   You know!

Morishige   I don't know what you're talking about.

He laughs and give the porn to **Tetsuhiko**. **Tetsuhiko** *opens the magazine and looks.*

Tetsuhiko   Morishige, have you ever . . . done it?

Morishige   What? Done what?

Tetsuhiko   Come on.

Morishige   You mean, bowling?

Tetsuhiko   With women.

Morishige (*laughs*)   Yes,

Tetsuhiko   Really?

Morishige   Yes, I have.

Tetsuhiko   Really?

Morishige   Yes.

Tetsuhiko   Wow. I see. Okay.

Morishige   What about you?

Tetsuhiko   What? . . .

Morishige   I see.

Tetsuhiko   When was it?

Morishige   I was thirteen.

Tetsuhiko   What the hell. What the hell! What the fucking hell!

He rampages for nothing and **Morishige** *laughs. They stay on the stage.*

Scene Twelve

At **Soga**'s. **Seiji** *and* **Kaneda** *are present. Continuation of Scene Ten.*

Seiji   We've been working on it for thirty years. We believed that we could co-exist. But now I think they should be our management. They're too emotional. We can't even hold a normal conversation.

Kaneda   The Nox isn't almighty or anything. Sometimes we feel small. You're afraid of your own prejudice sentiments but that just shows that you're keeping your head clear. The almighty feeling of the Nox tends to focus on elitism. If you are worried about it, I would recommend taking counselling.

Seiji (*sighs*)   You're right . . .

Kaneda   Why don't you take some time off?

Seiji   Yes. Well, there's Reiko, too, you know.

Kaneda   I'm very sorry.

Seiji   No. Yes. I lost my temper. I can't believe it. I was blood-obsessed. Shit! I'm getting older. Getting stubborn. There are more and more things I cannot forgive.

Kaneda (*laughs*)   When I became a Nox, I thought I became a superman. I was never tired, never caught a cold and my thoughts were clear. But we're not perfect. We've definitely lost something. Why don't you read books? Curios' works are amazing. The sun inspires them. Curios are weak but their vulnerability is the very source of their imagination.

Seiji   Thank you.

Kaneda   Seiji.

Seiji   Yes?

Kaneda   Adopt a Curio child.

Seiji (*laughs*)   That's not possible. I think I'm a supremacist.

Kaneda *laughs*.

They exit.

Scene Thirteen

In front of the checkpoint. Continuation of Scene Eleven. **Katsuya Okudera** *with a bag is on the bridge.* **Tetsuhiko** *and* **Morishige** *don't notice him.*

Katsuya   Hey! Hey! Could it be Tetsuhiko?

Tetsuhiko   Yes . . . Who are you?

Katsuya   Ha! Have you forgotten your uncle's face? Eh?

Tetsuhiko   My uncle?

Katsuya   Yes, I am. (*Approaches him.*) You've grown. (*Laughs.*) Hey, who do you think you are! Taller than me?! Who do you think you are? You're eating rubbish and still you've grown like this. It proves that you're a real idiot. But you look well. That's good.

He smiles and bashes **Tetsuhiko**. **Katsuya** *gives a glance to* **Morishige**.

Katsuya   Were you in some trouble just now?

Morishige   No, no. It's not like that.

Katsuya   Was my nephew troubling you?

Morishige   No, not at all.

Katsuya   Well, he has been stuck here, this one. No wonder he knows nothing. Please excuse him for his ignorance.

Morishige   Please. It's not like that.

Katsuya *bows.* **Morishige** *is shamed and approaches him.*

Katsuya *quickly cuffs* **Morishige**'*s wrist and attaches the chain to a steel bar. At this moment,* **Morishige** *does not know what is happening.*

Morishige   What, why? What is this?

Katsuya (*laughs*; *to* **Tetsuhiko**)   You were in trouble, right?

Tetsuhiko   What . . .?

Katsuya   He was giving you trouble, right? Right? What's the matter?

Tetsuhiko   It's not like that. There is no trouble.

Katsuya   Really? I thought this village was free now. But then, why do you have a checkpoint guard?

Morishige   Please. Could you unlock this?

Katsuya   What are you doing then? Monitoring?

Morishige   It's not like that at all. I'm just like an information guide.

Katsuya   Is that right?

Morishige   Did you come from Matsumoto? May I see your ID just in case?

Katsuya *takes out his ID and holds it where* **Morishige** *cannot see.*

Morishige   I'm sorry, I can't see it. I'm sorry. Could you?

Tetsuhiko   Take them off.

Katsuya   Hmm . . .

Tetsuhiko   Please. Come on! He's my friend.

Katsuya   A friend? (*To* **Morishige**.) Are you friends?

Morishige   Yes.

Katsuya (*to* **Tetsuhiko**)   Friend with him?

Tetsuhiko   Yes. He's different from other Nox.

Katsuya   Hey, hey, you have to be careful. Don't be deceived. Actually, don't tell me you're that stupid.

Teruo   What do you mean?

Katsuya   He is looking down on you. You're too stupid to notice.

Morishige   That's not right.

Katsuya   I know. You just want to tell others that you have a Curio friend. That's sort of cool among you guys, isn't it? Yeah, I know. I've heard about that. We're not your pets, you fool.

He takes **Morishige**'s *stick.*

Katsuya   They're the ones who ruined this village. You're too naïve.

He pokes **Morishige** *with the stick.*

Morishige   That's not true. We'd never do such a thing.

Katsuya   Don't be fooled. They're smooth talkers. (*He puts out the stick as a warning and it hits* **Morishige**'s *face.*) Sorry. I didn't mean to.

Morishige *bleeds from his mouth. He covers it with his hand.*

Katsuya   Hey, careful. Blood is bad news. Be extra careful. Tetsuhiko, be careful, the blood is super-infectious. Ah that was close. Porn! Holy shit! Here's porn!

He picks up the porn. **Tetsuhiko** *takes the stick and holds it against* **Katsuya**.

Katsuya   What do you think you're doing?

Morishige   Tetsuhiko, it's fine. Stop it, okay? Violence is never good.

Katsuya   There! Yes, we shall "discuss" it, as you always do.

Morishige   I think you misunderstand. We are trying to make this village—

Katsuya   No, no, no, no. I know you're going to brainwash us.

Morishige   Okay. I see. Then do as you wish. Go wherever you want. But can you uncuff me before that? I will not tell anyone about it.

Katsuya   Look. He's still talking down to me.

He checks his watch.

The dawn will be breaking in less than an hour. Enjoy.

He takes his bag and the porn and exits.

Tetsuhiko   Hey! Come on, take them off! Hey! Hey! What the hell! What the hell was that?

Morishige *tries to pull them off several times but all in vain.*

Morishige   Shit! It hurts. There's no use.

Tetsuhiko   What should we do? Shit!

Morishige   Calm down. Calm down.

Tetsuhiko   What should we do?

Morishige   Go find some cutters.

Tetsuhiko   Okay.

Morishige   Nothing small. Something that can cut through wire.

Tetsuhiko   Okay.

Morishige   Tetsuhiko. We don't have much time.

Tetsuhiko   Okay . . . Fine.

Morishige   I trust you.

Tetsuhiko *runs off.* **Morishige** *is still chained to the steel bar.*

Scene Fourteen

At **Ikuta's**. **Sōichi** *runs in to where* **Yū** *is.*

Sōichi   Yū! Yū! There you are. Okay. Calm down.

Yū   I am calm.

Sōichi   The result of the lottery came out. This year, you won!

Yū   What?

Sōichi *give a small envelop to* **Yū**. *Inside is a piece of folded paper, the notice.*

Sōichi   Congratulations. It was delivered to Junko's earlier. But she told me not to tell Tetsuhiko yet. Because he'll sulk.

Yū   Sure

Sōichi   What's the matter?

Yū   Erm . . . I haven't decided. It came so soon. It's hard to decide.

Sōichi   You're still young. But youth is not forever. Some can't cope by their late twenties. You should go while you can.

Yū   But are you going to be okay, Dad?

Sōichi   What?

Yū   Without me. Will you manage?

Sōichi   When you were small, I did everything on my own.

Yū   But you're getting older. Things will become harder.

Sōichi   I may be old but not that old.

Yū   I was thinking . . . I don't mind staying here.

Sōichi   Nonsense. That's dreadful.

Yū   Is being a Nox that great?

Sōichi   Of course.

Yū   But you hate the Nox.

Sōichi   Not if it's you.

Yū   You're not making sense.

Sōichi   I want you to have a better life. Many of us were killed by the virus. I want you to live even if that means you have to become a Nox.

Yū   You just want to get rid of me.

Sōichi   Why would I?

Yū   Because then you can live with Junko.

Sōichi   What are you saying?

Yū   It's fine, Dad. Why don't you marry Junko? Then I'll stop worrying and leave this village.

Sōichi   It's not like that.

Yū   I know you like Junko.

Sōichi   Shut your mouth! I just want my daughter to have a healthier, better life. That's all.

They remain on the stage.

Scene Fifteen

In front of the checkpoint. Continuation of Scene Thirteen. **Tetsuhiko** *and* **Junko** *come to* **Morishige** *who is still chained to the steel bar.*

They have a machete and umbrella.

Morishige (*looking at the machete*)   Hey, what's that? You're scaring me.

Tetsuhiko   This was the only thing I could find.

Junko   What's this? What's going on?

Morishige   I'm sorry. Nothing to worry about.

Tetsuhiko   No, it's just . . .

Morishige   It's fine.

Junko   Where's the key?

Morishige   We can't find it. Wow!

Tetsuhiko *tries to chop the chain.*

Morishige   What are you doing? You could have hurt me! Don't start without telling me.

Tetsuhiko   Sorry. (*He tries to chop again.*)

Morishige   Wait, wait, wait. Tetsuhiko, tell me, which one are you trying to chop? The chain? Or my wrist?

Tetsuhiko   The chain. What else?

Morishige   Okay, in that case, do it with care.

Tetsuhiko   Okay.

Junko   We don't have that much time. Actually, in the worst-case scenario, we'll have to chop off your wrist to release you. But you're a strong man, right?

Morishige   Oh no. I may be strong but not to that extent.

Tetsuhiko *bangs down the machete but he cannot quite find the good spot to chop it.*

Junko   Give it to me now!

She takes the machete and start chopping. **Tetsuhiko** *opens the umbrella and holds it above* **Morishige***.*

Morishige (*looks at his umbrella and laughs*)   That is very kind of you but I'm afraid that won't do.

Junko   Oh. The blade is chipped. The chain is stronger than it looks. It's harder than I expected.

Tetsuhiko   Hurry up! Dawn is breaking.

Junko   I know!

Morishige *looks in the direction where the sun is about to rise.*

Tetsuhiko   Hurry up!

Junko   Shut up!

Morishige   Tetsuhiko, there's the schlaf in the hut. Can you go and get it?

Tetsuhiko   The shelf? What do you mean the shelf?

Morishige   No, it's a sleeping bag.

Tetsuhiko   Okay.

Morishige   Go, go!

Tetsuhiko *runs to the hut.*

The sound of **Junko** *trying to chop the chain echoes.*

Scene Sixteen

At **Ikuta***'s.* **Yū** *and* **Sōichi** *are here. Continuation of Scene Fourteen.*

Yū   Is it that bad living here?

Sōichi   If you stayed, there's no future.

Yū   If that's what you think, then why are you here?

Sōichi   Where can I go? Wherever I go, it would be the same for me.

Yū   I understand why Junko is stuck here. But you don't have to stay here.

Sōichi   I can't run away just like that.

Yū   If you're staying here for Junko, then there's something else you need to be doing.

Sōichi   What do you mean?

Yū   I don't know.

Sōichi   If you don't know, then don't be pretentious like that!

Yū   I don't need to become a Nox. But we don't need to stay here either.

Sōichi   Then go wherever you want. You're free.

Yū   So are you, Dad. And Junko.

Sōichi   It's not that easy.

Yū   What do you mean?

Sōichi   It just isn't.

Yū   What isn't? You're always like that. That's nonsense. It's easy. It's easy!

Sōichi   If you don't want it, then give it to Tetsuhiko.

He throws the envelope and exits the room. **Yū** *picks up the envelop and exits.*

Scene Seventeen

In front of the checkpoint. **Morishige** *and* **Junko** *are present. Continuation of Scene Fifteen.*

Junko   No . . . This is not the best tool for it, is it? What he said sounded like gibberish. I didn't get what he wanted.

Morishige   I'm sorry about all this.

Junko   No, It'll be fine. I'll make sure about it.

Morishige   Please.

Junko (*banging on the chain desperately*)   It reminds me of ten years go.

Tetsuhiko *comes back with a sleeping bag.*

Tetsuhiko   Is this the one?

Morishige   Yes it is! Spread it.

Tetsuhiko *spreads the sleeping bag and brings it to* **Morishige**.

Morishige (*to* **Junko**)   I'm sorry. But as the situation is not looking good, I'm going in here.

Junko   Good idea.

Tetsuhiko *and* **Junko** *help* **Morishige** *go into the sleeping bag. Only his hand attached by the chain to the steel bar is sticking out from the sleeping bag.*

Morishige   Please continue. Please.

Junko   Okay,

Morishige (*looking at the direction of the sun which is blinding him*)   Hmm . . . I might not make it.

Junko *puts even more force into banging the chain.* **Tetsuhiko** *is restless.*

Tetsuhiko   Why the hell! Shit!

Morishige   Ouch . . . Ahh . . . .

Junko   Nearly there. Nearly there! You can do it.

Morishige   Erm . . . Thank you. Thank you. But . . . Just cut off my wrist, I'll be fine.

Junko   What are you saying?

Morishige   Please. I'll heal quicker than getting the sunlight.

Junko   But . . .

Morishige   Please. Now!

Junko   . . .

Morishige   Please. It'll be fine. I'm a Nox. I'm strong.

Junko *cannot put herself together to do it.* **Junko** *looks at* **Tetsuhiko**. **Tetsuhiko** *looks determined. He covers his mouth with a towel.* **Tetsuhiko** *takes the machete from* **Junko** *but he hesitates.*

Morishige   Do it! Now!

Tetsuhiko *bangs the machete down to* **Morishige**'s *wrist.* **Morishige** *screams.*
Tetsuhiko *bangs the machete down many times.* **Morishige**'s *wrist is now cut off and he pulls his arm into the sleeping bag.* **Tetsuhiko** *zips the sleeping bag.* **Junko** *wraps the wrist with a piece of fabric.*

The sun rises. **Junko** *wipes the blood that splatters back on* **Tetsuhiko**.

Junko   You don't have any scratches or anything. Right?

We can hear **Morishige** *getting his breath together inside the sleeping bag.*

Sōichi *and* **Yū** *enter. The steel bar is blood stained.*

Scene Eighteen

The same as the previous scene. We see **Junko** *and* **Tetsuhiko** *and* **Sōichi** *with* **Yū**.
Morishige *is in the sleeping bag.*

Katsuya *enters. Everyone notices* **Katsuya**.

Katsuya   I couldn't find my house. Have you moved?

Sōichi   Is that what you wanted to tell us first?

Katsuya   Long time no see. Katsuya Okudera is back now.

Sōichi   Not that.

Katsuya   I'm sorry. Sorry for all the inconvenience caused.

Junko   Why did you come back now?

Katsuya   What? Oh, I read about the village in the paper. You were in the photo, sister. That's how I found out that you're still here. So I came all the way to see you.

Sōichi   You bastard!

Katsuya   I didn't know. I didn't know what had become of this village. There was no information. Of course I was worried. I found out about the economic blockade when I found you in the paper.

Sōichi   Of course you knew.

Katsuya   I'm not lying. What is it? Don't talk to me like that!

Sōichi *approaches* **Katsuya**. **Katsuya** *gets alarmed and keeps a distance.*

Katsuya   What? (*Laughs.*) Am I the villain? (*Laughs.*) I am really sorry, I apologize. I'm sorry. It's all my fault that this village ended up like this. That's why I'm back.

Sōichi   Ten years. Eh?

Junko   What are you planning to do now?

Katsuya   Oh, I want to help.

Sōichi   Help? Look at this village. It's too late. This place is totally ruined. It's your fault.

Katsuya   Where's Dad?

Junko   Dead.

Katsuya   What? When?

Junko   Eight years ago.

Katsuya   How did he die?

Junko   He committed suicide.

Katsuya   What? And that is my fault as well?

Junko   Yes.

Katsuya   I see.

Sōichi   You did that much harm

Junko   It's too late. Way too late.

Katsuya   I also struggled a lot.

Sōichi   You reap what you sow.

Katsuya   If they found me, they would have killed me. That's why I couldn't come back here. Of course, I was worried about you.

Sōichi   You have no idea what we had to go through.

Katsuya   Yes, I do.

Sōichi   No, you don't.

Katsuya   You didn't have to stay here. You could have gone to Shikoku.

Sōichi   You just don't get it, do you? Junko can't leave until the last villager leaves. She is getting all the blame since the day you ran away. This is the kind of society we live in. You've ruined ten years of our time.

Katsuya   "Our" time? I never asked you to do anything.

Sōichi *steps towards* **Katsuya** *but as* **Yū** *speaks, he stops.*

Yū   Dad. Don't.

Katsuya   I see. You were stuck here all this time. That's why the way you think is ancient. Sister, you didn't have to stay here. You're too honest. To the extent that makes me think that you might be stupid. We can walk in the sun freely. The Nox will never get us. Why didn't you take any action for ten years letting the village go to like this? The Nox went mad here. Pathetic! Take revenge. We'll get them during daytime. It'll be easy. As easy as stealing a watermelon from a field.

Junko   Why did you come back?

Katsuya   To free this village? I'll teach you how to fight.

Morishige (*from inside the sleeping bag*)   We'll never fight with you!

Katsuya *notices who is speaking. He looks at the sleeping bag and laughs.*

Katsuya   Hey, hey. (*Laughs.*) Are you the chap from earlier on? (*Laughs.*)

Tetsuhiko *roars.*

He takes **Morishige***'s stick and goes at* **Katsuya***.* **Katsuya** *moves aside just in time.*

Katsuya   What the hell are you doing?

He faces **Tetsuhiko** *who is holding the stick.* **Tetsuhiko** *tries to corner* **Katsuya***.* **Yū** *cuts in to stop* **Tetsuhiko** *and now she is facing* **Katsuya***.*

Yū   It's not the Nox who ruined this village.

Katsuya   What?

Yū   It was Curios.

Katsuya   Are you calling yourselves Curios now? That's not good, is it?

Yū   We are called Curios because of you lot. Curios burnt your house. They were searching for the criminal, started doubting each other, and then screwed up. The Nox did nothing.

Sōichi   Shut up!

Yū   Curios as stupid as you ruined this village.

Katsuya   So what? Eh? So what? Can you stand this shit? Eh? Why do they have a better life?

Tetsuhiko *roars.* **Katsuya** *makes to attack him but* **Yū** *stops him.*

Yū   Don't, Tetsuhiko. Not so savage, you're different from him.

Morishige (*from inside the sleeping bag*)   That's right, Tetsuhiko. Don't!

Katsuya (*laughs*)   What's going on? (*Laughs.*) This is funny.

Tetsuhiko   Don't laugh at us! He did this to Morishige!

Junko (*to* **Katsuya**)   Is that right?

Tetsuhiko   Yes, that's right.

Morishige   It's fine.

Tetsuhiko   It's not fine.

Junko   Really?

Tetsuhiko   It was him. This bastard did it!

Junko *looks at* **Katsuya**. **Katsuya** *is unapologetic.*

Katsuya   What? What? (*Referring to* **Morishige**.) He'll be fine.

Tetsuhiko   What the hell!

Katsuya *snorts.* **Sōichi** *moves behind* **Katsuya**. *This way,* **Katsuya** *ends up being in between* **Tetsuhiko** *and* **Sōichi**.

Sōichi   You haven't changed then.

Yū   Dad. Don't. Tetsuhiko, don't do it. Junko, stop them.

She stops **Tetsuhiko** *who is about to attack him.*

Tetsuhiko (*to* **Junko**)   You won't stop me. (*Shakes* **Yū** *off.*) Right?

Everyone waits for **Junko**'*s decision.* **Junko** *nods.*

Tetsuhiko *goes at* **Katsuya** *and they start fighting.* **Yū** *tries to stop them but* **Sōichi** *holds her back.*

Tetsuhiko *roars.*

Yū   Let go of me!

Sōichi   It's fine. It's fine.

Tetsuhiko *bashes* **Katsuya** *with the stick and gets attacked.* **Katsuya** *is more used to fights.* **Tetsuhiko** *is not doing well.* **Sōichi** *joins them. They both attack and kick* **Katsuya**. **Yū** *begs* **Junko** *to make them stop but she does not move.*

Yū   Stop! Please, Dad, stop! You're repeating the same thing. It's the same as before. This doesn't take us anywhere. Stop!

Junko *does not move. No one is listening to* **Yū** *plead.*

Katsuya *makes to run away but slips on a pool of blood from* **Morishige**'*s wrist.* **Katsuya** *sees the bloody steel bar and realises that it is* **Morishige**'*s blood. Everyone understands how serious this is.*

Katsuya   What? Whaat? What's this? Don't tell me it's his blood. Yuck! Shit! (*Laughs and wipes the blood on his hand and face.*) Shit. Shit! (*Looks at* **Junko** *to ask for help.*) Help me, sister.

Sōichi *removes* **Katsuya** *from* **Junko**. **Katsuya** *gets the virus and starts coughing. He gets sharp pains immediately and starts to rampage. He screams.*

Katsuya *screams.*

Junko   Katsuya! Katsuya!

Sōichi *holds* **Junko**. **Katsuya** *keeps rampaging and after a while he dies.* **Junko** *collapses in front of* **Katsuya**'*s body.*

Sōichi   Junko. You've done everything you can. No one will blame you. Let's leave this village together. You don't have to be stuck here.

Junko *sheds tears. Blackout.*

Scene Nineteen

At **Soga**'s. **Seiji** *and* **Reiko** *are here.* **Yū** *is in a different room.*

Reiko   We had a chat for only a few minutes but she figured that I'm her mother. Isn't it amazing? It's true what they say. Blood relations are fascinating.

Seiji   How did she know?

Reiko   She just knew, no reason. She felt it. She just felt it . . .

Seiji   That's great. And how is it for you? What did you feel?

Reiko   I was hoping to feel something. But surprisingly, I felt nothing. Absolutely nothing. It was an illusion. Just as you said. What I saw was just a Curio girl. A poor, filthy girl.

Seiji   Were you disappointed that this girl was your daughter?

Reiko   No. No, I found it attractive. Didn't you find it attractive?

Seiji   I did.

Reiko   It is attractive.

She goes to the separate room and talks to **Yū**. **Seiji** *is watching them at the door.*

Reiko   You can stay here forever.

Yū   No, no . . . Sorry.

Reiko   If I apply, you can become a Nox right now. It's a fact that we're blood-related.

Yū   No, I mean . . . I haven't thought that far yet.

Reiko   You're fed up with Curios, right?

Yū   I can't suddenly call you Mother.

Reiko   In time you will. Love is unconditional, you know.

Seiji   When you're a Nox, you'll see what we mean.

Reiko   You guys are blood-obsessed. Curios even kill for family. But we're different. All human beings are our family. And we'll never attack them. There's no reason to hesitate.

Yū   I know, but . . . I'm sorry.

Seiji   You're upset, aren't you? You meant well but all in vain. The reason for that is always your own weakness.

Reiko   Then become strong.

Seiji   Only then you can face your problems. Don't mistake strength for evil. You must become strong even if that means that you have to turn your back on the sun.

The three stay on stage.

Scene Twenty

In front of the checkpoint. **Morishige** *is standing.* **Tetsuhiko** *comes out.*

Tetsuhiko   Is your hand okay?

Morishige   Kind of. I can't quite move my fingers though.

Tetsuhiko   Sorry.

Morishige   Not your fault. It's getting cooler these days.

Tetsuhiko   Yes.

Morishige   It's good for us to have longer nights.

Tetsuhiko   I heard that there's a place in the world where the sun barely comes out.

Morishige   In Northern Europe, yes.

Tetsuhiko   Have you been there?

Morishige   No. It's far away.

Tetsuhiko   Further than Okinawa?

Morishige   One hundred times further. Far and cold.

Tetsuhiko   I see. Which one do you like better? Cold weather or hot weather?

Morishige   Cold weather. You?

Tetsuhiko   I like normal weather.

Morishige   Like now?

Tetsuhiko   Yes.

Morishige   You didn't give me that option, you know.

Tetsuhiko   What?

Morishige   It's fine. Can you drive?

Tetsuhiko   Yes, I can.

Morishige   Great.

Tetsuhiko   I don't have a driving license though.

Morishige   Why don't we go somewhere next holiday?

Tetsuhiko   Where?

Morishige   Wherever. Anywhere far from here. You have never got out from here, right? I will drive at night. And you'll drive during daytime. We'll keep driving non-stop like twenty-four hours of Le Mans. And go as far as we can. It's fun to check maps as we go.

Tetsuhiko   But the sunshine will come into the car.

Morishige   I bought a new sleeping bag. It's like a sun-proof coffin.

Tetsuhiko   I don't fancy carrying a coffin.

Morishige   If you open it even a little, I will be seriously hurt. But I trust you completely.

Tetsuhiko   Right.

Morishige   What do you think? Doesn't it sound like fun? Nox and Curio have never traveled together like this.

Tetsuhiko   Travel?

Morishige   You don't fancy it?

Tetsuhiko   Well, I . . .

Morishige   What's the matter? Cheer up.

Tetsuhiko   I . . . I mean . . . I didn't win the lottery. I lost.

Morishige   I see.

Tetsuhiko   Shit. I thought I'd win.

Morishige   You had a big chance but it was still a lottery.

Tetsuhiko   Shit.

Morishige   There'll be other opportunities.

Tetsuhiko   I know. But still, I need to wait one more year.

Morishige   It'll be fine.

Tetsuhiko   It's not fine.

Morishige   Why don't you enjoy the sun while you can?

Tetsuhiko   I want to go to school. I want to learn all sorts of things.

Morishige   You know a lot more than I do.

Tetsuhiko   You don't understand.

Morishige   What they teach at school is nothing. Life gives you real knowledge. You'll see it yourself when you go to school.

Tetsuhiko   Then I need to go to school to find out about that. You can say that because you went to school.

Morishige   School is rubbish. What they teach at school is only knowledge. What you really need is wisdom. And you already have it.

Tetsuhiko   That shit again? You can say that because you went to school. You praise me often but that has never made me happy. Because I'm too stupid to understand what you are praising.

Morishige   You have something wonderful.

Tetsuhiko   If I am that wonderful, then why am I so unhappy? Why do so many people want to become Nox?

Morishige   Okay . . . Then you'll find out how great you are when you go to school. I'm just telling you to be patient. Yes, the Nox are free from aging or diseases. But the sun, the very core of the world, abandoned us. You can enjoy both day and night. For us, that in itself is an amazing thing. So try to enjoy the life you have now.

Tetsuhiko   I can't when I'm stuck here.

Morishige   You can move twenty-four hours. You can go anywhere. Let's go on a trip. We'll be the best pair traveling non-stop. They say that the Nox should not interfere with the Curio. But I don't think that's true. We can complement each other. Let's quit what we're doing and set off on a journey together. We'll do a campaign against discrimination. We'll even find a sponsor. What do you think? Isn't this a great idea?

Tetsuhiko   Don't call me a Curio . . .

Morishige   How you're called isn't a big matter. Sulking doesn't help. I'll represent the Nox and you'll represent the Curio. You can raise the value of the curious antique yourself.

Morishige and **Tetsuhiko** *remain on the stage.*

Scene Twenty-One

At **Soga**'s. **Seiji**, **Reiko**, *and* **Yū** *are present. Continuation of Scene Nineteen.*

Yū   I still don't understand what you are saying.

Reiko   Right. Nothing we can do about that. Because that is the very symptom of being a Curio. You just feel it that way, right? You don't feel like hating us.

Yū   What do you mean by "symptom"?

Reiko   The point about Curio is that you cannot think logically. So it makes perfect sense that you can't understand what I'm saying. You'll get it all when you become a Nox.

Yū   Then that means I'll never be able to understand it then.

Seiji   As long as you keep being curious antiques.

Yū   Don't make fun of me like that.

Seiji   There, look! Suddenly a victim.

Reiko   You'll get it when you're a Nox. You'll see how you were filled with unreasonable preconceptions. It's laughable.

Yū   I can't believe it.

Reiko   That's just how it is.

Yū   I want to go to Shikoku before I make a decision. I heard that Shikoku has a great city that is as good as Nox's city. They have good people and good society. So, could you lend me some money? I want to see Shikoku before I decide.

Seiji   Shikoku . . . Sure, money is not a problem. But, I wouldn't recommend it.

Yū   Why?

Seiji   I paid a visit two months ago. You'll be disappointed. They have a sort of a government. But it's dictatorial and old-fashioned. There's severe polarization and the cities are filthy. On top of that, they're educating their children to hate the Nox. I understand that they don't want their children to leave the place but, nonetheless, it's not a nice thing to do.

Yū   You're lying.

Seiji   No, I'm not. I was deeply disappointed myself. Do you still want to go?

Yū *collapses on the floor.* **Seiji** *and* **Reiko** *exit.*

Scene Twenty-Two

In front of the checkpoint. **Morishige** *and* **Tetsuhiko** *are present. Continuation of Scene Twenty.*

Morishige   I chose this job because I wanted to know more about the Curios. Actually, there are some people who don't like it when I become friends with Curios. They say that the Nox are clever but they have prejudice at the core.

Tetsuhiko   Would I become prejudiced if I became a Nox?

Morishige   I don't know.

Tetsuhiko   How is it for you?

Morishige   I don't hold any prejudice. That's why I'm here with you. Nothing will change.

Tetsuhiko   It will.

Morishige   No, it won't.

Tetsuhiko   No.

Morishige   No, it won't.

Tetsuhiko   I don't understand why you say that. Because we're so clearly different. Why do you say it's the same when it clearly isn't the case?

Morishige   The essence is the same.

Tetsuhiko   What's the "essence" then?

Morishige   We're all the same human race.

Tetsuhiko   That's what I'm saying. We're not the same. You had mentioned that before essence. And I thought about it, but I couldn't find anything like essence anywhere. You're confusing things with that word. You're making things confusing, thinking I don't know words.

Morishige   I'm not confusing things. Okay, so let's say there's a difference, but that doesn't make one superior over the other.

Tetsuhiko   You are superior. Why does everyone want to become a Nox? You make fun of Curios yourselves.

Morishige   There are people like that, but that's why I want the Nox to know more about the good things about Curios.

Tetsuhiko   There's nothing good about us.

Morishige   You guys are great. Animals, plants, water, the wind . . . They're all the most beautiful under the sun. I've only seen that on the screen, but I think Curios who live in such a world are wonderful.

Tetsuhiko   You're only looking at the good side.

Morishige   You're only looking at the good side of the Nox. I was against you becoming a Nox. The number of Curios is decreasing. Curio's culture should be preserved. I want to protect the Curios!

Tetsuhiko   Rubbish! It's just the same as what you said about the school. You can say such a thing only because you're a Nox. You're looking down on me. You say school is nothing great, the Nox is not special. But you can say that because you have everything! You have the knowledge and the mighty body and you want to keep them to yourself. I want to get out from this tiny world. I don't want to get sick or grow old. I want to be a Nox now.

Pause.

You want to protect the Curio? It's not fair. In the end, you're discriminating against us, too.

Morishige   No, I'm not.

Tetsuhiko   Yes, you are.

Morishige *hits* **Tetsuhiko** *on the cheek. He hits him again.*

Tetsuhiko *tries to fight back but obviously* **Morishige** *is stronger than him.*

Morishige   It's your own fault you're so weak.

Tetsuhiko *rushes to* **Morishige** *only to be beaten. He tries again and again but all in vain.* **Tetsuhiko** *collapses on the ground.*

Morishige   Becoming a Nox won't solve that.

Tetsuhiko *cries like a child.* **Morishige** *exits.*

Scene Twenty-Three

In a room in a hospital. **Kaneda**, **Seiji**, *and* **Reiko** *enter.* **Yū** *is in a different room.*

Kaneda *puts his bag on the table.*

Kaneda   I need to see Sōichi's signature.

Reiko *gives* **Kaneda** *the document with* **Sōichi**'*s signature.* **Kaneda** *checks it.*

Kaneda   Seiji, does it really need to be her?

Seiji   She's Reiko's daughter. It's only natural.

Kaneda   No, you were struggling over that fact.

Seiji   You're right . . . Yes. That's why. I felt it necessary to overcome my reservations. Accepting her would lead to my own maturity.

Kaneda   That's nothing to do with her.

Seiji   Right.

Kaneda   Right?

Seiji   And? So what?

Kaneda   You should not use her for such a purpose.

Reiko   Why? It's mutually beneficial.

Kaneda (*to* **Reiko**)   You didn't feel anything special toward her either, did you?

Reikok   You're right.

Kaneda   Do you need to be so hung up on blood relations?

Reiko   I'm not hung up on it. But neither is there a reason to avoid her. This is fate. This is a connection we found.

Kaneda   Perhaps.

Reiko   She wants it. What? Are you against it?

Kaneda   It's not like that.

Reiko   Then, what?

Kaneda   I knew her when she was a child.

Reiko   Are you saying you know her better than I do?

Seiji   Perhaps you're the one hung up about it.

Kaneda   Yes, you're right. I'm opposed.

Reiko   Why?

Kaneda   I don't know.

Reiko (*laughs*)   What do you mean you don't know?

Seiji   She's suffering. From being a Curio.

Reiko   We want to help her.

Seiji   I don't want to call foolishness a crime, but it's infinitely close to criminal in reality. And she knows it.

Kaneda   That's their problem.

Reiko   You're cruel. You're okay with leaving her in such a place?

Kaneda   That's a problem they have to overcome themselves.

Seiji   We are the ones who overcame it. Kaneda, why are you saying this at this stage?

Pause.

Kaneda   Exactly.

Seiji   We need to save her.

Reiko   Being a Curio is a disease. It can be cured with medicine.

Kaneda *goes to a separate room and looks at* **Yū**.

Kaneda   Why are they so willing to give up the sun? That is the very symptom of being a Curio!

As he gets excited, **Seiji** *and* **Reiko** *enter.*

Seiji   Perhaps I should ask a different doctor to step in.

Kaneda (*to* **Yū**)   Are you really sure?

Yū   Yes.

Kaneda   . . .

Seiji   You're a third party. You can oppose all you want, but it doesn't carry any weight.

Kaneda   That's right . . . Let me do this.

He takes out a set of injection with vaccine and puts it on the table.

Reiko *takes* **Yū**'s *jacket and rolls up her sleeve.* **Kaneda** *continues his preparation.*

Kaneda   First, I'll administer a vaccine. And then the blood of a Nox. Which or you are going to do it?

Reiko   I'll do it.

Kaneda (*to* **Yū**)   Give me your arm.

Yū *offers her arm to* **Kaneda**, *who administers the agent.* **Yū** *is scared but* **Reiko** *comforts her.*

Kaneda *administers the vaccine.*

Kaneda   You'll be fine. Reiko, get ready. I'll draw your blood.

Reiko   That won't be necessary.

Reiko *makes* **Yū** *stand, touches her gently and then kisses her.* **Yū** *is surprised and resists but* **Reiko** *forces her to continue. When they are separated, both of them have blood around their mouth. The infection is done with* **Reiko**'*s bloody kiss.*

Reiko   Do you think that was enough?

Seiji (*to* **Kaneda**)   Sorry. She wanted to do this.

Reiko *steps away from* **Yū** *and wipes her mouth with her handkerchief.*

Yū' *starts breathing heavily. She starts coughing. Three of them observe* **Yū.**

Kaneda   She's going to thrash about. Tie her to the bed.

Yū *starts suffering and roars like an animal. She starts getting wild.*

Reiko *and* **Seiji** *are watching this as if they are looking at a new-born baby.*

Yū *thrashes around on the floor and tries to get* **Reiko.** **Reiko** *accepts her.* **Yū** *struggles in* **Reiko** *and* **Seiji**'*s arms then eventually loses consciousness.* **Reiko** *and* **Seiji** *take* **Yū** *to a different room to exit.*

Kaneda *puts his tools back in his bag and then sinks onto a chair.*

Scene Twenty-Four

In front of the checkpoint. Night. **Kaneda** *and* **Sōichi** *are present.*

Sōichi   We're going to try and build a life that's independent from a Nox town. We've been fine for ten years. It'll be fine.

Kaneda   Sure.

Soichi   We'll do everything on our own. We won't let you bastards call us thieves anymore.

Kaneda   Where will you go?

Sōichi   I don't know. We'll go down to Okinawa for starters.

Kaneda   Okinawa? I won't be able to visit you so easily.

Sōichi   Don't visit.

Kaneda   You really don't like me.

He stares at **Sōichi.**

Kaneda   When I saw you after all those years, I was overwhelmed by an indescribable feeling. Of time. Time is curved into your body.

Sōichi   Shut up.

Kaneda   Even though we have lived the same amount of time.

Sōichi   Are you bragging now?

Kaneda   No. I felt like I was left behind. You're the only one moving forward in time.

Sōichi   Of course, you bastards don't have dawn.

Kaneda *laughs. He keeps laughing.*

Sōichi   You're laughing too much . . .

Kaneda   No, it's just that you're so right.

Sōichi   The sun rises and sets. That's one day.

Kaneda   We have the moon.

Sōichi   The moon reflects the light of the sun. Did you know?

Kaneda   That's right. There's no way we can win. If everyone becomes thieves or pirates, then the society is done for. It doesn't matter how heroic you are, you are still parasites.

Sōichi   That's right. So, I'm not going to depend on you.

Kaneda   Right. You can be independent. Sōichi. I'll tell you a secret. The Nox's birth rate has not improved. Not at all. It's written on the paper that the birth rate is increasing and we're overcoming the issue with the sun but they're nothing but wishful thinking. The media is hiding the truth. Only 1 percent of the babies are born Nox. Others purchase Curio children. The Nox cannot be independent. It's us who are thieves.

Sōichi   Still, you're ruling the world now.

Junko *and* **Tetsuhiko** *come out.* **Yū**, *who is now a Nox, is coming to visit them.* **Morishige** *comes in from the bridge.*

Kaneda (*checks his watch*)   It should be anytime now. I'm so sorry to call you out so late.

Junko   It's fine.

Sōichi *gives an envelope to* **Junko**, *who hands it to* **Tetsuhiko**.

Sōichi   Tetsuhiko, you can have this. It's the right that Yū won. Do as you please.

Junko   You have one year. Think about it carefully.

Kaneda   Are you sure?

Junko   Yes.

Yū, **Reiko**, *and* **Seiji** *enter.* **Reiko** *and* **Seiji** *go to see* **Yū** *who is waiting for them.*

Yū *walks up to face* **Sōichi**.

Sōichi   You okay?

Yū   Yes. I'm fine. I still have a bit of a headache, though.

Kaneda   Sure.

Yū *observes* **Sōichi**.

Sōichi   What does it feel like?

Yū   Like I've been cleansed? It's like, it seems so silly I was struggling like that.

Sōichi   Right. That's . . . good.

Yū   Yes. I feel that I'm free. So are my body and thoughts. Thinking back, I think I could have done more in those ten years. I'll study hard and make sure that nobody has to go through what we went through in this village. The years we spent here were a total waste of time.

Junko   I don't think it was a waste of time.

Yū   But this whole thing happened because we did nothing. I think it is very important for us to take action. I wonder why I never took action when I always thought I should be doing something. So I've decided that I'll spend my time so that someone like Dad or Junko can live in a more convenient and healthier environment. I will help this village. I think I can do it now. This village has to change.

She sounds very articulate and strong compared to before. **Sōichi** *starts sobbing.*

Yū   Hey! Dad? What? Are you crying?

Sōichi   Huh? Oh, yeah, ha ha, what's with me? (*Laughing and crying at the same time.*)

Yū   What? What's with you?

Sōichi (*crying*)   No, ha ha, I'm happy you've become so grown up. (*Laughs.*)

Yū   You're funny (*Laughs.*)

Sōichi *sobs on the ground.*

Yū   Don't exaggerate it.

Junko   Thank you for coming. Thank you for coming to say hello. But it's probably enough. Enough for today.

Yū   Okay.

She goes back to **Reiko** *and* **Seiji** *who are waiting on the bridge. They exit.*

Junko *comforts* **Sōichi**.

Sōichi   Oh, ha ha, sorry, I'm sorry, ha ha, oh, did Yū leave? Did she . . .?

Pause.

Kaneda *takes off his jacket and puts his forehead on the ground to apologise.*

Kaneda   I'm sorry.

Sōichi ...?

Kaneda I'm sorry.

Sōichi What are you doing? (*Laughs.*) Stop it.

Kaneda I'm sorry. I'm sorry! I'm sorry.

Sōichi It's okay.

Kaneda *looks up.*

Sōichi Go home. Dawn is breaking.

Kaneda *throws away his jacket, takes off his tie, and crosses his legs.*

Sōichi What are you doing?

Kaneda Sit here with me. I'm going to watch the sunrise here.

Sōichi (*laughs*) You fool.

Kaneda This is going to be the last sunrise I see in my life and I want to see it with you.

Sōichi (*laughs*) What are you talking about it?

Kaneda We can never live turning our backs to the sun.

Sōichi Come on. Stop it. (*Laughs.*) You're causing a trouble.

Kaneda Sōichi, being a Nox is a disease.

Sōichi That's what I've been telling all along.

Junko *starts laughing.* **Kaneda** *lies down on the ground and spreads his arms and legs.*

Sōichi Bye. Please go home. Okay?

Sōichi *and* **Junko** *exit.* **Kaneda** *is still on the ground.*

Tetsuhiko *and* **Morishige** *look at each other.*

Tetsuhiko *holds the envelope high and tears it. He tears it in pieces and scatters them.*

They give each other a big smile and step closer. Blackout.

Curtain.

Notes

* The first edition of *The Sun* translated by James Yaegashi is included in ENGEKI: *Japanese Theatre in the New Millennium 1* published by the Japan Playwrights Association.

Carcass

Takuya Yokoyama

Introduction to the Playwright and the Play

Youichi Uchida (*cultural journalist*)

Translated by M. Cody Poulton

The term "carcass" of the play's title refers to the sides of meat of a slaughtered cow or pig after its head, blood, skin, and internal organs are removed and it is sliced in two down the back. This drama, which features three men who work in an abattoir processing carcasses, won the 2009 Japan Playwrights Association New Playwright Award, a major benchmark signifying the debut of a ground-breaking new dramatist. For a writer who consistently portrays oppressed and nameless people, this was a major achievement.

Prior to the opening of Japan with the Meiji Restoration, the consumption of four-legged animals was prohibited. This was due to ancient practices that avoided the shedding of blood as a form of ritual pollution, as well as to the influence of Buddhism, which forbade the killing of living creatures. Groups responsible for the slaughtering of cows and horses, or those who dealt with corpses, existed at the very bottom of the premodern social hierarchy. Even after the prohibition against eating animal flesh was lifted in the nineteenth century, such people were discriminated against and segregated into ghettoes; they were called *burakumin*, which literally means "village people." Their history of engaging in such dangerous jobs as the slaughtering of animals also coincides with the immigration of labourers from the Korean peninsula during Japan's colonial period.

Given this complex history, surely no play in Japan has ever been set in a slaughterhouse. The writer himself was able to observe the slaughtering and processing of carcasses in an abattoir thanks to the introduction of a classmate from middle school who worked in one. What he witnessed and heard about labour conditions in such a place are vividly reflected in this text, portraying a side of Japan that has hitherto remained unknown.

Imai, a customer who has come to inspect the abattoir, relates how his cattle resist being led to slaughter. He stresses that producers like him are sending "lives" to the abattoir. Genda, one of the workers there, objects strenuously to this charge. He cannot bear it being thought that he is taking the life of anything. His objection underscores what is a fundamental example of prejudice against those who work in abattoirs. Slaughterhouses exist because consumers want to eat meat. Those who work there do not want to be told that they are in the business of killing.

The dialect Genda speaks (he has come to work in the Tokyo region from Osaka) plays an important role in the Japanese production of this play. His dialect has a unique charm to it in contrast to the standard Tokyo Japanese that Imai and Sawamura speak. The Osaka dialect carries with it a certain tenor and nuance, conveying degrees of pathos and irascibility that transcend the prosaic qualities of the standard tongue.

It would not be wrong to say that Genda's Osaka-inflected invective against Imai's feelings of prejudice presupposes the existence in the Osaka region of a great number of communities that are still disciminated against. And though he does not actually appear in the play, one can surmise by his surname that a character called Yanagi, whom Genda defends, is a member of the so-called *zainichi* Korean community who remained in Japan after the Second World War. (Yanagi is transliterated as Yoo, Yu, or Ryu in Korean.) The slaughterhouse presents as it were the shadow side of Japanese society.

Until 2010 the part of the brain known as the medulla or brainstem was essential to testing for BSE (bovine spongiform encephalitis, or mad cow disease). The little-known fact that the loss of a brainstem could spell a financial loss signals to us just how precarious and insecure were the jobs of those who were working in the dregs of this industry. A laborer who was laid off from working in a slaughterhouse had literally nowhere else to go. This Osaka-born playwright, who consciously uses the Osaka dialect to great effect, portrays an unknown class of people forced to live in oppression. One might say that Yokoyama uses language here like music.

Playwright Biography

Takuya Yokoyama

Born in Osaka on January 21, 1977, Yokoyama is a playwright, director, and head of theatre company iaku (founded in 2012). He is known for writing plays structured in precise conversational layers that, like a spiral stairway, lead the audience unexpectedly into moments of conflict among his characters. The rich dramaturgy of his plays invites repeated production. Furthermore, he aims to create plays that entertain and stand up to critical viewing by adult audiences. Yokoyama has garnered numerous awards including the 15th Japan Playwrights Association New Playwright Award for *Carcass* (2009), 1st Sendai Short Drama Award for *Not Knowing How Others Feel* (2013), 72nd Agency for Cultural Affairs National Arts Festival New Artist Award (Kansai district) in 2017, Osaka City Sakuya Konohana Award (2018), and others.

Carcass

Takuya Yokoyama

Translated by Mari Boyd

Characters (in order of appearance)

Sawamura
Genda
Toru Imai

A meat processing plant is a factory where livestock is slaughtered and processed.

Meat culture in Japan became popular after the Meiji era (1868–1912). In those days, the slaughter of cattle and horses was seen as an impure act, and those who engaged in it were regarded as "polluted" and segregated from the general public. Although there are regional differences, the issue of buraku[1] discrimination is also involved, and to this day, some people still look at such processing sites in a discriminatory way.

Marumoto Meat Center is a small-scale meat processing plant in a town near Tokyo.

A day at the meat processing plant begins at 8:00 am. At Marumoto, the early shift A starts at 7:30 am and shift B at 8:00 am. Both continue non-stop until 2:00 pm. The workers take a break when their work is finished. After that, they spend time on equipment maintenance, leftover duties, and physical training. Shift A leaves at 3:30 pm and Shift B, at 4:00 pm.

The setting is the grinding room at the Marumoto Meat Center.

The grinding room is mainly for workmen to sharpen knives. As many of the workers also take their break there, the room de facto functions as a rest area.

Sofas and stools, etc. are placed in a haphazard manner. There are magazines and newspapers on a long table. In the corner of the room is a grinding machine for utility knives. There is also an intercom.

One winter day.

It is after 2:00 pm and time for a break. **Sawamura** *comes into the grinding room with a container of instant* yakisoba[2] *noodles in one hand. The hot water has been drained out. Sitting down on a chair and removing his mask, he pours sauce on top of the yakisoba. The sauce is in powder form, rare for yakisoba.*

With a dubious look on his face, **Sawamura** *mixes the sauce and noodles. At that moment,* **Genda** *enters with a convenience store bag. He smells the sauce.*

Genda Amazing.

Sawamura Mr. Genda.

Genda The smell fills the air.

Sawamura Huh?

Genda *sits on a chair nearby.*

Genda You did good, today.

Sawamura Thanks, so did you.

Genda Oh, what a day. That sire pig was a real tough call. It was this huge (*indicating with his hands*).

Sawamura I fired three shots with the slaughter gun.

Genda   It held out for too long.

Sawamura   I was once screwed good and proper by a sire pig and its tusk. It bored right into my thigh.

Genda   Scary . . . Why the hell does it stink so much even before it's brought into the chamber?

Sawamura   It's got balls.

While talking, **Sawamura** *is still struggling to mix the sauce into the noodles.* **Genda** *eyes* **Sawamura**'s *noodles as he himself rummages in his store bag.*

Genda   Sawamura, day after day you eat that shit.

Sawamura   Huh?

Genda   Always the same instant yakisoba.

Sawamura   It's boiled. It's not fried at all.

Genda   Oh yeah, that's true.

Sawamura *reaches the height of his frustration.*

Sawamura   Aw, fuck.

Genda   What's up?

Sawamura   Could you listen to my story?

Genda   Huh?

Sawamura   It's the pits.

Genda   What is?

Sawamura   I'm going to spread the sauce evenly over the noodles from now on.

Genda   Huh? What kind of declaration is that?

Sawamura   There's no this way or that way about it.

Genda   I don't get your this way or that way, but how come?

Sawamura   Can you believe it?

Genda   I mean, what are you going on about? We're not getting anywhere.

Sawamura   May I put my trash in your, uh . . .

Genda   Yeah.

Sawamura *drops the vinyl packaging of his instant yakisoba and the sauce container into* **Genda**'s *vinyl bag. He starts talking methodically.*

Sawamura   You know, in junior high school, I . . .

Genda   There you go again, topic hopping.

Sawamura   Hear me out.

Genda, *signaling his acknowledgment with his eyes, takes out a rice ball from a vinyl bag.*

Sawamura   Kato, an upper classman in the same club, was my hero.

Genda   Huh, what kind of club were you in?

Sawamura   Soft tennis.

Genda   You played soft tennis? You're kidding.

Sawamura   I'm going to go off track here.

Genda   Is there a through-line to your talk? Going off track can only happen when you have a through-line.

Sawamura   So you see, when my hero, Kato, ate instant yakisoba, he would trickle the sauce smack in the center of the noodles. He was that type of guy.

Genda   Uh-huh . . . Huh?

Sawamura   So you see, (*turning his hand around above the noodles*) not doing this but zooming in on one spot. That type.

Genda   Oh yeah? So there are rival cliques over things like that.

Sawamura   That was so cool, you know. At that time.

Genda   I don't really get that but . . .

Sawamura   Uh, you don't think it's cool? With the sauce pooled in one spot? Isn't it so daring?

Genda   Daring . . . I won't say it isn't.

Sawamura   He doesn't pander to yakisoba, see.

Genda   You're talking without knowing the true meaning of pander.

Sawamura   All through junior high, I belonged to the clique that pooled the instant yakisoba sauce in one spot.

Genda   So then? What are you going to do from here?

Sawamura   I'll spread it all over the noodles.

Genda   Why? Why does it matter? You mix it all together, anyways.

Pointing to **Sawamura**'s *yakisoba.*

Sawamura   Well, you see, if I had the usual UFO yakisoba, there wouldn't be any problem . . . No, even if it wasn't UFO, if it were simply the same kind of yakisoba, I could deal with it. But this . . .

Genda   Oh, don't you have a UFO. today?

Sawamura   They were sold out.

Genda   Oh, yeah,

Sawamura   Now this, I bought it today. It turned out to come with sauce powder. I don't know what I was thinking about, but I got carried away.

Genda   . . . got carried away . . .

Sawamura   See this? This sauce powder makes it all lumpy. See?

Genda *looks.*

Genda   Ahh, you're right.

Sawamura   As if it were sneering at how I'd always collected the sauce in one spot.

Genda   Humph.

He proceeds to feed his face with a rice ball and spreads out a magazine.

Sawamura   Mr. Genda, are you listening?

Genda   Yeah, but I'm getting bored.

Sawamura   What did you say?

Genda   I mean, you'd better eat up or the noodles will get soggy.

Sawamura   I know.

He stops mixing the sauce and noodles and starts eating.

Genda   Sawamura, haven't you been eating instant yakisoba for lunch ever since I came here?

Sawamura   I have been even before you came to work here.

Genda   UFO.

Sawamura   Right.

Genda   You know, if they're out of UFOs, you could try something else for a change.

Sawamura   Huh?

Genda   There are lots of varieties, like Cup Noodles.

Sawamura   No way, I reset myself this way.

Genda   Reset yourself?

Sawamura   I use UFO as it has the strongest effect, but if it's sold out, I do try other types.

He continues to eat. Closing his magazine, **Genda** *speaks.*

Genda   Sawamura, how long have you been working here?

Sawamura   Thirteen years.

Genda   Doesn't the smell bother you?

Sawamura   Ohh . . .

Genda   Uh, that's right. You're wearing a mask when you work.

Sawamura   The mask is protection against splatter. Sometimes, blood gets into your mouth, right?

Genda   Yeah, that gets me down.

Sawamura   I don't have a problem with the smell any more. The UFO sauce revives my normal sense of smell. It resets my ability to smell.

Genda   Uh, is that why you've been taking a shower after work recently before going home? Is that resetting, too?

Sawamura   If we got used to the smell here and forgot what our natural body odor was, that would be scary.

Genda   I get it. It's this.

He raises his little finger.

Sawamura   Excuse me?

Genda   You're seeing a woman.

Sawamura   Are you stupid?

Genda   Confess

Sawamura   I have a wife and child.

Genda   That has nothing to do with it. Aren't you dropping by a woman's place on the way home?

Sawamura *takes a breath.*

Sawamura   It's my son.

Genda   Huh?

Sawamura   Nowadays, Shota won't come to me.

Genda   Humph.

He draws himself together slightly.

So, he doesn't want to get close. Is that really because of your BO?

Sawamura   Weeell, my wife suggests that in a roundabout way.

Genda   How old is Shota?

Sawamura   He's in third grade.

Genda   Have you told him what your job is?

Sawamura   I usually say I'm a butcher.

Genda   Kids usually start worrying about what others think during puberty. At least, from my personal experience, that is.

Sawamura   Uh-huh. I don't think he was teased at school. It seems to be more specifically about my body odor.

Genda   You don't smell. Not a bit.

He tries sniffing himself.

Isn't it all in your imagination?

Sawamura   I don't know. Among human senses, smell is the first thing to go, don't you think?

Genda   Is that how it is?

Sawamura   Mr. Genda, have you ever traveled abroad?

Genda   What makes you say that? Sure, I have, even me.

Sawamura   I haven't.

Genda   Why not?

Sawamura   You know how they say that when you get off at the airport in South Korea, you can smell kimchi?

Genda   Uh-huh, I've heard that one.

Sawamura   But that smell fades very quickly. You get used to it.

Genda   Humph.

Sawamura   If you work every day, you get used to the smell.

Genda   I suppose.

Sawamura   I want to be aware of my own odor. I want to start there.

Genda   Couldn't you just use Febreze spray or such.

Sawamura   No, it's too much trouble to carry around.

Genda   How about perfume?

Sawamura   Not my thing . . .

Genda   Uh, so. So your only choice is yakisoba?

Sawamura   Well.

Genda   You're weird.

Sawamura   I simply like yakisoba.

He holds up his yakisoba container.

Genda   Yeah, of course, you can't eat it everyday unless you like it.

Sawamura   That's the bottom line.

Genda   Really. It's for Shota's sake.

The intercom buzzes. **Genda**, *who is sitting near it, picks up the receiver.*

Hallo.

The call is from the cattle processing and dressing chamber. The staff need reinforcement.

We just started our break. What's up?

The caller says that one swine's brainstem is missing.

Brainstem?

Sawamura   Huh?

Genda   Again? That's incredible.

The caller says that help is needed but they don't have to come right away.

Genda   We'll come straight after lunch. Get a grip on yourself and fix your own problems or else you're in for real trouble.

He puts down the receiver.

What kind of a place is this?

Sawamura   Has another brainstem gone lost?

Genda   They've halted the line and the whole team is searching for it.

Sawamura   Have they made an assembly announcement?

Genda   He said we could take a short rest first and then join them.

Sawamura   All right.

Genda   I can't believe it. Are they stupid or what?

Sawamura   Who is the chief of the swine processing chamber?

Genda   Dunno. Some young guy.

Sawamura   Umph. Laying off the veteran workers really isn't a good idea. even in a recession.

Genda   Then the remaining workers fuck up on the line. That's a glaring case of getting your priorities wrong. The company's already in a tight situation and someone messes up. Who the hell was it?

Sawamura   Probably the guy who does the decapitation.

Genda   A real pisser.

At this moment, **Imai** *enters.* **Sawamura** *and* **Genda** *look at him.*

Imai   Oh, how d'you do.

Sawamura *and* **Genda** *do not return the salutation.* **Sawamura** *gives a faint bow.*

Imai   Is this the grinding room?

Sawamura   It's the alternative processing chamber.

Imai   The alternative processing chamber?

Genda   It's an especially high-grade processing chamber.

Imai   Oh, wow.

Genda   What's with your "wow"?

Imai   Oh, excuse me.

Sawamura (*appeasingly*)   Mr. Genda.

Genda   Anyways, who are you?

Imai   Well, my name is Imai.

Sawamura   Are you a livestock farmer?

Imai   Um, something like that. I was told to wait over here.

Genda   By who?

Imai   My company president and your director.

Sawamura   You new?

Imai   Yes, sort of.

Sawamura   Sit over here.

Imai   Uh, thank you very much.

He ends up sitting down on the indicated chair. A slightly uncomfortable feeling pervades the room. **Sawamura** *and* **Genda** *return to their meal.*

Genda   Wolf it down and then get going, OK?

Sawamura   Uh-huh.

Imai (*leisurely*)   It's a nice scent.

Sawamura   Huh?

Imai   Yakisoba is like—if someone is eating it, you want some, too.

Sawamura   Oh yeah?

Imai   Yes.

Sawamura *holds out his yakisoba container.*

Sawamura   Help yourself. There isn't much left.

Imai   Oh, no. It's OK.

The only sound is of food being eaten.

Genda   Still, why do they have to call on workers in the alternative processing chamber?

Sawamura   Well, it's a problem that concerns the whole company.

Imai   Excuse me.

Genda   What?

Imai   Could you explain the meaning of alternative processing chamber?

Sawamura *and* **Genda** *look sharply at* **Imai**.

Imai   It's alright if you don't want to.

Genda   Sawamura.

Sawamura   Yes.

Genda   You teach him.

Sawamura (*not pleased*)   Yeah . . .

Genda   Spreading the word on meat processing is part of our work.

Sawamura   I know, but . . .

Imai *is looking with great anticipation at* **Sawamura**, *who begins to feel that he must speak.*

Sawamura   Did you see the processing chambers of the cattle and swine?

Imai   I don't understand what "processing chamber" means.

Sawamura   It's where the cattle and swine are killed and dressed.

Imai   Ohh, I just passed that area.

Sawamura   In that chamber, a belt conveyor takes the cow, for example, to the worker who shoots it in the head, then to the one who cuts its throat and does the bloodletting, on to the one who does the pithing, then to the one who shackles and hangs it and further on to the decapitator, etc. There are many steps to the process and many workers are lined up to dress the carcass.

Imai   Uh-huh.

Sawamura   Think of it as the reverse of an automobile factory. Instead of putting parts together, you break up the vehicle into parts.

Imai   Ahh.

Sawamura   Oh. You don't get it?

Imai   Oh, I do.

Sawamura   Uh-huh. The alternative processing chamber is for sick animals that can't go on the conveyor belt.

Imai   Sick animals?

Sawamura   Sick animals.

Imai   Animals that are diseased?

Sawamura   Well, some are actually ill, but others could have broken a leg during the transfer and can't walk, or are outsized swine like seed pigs. There may be more of that kind of thing.

Genda   Do you have to explain all that?

Sawamura   Well, he's new.

Imai   I'm sorry.

Sawamura   Then, there are the fancy brand pigs that clients request personalized processing for.

Genda   Those are the troublemakers.

Sawamura   This alternative chamber is where us two conduct the processing of the brand cattle and pigs.

He points in the direction of the alternative processing chamber.

Imai   Just the two of you.

Genda   Us two do *everything* that's done in the other line.

Imai   That's amazing.

Genda   Not really. Until recently, paired workers took turns with the weekly duty at the alternative chamber. It came to a bimonthly session for each pair. But with the large scale lay-off of the freelancers we were put in charge. I guess you wouldn't get the significance of that.

Imai   No, I don't.

Genda *is shocked by* **Imai***'s quick, thoughtless response.*

Sawamura   Just for the record, freelance refers to workers who can handle the whole disassembling process.

Imai   Aha. The pros.

Genda   Of course. That's how they make their living.

Imai   It must be so.

Genda *finishes his meal, ties the mouth of the store bag he is using for trash.*

Genda   Now, here goes. I'm off on a journey to find the missing brainstem.

Sawamura   Hey, wait. I'm going too.

He shovels the rest of the yakisoba into his mouth.

Genda   Not to worry. Not to worry. I'm your junior, remember.

Sawamura   There you go again.

Genda   Today, Sawamura, you're on shift A and I'm on B.

Sawamura   Come on. There's only a 30-minute difference.

Genda   You have to take a shower and go off to your you-know-what.

He raises his little finger suggestively.

Sawamura   Look here.

Genda   Just kidding ya. Sawamura, you take care of that youngster over there.

Sawamura   Huh?

He looks at **Imai**.

Genda   We can't leave him alone. We can't have him nosing around, either.

Sawamura   Uh-huh.

Imai   I wouldn't do that.

Genda   He wouldn't like to be left all alone.

Imai   Well, that's true.

Genda   So, see ya later.

He exits.

Sawamura *shouts after him.*

Sawamura   Hey, thanks for subbing for me

He then opens the bag from the store and tosses in the empty yakisoba container. He takes a breath and looks at **Imai**.

Sawamura   You know?

Imai   Yes?

Sawamura   How do you pour sauce on your yakisoba?

Imai   What?

Sawamura   Forget it. It's nothing.

Imai   Oh, uh.

Sawamura   How about some coffee?

Imai   Uh, oh yes. Is it alright?

Sawamura   Sure. The coffee maker's in the kitchenette. Go help yourself if you want some.

He points to the kitchenette where the boiler is.

Imai   Ah, then, maybe later.

Sawamura   Was there a lot of stuff going on over there.

Imai   Over where?

Sawamura   The cattle processing chamber.

Imai   Oh, the cattle. There certainly was. People were everywhere.

Sawamura   They lost a brainstem, I hear.

Imai   Brainstem?

Sawamura *points to the back of his neck where it joins the head.*

Sawamura   Right here.

Imai   I see. That's the brainstem

Sawamura   It's unbelievable.

Imai   Is it so important?

Sawamura   Because it's what's sent off to the screening test. That's the so-called BSE test.

Imai   Oh really.

Sawamura   "Oh really." Do you know what BSE refers to?

Imai   I do.

Sawamura   It's mad cow disease.

Imai   Right. I mean, so the brainstem of each cow has to be removed and tested.

Sawamura   Ever since BSE became a major problem, that's been the policy. Hey, are you really a livestock farmer?

Imai   We are now speciality swine breeders.

Sawamura   Maybe so. But to get ahead in this industry, you should know that much at least.

Imai   You're certainly right.

Sawamura   On rare occasions, the brainstem is lost. When that happens, we stop the line and everyone pitches in to find it. This year it's happened twice already. Twice in the three months since the large-scale firing of freelance workers.

Imai   So then, if you can't find it, what happens?

Sawamura   That's the end. If we can't make the shipment, we have to compensate for the loss.

Imai   Wow. No wonder everyone joins in the search.

Sawamura   Last time, it didn't turn up, and those on the floor were extremely nervous.

Imai   Uh-huh.

Sawamura   Genda was really pissed, saying it was unthinkable. Oh, Genda is that peculiar guy who was here earlier.

Imai   Why does he speak with an Osaka accent?

Sawamura   He's from Osaka, you see.

Imai   I get it.

Sawamura   He worked at an Osaka meat processing plant for twenty years. He's built a solid career for himself. I'm no comparison.

Imai   Why did you call him your junior then?

Sawamura   Oh, that's because he joined us last year. So in that sense, he is a junior employee. As far as we're concerned, it's a huge help to have someone like him with us.

Imai   Hm.

He asks a thoughtless question.

Why join this company?

Sawamura   Me?

Imai   No . . .

Sawamura   You mean Genda?

Imai   Right.

Sawamura   Well . . .

Imai   Is the salary better here?

Sawamura   That's not the issue. Our company has been hit hard by the recession.

Imai   Why should a native Osakan come here?

Sawamura   Is that strange?

Imai   You see, one of my college friends was from Osaka. He was always going on about how wonderful Osaka was.

Sawamura   Genda's not like that.

Imai   He must have had some special circumstances.

Sawamura   What do you mean by that?

Imai   Well, I don't really know, but I sense there's something going on.

Sawamura   You sense something?

Imai   Something about him bothers me.

Sawamura   Like what?

Imai   I can't tell. We could ask him why he left Osaka.

Sawamura   Why do you suggest that?

Imai   Why not?

Sawamura   Do you have a grudge against him?

Imai   What do you mean by grudge?

Sawamura *takes a hard look at* **Imai**.

Imai   Huh?

Sawamura   What's your name again?

Imai   Imai.

Sawamura   Now listen, Imai, I'll let that innuendo go. But don't say or do anything you'll regret later

Imai   Oh, no. Please excuse me.

Sawamura   You don't get it, do you?

Imai   No, I don't.

Sawamura   Am I hearing an echo.

Imai   No, I don't mean it like that.

Sawamura   Well, whatever. In an occupation like this, we have to be sensitive to external criticism.

Imai   Oh really . . .

Sawamura   The roots of discrimination are deep. I hope you are aware of the historical background of meat processing places.

Imai   Uh. Well, somewhat.

Sawamura   "Somewhat" means how much?

Imai   Oh, excuse me. I haven't studied the subject very much.

Sawamura   It's dangerous to make careless comments.

Imai   I see. I am sorry.

Sawamura *deliberately looks shocked and gives a big sigh.*

Sawamura   Why did this young man so uninterested in this occupation think to work in livestock farming?

Imai   My destiny, I guess.

Sawamura   As one in a similar occupation, I take issue with your "destiny."

Imai   Oh.

Sawamura   Excuse me. I didn't mean to sound pompous.

Imai   No, not at all.

Sawamura   Then, I retract the destiny bit.

Imai   Yes.

Sawamura   If not destiny, what drove you?

Imai   Well, then, let me think. It was the right time for a change—that may sound better.

Sawamura   Go on. The right time for what?

Imai   I realized it would be no good to go on having a good time.

Sawamura   How long were you having a good time?

Imai   Until quite recently. Yeah that's it.

Sawamura   That's it. I thought you lacked the feel of a laborer. You're a Neet? Right on the nail, a Neet.

Imai   I was but I gradually got sick of being called by that word.

Sawamura   No, no. Imai, you got it wrong.

Imai   Huh?

Sawamura   You should get sick of yourself being a Neet.

Imai   Aha, that's a good one.

Sawamura   No it isn't. Hey, how old are you?

Imai   I've just reached thirty.

Sawamura   Thirty? You're only three years younger than me? Hey, I thought you were younger than that.

Imai *speaks in a matter of fact way.*

Imai   I've never had any bad experiences.

Sawamura   Oh no. You feel no hesitation to admit that you've been a Neet 'til age thirty?

Imai   That's right.

Sawamura   You've never been employed? Not once?

Imai   Wait, I've worked parttime. But I felt that if I worked seriously, I would lose out to society.

Sawamura   I saw someone on TV who said the exact same thing.

Imai   But now it's different. I was definitely a Neet until a short time ago, but now that I'm thirty, I've decided to change my ways.

Sawamura   It's fine to make a declaration like that but ordinary people think like that around age twenty, when they graduate from high school or college.

Imai   I realize that, but . . .

Sawamura   I am thirty-three and supporting my wife and a son in grade school.

Imai   Wow, that's really something. It sure is.

Sawamura   It's average.

Imai   I can't imagine myself like that at all.

Sawamura *shows* **Imai** *his cell phone standby display, which is of his family.*

Imai   Your kid?

Sawamura   When he was younger. This is my wife.

Imai   Uh-huh.

Sawamura *puts his phone away after a while.*

Sawamura   You have to work hard at it.

Imai   Huh?

Sawamura   You've got a good frame. You'll do fine once you get some training. The line work is all about stamina.

Imai   I'm thinking of joining the management if possible.

Sawamura *is completely floored by* **Imai**'s *reply.*

Sawamura   Dreamer. A total dreamer.

Imai   Huh?

Sawamura   Having dreams is fine. But it's not the kind of thing a guy just starting work says.

Imai   Oh.

Sawamura   Why do young people want to take the easy road?

Imai   Management isn't all about easy work, you know.

Sawamura   You say this, I say that. You're way too easygoing. Oh, excuse me. I didn't mean to be pushy.

Imai   No problem.

Sawamura   You just want to sit on your butt. It's completely obvious you're shirking physical labor. So obvious, too obvious.

Imai   I don't deny that's a part of it.

Sawamura   See, it's obvious. So obvious, too obvious. After you've done your share of the line work and all, you can talk about your dreams.

Imai   Ah.

Sawamura   After all is said and done, this industry is for physical types. Are you aware of how many workers are into body building and martial arts?

Imai   Not really.

Sawamura   Well, never mind that. I hope that something in you will be ignited by having met me. I want you to put in the hard work that'll allow me to say, "Hey, you look leaner and sharper," or, "You're moving like a practiced worker," the next time I see you.

Imai   Ah.

Sawamura   Then I say, "You talked about doing management and such stupid things." You'd say, "Mr. Sawamura, please stop going on about that. It was just youthful enthusiasm." Then we get to the "Let's go for a drink. It's on Imai." You say, "Why do I have to treat you all?" I hope it happens. That's all.

Imai   Yes, thank you very much.

Sawamura   There you go again. (*Mimicking* **Imai**'s *voice.*) Another hollow "thank you very much."

Imai   I don't talk like that.

Sawamura   I don't want to be put in the same "youth" category as people like you. Oh, I'm sorry. I just said "people like you."

Imai   No problem.

Sawamura   This is love. I'm talking out of love.

Imai   I understand.

Sawamura *makes another deep sigh.*

Sawamura   You see, saying this kind of thing has an underside.

Imai   An underside?

Sawamura   I envy you. I married at about twenty and had a kid. To support my wife and boy, I had to work hard all the time. The only period of time I had good fun was, honestly, back in grade school.

Imai   Umm. I must say you lost an opportunity in life.

Sawamura *glares at* **Imai**.

Sawamura   Now that pisses me off.

Imai   Huh? Oh. I didn't mean to.

Sawamura   I agree that I lost a chance in life. But when some stranger tells me that, I lose it.

Imai   Uh, excuse me. I am sorry.

Sawamura   Well, never mind. It's true anyhow.

Imai   Uh-huh.

Sawamura   Hey then, tell me of a time in your Neet period when you said to yourself, "That was fun! I had a wild time."

Imai   Uh.

Sawamura   Look, you've had ten more years for personal pleasure than me. You must have a success rate of fab experiences that I could never catch up with however hard I tried.

Imai   Oh.

Sawamura   Tell me about them.

Imai   Occasions when I thought I had a wild time

Sawamura   Uh-huh. Including criminal acts and such. The whole lot.

Imai *ponders.*

Imai   Well, let's see . . . Umph.

He recalls something suddenly and laughs out loud.

Sawamura   Now we have it!

Imai   Yeah, it happened about two years ago.

Sawamura   Uh-huh.

Imai   Is that alright?

Sawamura   Sure.

Imai   I was really into karaoke about two years ago.

Sawamura   Karaoke.

Imai   You know, I've been to Utahiro[3] three days in a row. Oh, three days in a row means I went home in the morning, slept until the evening, and then went out again at night. But my friends changed every day, and I was the one always there. I've mastered all the Kobukuro[4] songs at Utahiro in three days. I gradually became hoarse. Oh, and on the third day, the Utahiro staff remembered me and said, "You've gone on three days running, that's amazing." I was like a legend. That was simply crazy.

Imai's eyes indicate that he is faraway in his memories. **Sawamura** *is disgusted by the underwhelming recollection he has just heard.*

Sawamura   Uh, is that it?

Imai   Huh?

Sawamura   That's your highest rating from your Neet period?

Imai   Huh? Don't you agree?

Sawamura *is flabbergasted.*

Sawamura   Wow, your ten years are . . .

Imai   Well, how about this one? My city legend: How I talked for eighteen hours nonstop at Denny's through four meals—lunch, dinner, midnight snack, and breakfast.

Sawamura *quietly shakes his head.*

Sawamura   Too-bad, too-sad, what a shame.

Imai   What is that about?

Sawamura   You are even now a too-bad, too-sad case as you don't realize that you've spent so many too-bad days.

Imai   No, no. I had a fantastic time.

Sawamura   Excuse me, but I was expecting to hear about a bicycle tour around Japan or a backpacking tour across Southeast Asia.

Imai   Really! What's the point of doing things like that?

Sawamura   The point? What's the point of Utahiro and Denny's?

Imai   It's a way of deepening friendship.

Sawamura   It's uninspiring.

Imai   No, it isn't. We had a good time having fun like that in the circles I moved in.

Sawamura   Hey, we are only three years apart. What is it with this generation gap?

Imai   Indeed.

Sawamura   Your parents must be disappointed.

Imai   Not really.

Sawamura   Yes, they are.

Imai   When I told them I was ready to work, they cried for joy.

Sawamura   Well, by this time they may have reached such a point.

Imai   They've given me plenty of time to enjoy myself. So, from now on, I will pay them back.

Sawamura   Humph. So, why are you working at a farmer's?

Imai   My parents are farmers.

Sawamura   Oh yeah? Uh, is that true?

Imai   Yes.

Sawamura   Then, your dad used his influence for you?

Imai   Well, I suppose you could say that.

Sawamura   To the end, you trouble your parents.

Imai   But I'm not troubling them.

Sawamura   Where did they get a foot-in-the-door for you? What's the name?

Imai   Imai Farm.

Sawamura's *mind goes blank for a moment. He says the name out loud.*

Sawamura   I-ma-i Farm.

Pause. He works it out in his mind.

Uh, Imai Farm.

Imai   Yes.

Sawamura   Uh, "i" as in "Izu" and "mai" as in "dance." That Imai Farm?

Imai   Yes.

Sawamura (*pointing to* **Imai**)   Imai.

Imai   Yes.

Sawamura (*beat*)   Mr. Imai.

Imai   Yes, with the correct term of address.

Sawamura   You are from the Imai Farm?

Imai   *That* Imai.

Sawamura   Are you the heir?

Imai   I will be eventually.

Sawamura   Oh, that's why you aim for management!

Imai   Eventually.

Sawamura *stares hard at* **Imai** *as if to mock him. Then he adjusts his posture.*

Sawamura   I must apologize, I had no idea who you were.

Imai   Wait a moment. What're you doing? You're suddenly doing the modest.

Sawamura   Please excuse me for getting carried away.

Imai   Stop that. Aren't you being a bit transparent?

Sawamura   Well, Imai Farm is one of our best clients. Right now, we are indebted to the Imai Farm for its business.

Imai   Oh, thank you, too. We appreciate your service.

Sawamura   Oh no, we are honored to have your continuing custom. Recently, Genda and I have been assigned the "butchering" of your Imai brand black swine.

Imai   "Butchering"?

Sawamura   That's the processing I mentioned in the alternative chamber.

Imai   Oh, I see.

Sawamura   Excuse me. I deeply apologize for the terribly rude attitude on the part of Genda and me.

Imai   Never mind the attitude.

Sawamura   I am Sawamura of Marumoto Meat Center.

Imai   And I am Toru Imai of Imai Farm.

Imai *brings out his business card with alacrity.* **Sawamura** *accepts it. He passes his hand over the pockets of his work uniform but cannot find a business card.*

Sawamura   I am sorry. My . . . my business cards must be in my locker.

Imai   No problem at all, Mr. Sawamura. I've remembered your name.

Sawamura *continues in his fawning frame of mind.*

Sawamura   Please don't remember in a negative way.

Imai   What do you mean by that?

Sawamura   You know, I got carried away . . . Well, I didn't really get carried away, but you know, I talked a whole lot of shit just now.

He suddenly bows deeply and continues.

I apologize. I retract all the improper remarks I made earlier.

Imai   Uh, wait a moment, some of them were factually correct. There haven't been many people who've been straight with me, so you've given me an opportunity to think about how to live.

Sawamura   I am very sorry. I was patronizing you.

Imai   Now just stop that.

Sawamura   I won't.

Imai   You must.

Sawamura   I won't quit until you forgive me.

Imai   Need for forgiveness isn't in the picture. Let's sit down, OK?

He makes **Sawamura** *straighten up.*

Imai   Oh, how about some coffee. Let's see, the kitchenette is where?

He looks towards the kitchenette.

Sawamura   I'll get some ready.

He heads to the kitchenette.

Imai   Oh, wait, that's not what I mean.

Left behind, **Imai** *has nothing to do but sit down. A long pause while* **Sawamura** *prepares the coffee beans and water for the coffee maker.* **Imai** *is leafing through a magazine or two on the table. Having started the coffee maker,* **Sawamura** *enters.*

Imai   Oh, thank you.

Sawamura   Well, well, well, well . . .

What he is referring to is not clear, but he repeats the word while he sits down.

But it's quite something to sing for three consecutive days at Utahiro.

Imai   Mr. Sawamura?

Sawamura   And Denny's as well. How long were you talking at Denny's?

Imai   Let's quit talking about my Neet days.

Sawamura   But really. I haven't been to karaoke for ages. I can really get into Kobukuro music, right?

Imai   Mr. Sawamura.

Sawamura   Oh, do you know why the band is called Kobukuro? One of the pair is Kobuchi and the other is Kuro-something.

Imai   Kuroda, you mean. I know.

Sawamura   You sure know that world, Kobukuro-freak.

Imai   Just stop going on like that.

Sawamura   Oh, you don't like Kobukuro talk?

Imai *doesn't reply.*

Sawamura   Uh-uh, are you irritated? Are you angry about what I said before?

Imai   I'm not angry.

Sawamura   Oh yes, you are. It shows in your eyes. Please forgive me.

Imai   Mr. Sawamura.

Sawamura   Yes.

Imai   It's not really a matter of forgiving or not forgiving. But I do forgive you.

Sawamura Really?

Imai Yes. So please be your usual self.

Sawamura OK. Well. I am my usual self.

Despite his claim, he is still feeling awkward. The conversation limps along.

Sawamura So, what's up today?

Imai Huh?

Sawamura Why are you here today?

Imai Oh, my dad's, I mean, I'm chauffeur for the president.

Sawamura So you are in his attendance?

Imai Uh-huh. In addition . . . Maybe it's not polite to say "in addition," but I wanted to observe the meat processing if I had the chance.

Sawamura Ah, in that case, you arrived way too late. I mean, sir, you were a little late.

Imai No need to strain to be polite. Ordinary language is fine.

Sawamura Ah, um.

Imai *looks at the clock.*

Imai Does work end around this time?

Sawamura It starts around 8 am sir. We're supposed to take breaks but to ensure efficiency, sir, we work right through until 2 pm. From 2 pm, there's a lunch break, and after than until the work day ends, we are free to do what we wish.

Imai Wow, that's a long break.

Sawamura Some use the free time to train in the gym, sir. Those are the guys who like to do body building as I said before.

Imai On average, is your actual work for about six hours?

Sawamura About five to six hours. Oh, that may seem like a short day, but it's actually quite tough, sir. The work is not just about physical stamina, but requires precision.

Imai *disregards* **Sawamura**'s *attempts at politeness.*

Imai How does processing feel like?

Sawamura Uhm, the line work itself you get used to. Injuries come with this job because we use knives. But . . .

Imai So you're on edge a lot? . . .

Sawamura Well, what's worse than injuries is that work failure is considered unacceptable.

Imai Work failure.

Sawamura   Blood stains on the carcass are not allowed. At the end, the carcass is split along the spine and is dressed. That splitting has to make two balanced parts or else it is considered work failure. Work failure means that we have to compensate for the failure. So you see . . .

Imai   That's tough.

Sawamura   I'm only half way to becoming a pro. But the work requires the matchless skills of experts, I assure you.

Imai   Aha.

He nods his head many times.

Thanks.

Sawamura   Um.

Imai   I know nothing about meat processing.

Sawamura   Well, that can't be helped.

Imai   My dad, no I mean, the president told me to make sure I knew what the business was like.

Sawamura   Well. It's probably better to know how your premium farm swine are distributed in the market.

Imai   Right.

Sawamura   Next time you have a chance, come along to observe the line work.

Imai   Yes, I'd like to do that. Please teach me more about meat processing.

Sawamura   Oh, I can't teach, you know. No way. I know next to nothing.

At that moment, the intercom buzzes.

Oh, excuse me.

Sawamura *takes the receiver.*

Hallo, Sawamura speaking. Oh, Mr. Kunimoto. Thank you for your hard work.

[The speaker at the other end is Kunimoto, chief of the cattle processing chamber.]

Sawamura   I heard about the missing brainstem.

[The speaker confirms that it is still missing.]

Sawamura   This is a disaster. Who did the decapitating?

[The speaker says a worker called Yanagi.]

Sawamura   Ohh, Yanagi, is it.

[The speaker says this Yanagi guy has gone missing, too.]

Sawamura   Huh, Yanagi is missing? From a sense of responsibility?

[The speaker says he doesn't know.]

Sawamura   Going into hiding won't do him any good. You know, well, the priority is the brainstem, not Yanagi.

*[The speaker says he wants **Sawamura** to cooperate, too.]*

Sawamura   Uh, what do you mean by cooperate? Wait, didn't Mr. Genda go your way?

*[The speaker says he hasn't seen **Genda**.]*

Sawamura   No, that's not possible. He went off cheerfully, saying he'd do my part of the search as well.

[The speaker says to hurry up as they really need more hands on deck.]

Sawamura (*looking at* **Imai**)   You see, there is an important visitor here right now.

[Kunimoto slams down his receiver violently.]

Sawamura   Hey. You—

Sawamura *puts down his receiver and sits down.*

Sawamura   Well, well, well, well.

Imai   Uh, is everything alright?

Sawamura   Yes, it is.

Imai   But . . .

Sawamura   Oh, crap. I forgot the coffee. I'll go take a look.

He goes to the kitchenette. **Imai**, *feeling bored, plays with his smart phone.*

After a while, **Genda** *enters. He is holding a nylon bag in his hand. He opens the door slowly and looks around first.*

Imai   Oh, hallo.

Sawamura   Hey bro, you're still around.

Imai   Excuse me.

Genda *eventually enters the grinding room.*

Genda   Where's Sawamura?

Imai (*pointing to the kitchenette*)   In there.

Genda *puts away the nylon bag in his locker.*

Imai   What are you doing?

Genda   What?

Imai   What's that?

Genda   Nothing to do with you.

Genda *heads toward the kitchenette, saying:*

Genda   Sawamura.

*He almost collides with **Sawamura**, who enters with two mugs of coffee on a tray.*

Genda   Whoa, you took me by surprise.

Sawamura   What is it?

Genda   What are you doing?

Sawamura   Serving coffee.

Genda   Ah, thanks.

He tries to take a mug of coffee.

Sawamura   No! (*Sidesteps **Genda**.*) *Tei!*[5]

Genda   *Chou!*

Sawamura   That's dangerous.

Genda   I thought you were holding the tray properly?

Sawamura   This isn't for you, Mr. Genda.

Imai   It's my mug.

Sawamura   I am borrowing it as there were no others.

Genda   What?

Sawamura   Oh, if you want some, there's more coffee in the hotpot. Oh, but no cups.

*He walks past **Genda** and readies to give **Imai** a mug of coffee.*

Sawamura   Here you are.

Imai   Ah, thank you.

Sawamura (*offering the mug*)   Here.

Genda *snatches away the mug in **Imai**'s hands.*

Imai   Oh?

Sawamura   What the hell are you doing?

Genda   Give me back my mug.

Sawamura   So I just asked you to lend me your mug, didn't I?

Genda   Why do you have to use my mug?

Sawamura You are so smallminded.

Genda Whaddaya say?

Sawamura (*to* **Imai**) I'm sorry.

Imai Not at all.

Sawamura (*handing* **Imai** *his own mug*) Please take this one.

Imai Oh, now I am sorry.

Sawamura *tries to admonish* **Genda**.

Sawamura Mr. Genda.

Genda Look here, Sawamura.

Sawamura What's up?

Genda What's happened?

Sawamura Huh?

Genda Why are you acting as if you've been brought to heel. What is this all about? What's happened in the last ten minutes?

Sawamura *gives a cough and points at* **Imai**.

Sawamura Can't you tell?

Genda What?

Sawamura This is Mr. Imai.

Imai How do you do?

Genda You told me his name before.

Sawamura His name is "Mr. Imai." Doesn't it ring a bell?

Genda Nahh.

Sawamura Dense. You are so dense, Mr. Genda.

Imai You know, Sawamura, this isn't the time to be talking about a name.

Sawamura Hey, now don't try to end this conversation.

Genda Huh?

Sawamura This personage is Toru Imai, the heir to the Imai Farm.

Imai Please don't call me the heir.

Sawamura Look, Mr. Genda's face is turning pale fast.

Genda What the heck are you going on about? That kinda stuff is totally unimportant right now.

Sawamura   Mr. Genda, this is a visitor from the Imai Farm, our best customer.

Genda   So what?!

Sawamura   So, let's pay respect.

Genda *clucks his tongue once and claps his hands twice in front of* **Imai**. *(Two claps, one bow.)*

Genda   Done.

Sawamura   Wait a moment, Mr. Genda.

Genda   Sawamura, this is worse than I thought.

Sawamura   So you've figured out how dumb you are at last. You and your silly antics . . .

Genda   No, I'm talking about the brainstem.

Sawamura   Huh?

Genda   No one can find it.

Sawamura   Oh, the intercom buzzed a while ago. Mr. Kunimoto is the chief of the cattle processing chamber, right?

Genda   Dunno.

Sawamura   You can't deny knowing that. Mr. Kunimoto told me about Yanagi. He's run away it seems.

Genda   What? Why did he run away?

Sawamura   Mr. Yanagi was the one doing the decapitation. I don't know but he may have felt responsible.

Genda   Maybe he rushed off to the toilet or somewhere.

Sawamura   No way. Mr. Kunimoto said so.

Sipping coffee, **Imai** *comments.*

Imai   Geez, you have a big problem.

Genda   Shut it, you.

Imai   Excuse me.

Sawamura   Mr. Genda.

Genda   Sawamura.

Sawamura   Yes.

Genda   Both Yanagi and Kunimoto would have trouble if they were fired.

Sawamura   That wouldn't happen. Not that I care.

Genda   The director will arrive here even as we speak.

Sawamura   Will he?

Genda   What can we do?

Sawamura   No good asking me what to do.

Genda   We're in big shit.

Sawamura   You've suddenly become genuinely concerned. Is it because Mr. Yanagi is involved.

Genda   No, nothing to do with him.

Sawamura   So, why are you back here? If he hasn't been found, you have to search him out.

Genda   So I'm here to get you over there.

Sawamura   Huh?

Genda   We switch. You go now.

Sawamura   No, I don't want to.

Genda   Why?

Sawamura   I have to talk with Mr. Imai.

Genda   'Bout what?

Sawamura   About the meat processing business.

Genda   This isn't the time for that!

Sawamura   He's an important customer.

Genda   This selfish pig farmer.

Imai   Selfish?!

Sawamura   Hold it, Mr. Genda. For our company Imai Farm is . . .

Genda   Which is more valuable, our workers or . . .

Sawamura   Both are. So, Mr. Genda, please take care of the workers. See, I am on shift A and close to knocking off.

Genda   You're gonna talk like that, are ya? You gonna betray your buddies, Sawamura?

Sawamura   Why do *you* talk like that? You left your buddy and came back here.

Genda   I came back here to get you. Kunimoto was calling out, "Where's Sawamura?" with a ferocious look on his face. You got his phone call, right?

Sawamura   Yeah . . .

Genda   There you are.

Sawamura   But. (*Looks at* **Imai**.)

Imai *has been sipping his coffee elegantly. He hurriedly puts down his mug.*

Imai   I'm doing fine over here.

Genda   Hm, See. If you don't show your face, they'll never stop badmouthing you.

Sawamura   Alright then, you come with me.

Genda   Why the hell should I?

Sawamura   'Cause if you two are alone together, you're going to give him a hard time.

Genda   I'm not gonna say things to him. But I can't leave when a pig farmer we do regular business is left here all by himself.

Sawamura   So I am saying that I'll take care of that part.

Genda   Sawamura, seriously, this isn't a time to harp on this. You'll find out when you get there.

Sawamura   Alright, I get it.

He starts to leave but then stops.

Sawamura   Don't blab.

Genda   What the hell do you think I'd blab about?

Sawamura   I'll find him right away. Oh, Mr. Imai, try to relax

Imai   Ah, thanks.

Sawamura *exits.* **Genda** *exhales deeply and then turns to* **Imai***.*

Genda   OK, go home.

Imai   Huh?

Genda   You can leave now.

Imai   Wait, you see . . .

Genda   Probably, the director isn't in a state to hold a conference. Your president has probably been told to leave for today, wouldn't you think?

Imai *checks his cell phone.*

Imai   I'm to get a call when the conference has ended.

Genda   How's that? Aren't you out of range?

Imai   I don't think so.

Genda   Why not go take a look?

Imai   Huh?

Genda   At the conference room.

Imai *looks hard at* **Genda**.

Genda   What?

Imai   Why are you trying to make me leave this room?

Genda   Huh?

Imai   Something strange is going on.

Genda   What are you talking about?

Imai *looks sharply at* **Genda**.

Genda   You get on my nerves.

Imai   I do?

Genda   This is the recess room. Let me rest.

Imai   You said this was the grinding room.

Genda   We take breaks here.

Imai *looks around suspiciously.*

Genda   What now?

Imai   Very well.

He takes out his cell phone.

I'll try phoning him.

He starts phoning, while looking at **Genda** *from time to time.*

Genda   You're starting to piss me off.

Imai   Oh, hallo. This is Toru. Is this a good time to talk?

Continuing to speak, **Imai** *exits the room.* **Genda** *sits down on a chair and holds his head in his hands. Raising his head, he kicks the door* **Imai** *used to exit. Then, from his locker he takes out the nylon bag and looks inside. The brainstem that everyone is wild to find is there.*

Genda   Tsk.

Making a small clucking sound with his tongue, he checks the brainstem without bringing it out of the bag. He wants to dispose of the bag and all somehow. He wanders around the room with it.

What the fuck can I do?

Sensing that **Imai** *is on his way back,* **Genda** *ties the mouth of the bag and returns it to his locker. He sits down.*

Genda (*muttering to himself*)   Shit.

Soon, **Imai** *returns talking on his cell phone.*

Imai   OK—I understand. Roger. Yes, ye-s. (*With these words, he sits down on a chair.*)

Genda   Why are you sitting down?

Imai   He said to wait a bit longer.

Genda   Who did?

Imai   The president. He's still in conference.

Genda   Then, why don't you go join them over there?

Imai   I can't do that. I'm brand new in the company.

Genda   Oh shit.

He drinks his coffee irritably. **Imai** *smells something.*

Imai   Something smells?

Genda   Huh?

Imai   A raw kind of smell.

Genda   I've been butchering animals. I smell.

Imai   Ohh. (*With a wry face.*) May I have another cup of coffee? Is that alright?

Genda   Do as you like.

Imai   OK.

He takes his mug and heads for the kitchenette for a refill. **Genda** *keeps an eye on* **Imai**'s *movements but cannot find an opportunity to take action.* **Imai** *returns shortly.*

Imai   You know, I've walked in here on an unbelievable day.

Genda   You got that right.

Imai   Yanagi, the one on the run—what's he like?

Genda   What's that got to do with you?

Imai   Oh, I see. Well how about a different topic?

Genda   Just stuff it.

Disregarding **Genda**'s *remark,* **Imai** *continues.*

Imai   About the brainstem. Do you go frantic searching for it?

Genda   What?

Imai   Well, it's a great loss, right?

Genda   Yeah, of course.

Imai   How much is the compensation for one cow?

Genda   Dunno.

The atmosphere grows increasingly uncomfortable.

Genda Hey you.

Imai Uh, yes.

Genda Are you really the heir to the Imai Farm?

Imai Well, in the future. I was talking with Mr. Sawamura earlier that as I've only just joined the company, I'm still a novice and know next to nothing.

Genda Humph. In that case, tell your boss from me . . .

Imai Yes?

Genda . . . to stop going out of his way to have his brand pigs butchered in the alternative processing chamber.

Imai What?

Genda I don't know what considerations you have, but it's much more efficient to put them on the conveyer belt. Especially now that so many workers have been fired.

Imai Oh.

Genda What's the problem? Can't you understand what I'm saying? Maybe you can't.

Imai Yes, I can in my own way.

Genda In your own way isn't good enough.

Imai I thought your company was very happy to have the Imai black swine for meat processing.

Genda Who'd be happy with them? Your swine are such a labor-intensive burden . . . The only one that's happy is the director. He lets you walk all over him with your demands for special treatment.

Imai But it seems that the Marumoto Meat Center stays in business because we give you business. I don't see why you can't take heed of some of our requests.

Genda That's not the point.

Imai But wouldn't you be in trouble if Imai Farm withdrew its business?

Genda I'm not talking about your withdrawing your custom from Marumoto. I'm just asking you to stop requesting the manual butchering of your swine.

Imai Excuse me, that expression you use, "butcher."

Genda What about it?

Imai Physiologically, I can't take it.

Genda That's not my problem.

Imai   Well, as far as we are concerned, we expect you to use manual processing or . . .

Genda   Or what? You're gonna withdraw? Humph. Talking like a professional negotiator . . .

Imai   I don't mean it like that, but we are selling premium swine after all. We need to raise the product value.

Genda   What's the difference between butchering on the line and by hand?

Imai   Think of how hand-woven sweaters and machine-made ones have a different natural feel to them.

Genda   Don't put pigs and sweaters in the same category. Oh shit, there's nothing fancy about raw meat. Even on the line, the whole animal is processed by hand. Get that?

Imai   That may be so, but we consider the added value of Imai black swine to lie in the clarification of responsibility at all stages of the meat processing through the identification of who bred the animal, who transported it, who processed it, and who packed it.

Genda   You're just parroting what someone else said.

Imai   Oh, can you tell? In the car on the way here, my father, I mean the president, told me about it.

Genda   That figures.

Imai   But I didn't know that only two workers were handling all our swine.

Genda   Only two were left who could process the pigs from snout to tail. Under normal conditions, we'd have our hands full with the sick swine. Now we're forced to process your swine as well. It's a real pisser.

He finishes his coffee.

Imai   You think "it's a real pisser."

Genda   Yeah.

Imai   Our poor swine are slaughtered by someone with that attitude.

Genda *is offended.*

Genda   Wait a moment.

Imai   Yes.

Genda   What was that you said just now? Why are you talking like that?

Imai   Oh, uh-oh, I shouldn't have used the word "slaughter." The correct word is "process." I am sorry.

Genda   Whatever. That kind of thing isn't important.

Imai   Oh.

Genda   What bothers me is the way you say "someone with that attitude." It's not a matter of feelings. You have to butcher the animal.

Imai   Ahh, but I object to our swine being processed by someone who's thinking "it's a real pisser."

Genda   There's no connection. Have you looked at the finished product? We do a fine job, you know.

Imai   It's not just about the results with Imai swine. We want to have an aesthetics informing the process.

Genda   So effing stupid. For example, when you have to do a job, any job, say for a moving or delivery company. Have you ever found yourself thinking, "what a hell of a bother," this is "a real pisser."

Imai   Your example is too far-fetched.

Genda   No, it isn't.

Imai   As livestock farmers, we want you to take pride in the processing of the Imai black swine brand.

Genda   That's what I am saying is so stupid. This conversation is getting nowhere.

Imai   From the Imai perspective, we are entrusting the life of our brand in you.

Genda   Life? Life? Are you really serious?

Imai   What's wrong with what I said?

Genda   You'd better study some more, kiddo. You shouldn't join this industry feeling like that.

Imai   I don't want you telling me how to feel.

Genda   There's no sense talking to the likes of you.

Imai   If I may go back to an earlier point . . .

Genda   I'm saying I can't get through to you.

Imai   Are you saying that you don't want to process our swine, Mr. Genda?

Genda   If I didn't have to, I wouldn't.

Imai   I see.

After a while, **Imai** *decides to reveal the true purpose of his visit.*

Imai   You might as well know.

Genda *glances at him.*

Imai   Shipments will increase.

Genda   Huh?

Imai   We have conducted research on breeding for many years. From next year, the shipments will triple.

Genda   Uh?

Imai   That's why they are holding a summit meeting.

Genda   If the amount triples, there'll be no way to handle the work except by using the line for all your swine.

Imai   You mean processing in the alternative processing chamber will become impossible.

Genda   Of course. It's not just a matter of the number of workers. A dedicated dressing chamber will become necessary.

Imai   If our company insists on manual processing, what would happen?

Genda   You'd have to go elsewhere.

Imai   I see.

He nods his head a few times.

Imai   I am glad to hear the opinion from the floor.

Genda   Wha—?

Imai   You know, there aren't many places with reasonably good workmen that will listen to our selfish requests—oh, though I hadn't thought of our being selfish till today—

Genda   We just happen to be a rare case.

Imai   Uh-huh. So, we have to expand resources.

Genda   Expand resources?

Imai   We need meat processing plants willing to accommodate our requests.

Genda   Do such unusual plants exist?

Imai   Actually, we found one in Chiba prefecture last week.

Genda   Oh?

Imai   It's larger in scale and has a higher efficiency rate than Marumoto.

Genda   Really

Imai   They do exist.

Genda *understands what* **Imai** *is implying.*

Genda   What about your business with us then?

Imai   That's the topic of today's conference.

Genda   Are you really a new employee?

Imai   I became a full-time employee last week.

Genda   It's not the kind of thing a new worker can talk about.

Imai   I was educated to be the heir to the business. As I majored in management in college, I have the basic knowledge, you see.

Genda   Now you're really pissing me off!

Imai   Oh, here is my business card.

He tries to give **Genda** *his business card.*

Genda   No.

Imai   I see.

He puts his card away.

There are various choices. Improving your facilities would be one of them.

Genda   You've seen our situation. How can you say such a thing.

Imai   For us, the issue is how to move on to mass production while maintaining the power of our brand.

Genda   This is what you'd call the mass production of "life"!

Imai   Breeding is a science.

Genda   Oh yeah? Don't talk to me about that. It has nothing to do with me.

Sawamura *suddenly enters in a hurry.*

Sawamura   Mr. Genda.

Genda   You're back fast, Sawamura.

Having run back, **Sawamura** *is breathless.*

Genda   What's up?

Sawamura   Mr. Yanagi . . .

Imai   The one who ran a way?

Genda   What happened to him? He was there, right?

Sawamura   Yes, he was, but . . .

Genda   What?

Sawamura   Yanagi took a slaughter gun with him.

Genda   Huh?

Sawamura   A slaughter gun. That's dangerous.

Genda   What's going on?

Sawamura   I don't know.

Genda   Where's Yanagi gone with a slaughter gun?

Sawamura   Mr. Kunimoto and his men are looking for him.

Genda   What the hell is he up to?

Imai   Excuse me, what is a slaughter gun?

Sawamura *does not intend to ignore* **Imai***, but has no time for him right now.*

Sawamura   As no one knows what Yanagi will do, we're supposed to stand by here until they find him.

Genda   Why do they say they don't know what he might do?

Imai   What's a slaughter gun?

Genda *half-sighing as he speaks.*

Genda   Shut it.

Imai   Well, I'm worried.

Genda   You really don't read the situation well, do you.

Imai   I ask questions about what worries me.

Genda   Think it out for yourself.

Imai   Uh-huh.

Sawamura   It's a device to shoot the cow in the head.

Genda   Wait, Sawamura.

Sawamura   We can't take any action right now, anyway.

Genda   Is this a time to be explaining things?

Imai   Then, is it really a gun as the name indicates? (*Making the shape of a gun with his hand.*)

Sawamura   It's a cylinder and you hold it like this. (*Gestures how to hold the cylinder.*)

Imai   Really.

Sawamura   When you knock it hard against the cow's head, the gunpowder explodes inside the cylinder, and a thick needle shoots out and makes a hole . . .

Imai   In its head?

Sawamura   Then it faints.

Imai   Wow. I mean, the gun must be dangerous if it's taken outside.

Sawamura   Of course, it is.

Imai   Is it so easy to run off with?

Sawamura   No, usually someone is in charge. A record is kept of who's using it and how many rounds of gunpowder have been issued. After use, the shell casings are supposed to be returned. This time, Yanagi took advantage of the general disorder.

Genda   Did Yanagi really take it with him?

Sawamura   I saw him. And they suspect he probably took the brainstem with him, too.

Genda   Why do they think that way?

Sawamura   Well, it's quite natural to think so.

Imai   Oh, no.

Genda *and* **Sawamura** *turn towards* **Imai**.

Genda   Now what is it?

Imai   You see. Withdrawal seems to be the best strategy after all.

Sawamura   What?

Imai   It doesn't look at all like your company is functioning in a satisfactory way.

Sawamura   What do you mean?

Imai   I will report this to the president as well.

Genda   Do what you like. We can't be taking care of you now.

Sawamura   What are you talking about?

Genda   Sawamura, where's Yanagi?

Sawamura   How should I know?

Genda   You must know.

Sawamura   Anyways, you shouldn't go where the others are right now.

Genda   Why not?

Sawamura   Because things'll get complicated. More important than that, what have you been talking about with Mr. Imai?

Genda   Nothing to do with us.

Sawamura   What does that mean?

Genda   He goes on about what the top level are talking about. It's not stuff a worker should interfere in.

Sawamura   Why is Mr. Imai telling you about it then?

Genda   'Cause he's got a loose tongue.

He points at **Imai**.

Imai   It's just the way the conversation went. It's also my job to find out what the workers on site are thinking about.

Sawamura   Huh?

Genda   Acting like a fucking spy.

Sawamura   What is this? What's happened?

Genda   Sawamura, I can tell you about that tomorrow. Right now, we should focus on Yanagi's whereabouts.

Sawamura   It's not for us to stick our necks into Yanagi's problems.

Genda   He's one of us.

Sawamura *turns to* **Imai**.

Sawamura   What do you mean by withdrawal?

Imai   Just as Mr. Genda says, I shouldn't have shared with a worker.

Genda   It's too late to say that.

Ignoring **Genda**, **Sawamura** *edges up to* **Imai**.

Sawamura   Are you saying that Imai Farm will withdraw its business from us, the Morimoto Meat Center?

Imai   At this moment in time, nothing has been decided. Eventually, your director will be speaking to you all.

Sawamura   You sounded just before as if it was all decided.

Genda   Sawamura, we can't do anything about what he's talking about.

Sawamura   That's why I asked you to watch your mouth with him.

Genda   I did.

Sawamura   If you had, such topics wouldn't even have come up. What are we going to do if the Imai black swine brand is withdrawn?

Genda   No problem. We'll be able to work without anyone getting special favors.

Sawamura   We won't have any work left to do. The company will go bankrupt. (*To* **Imai**.) We are probably the only plant that still does manual butchering. What are you going to do with your Imai black swine?

Imai   We've found a meat processing plant that's willing to accept our requests for differential treatment.

Sawamura   But we already meet your special requests, right? What is this about?

Imai   I am just a new employee.

Genda   Considering your entry position, you sure sounded pompous

Imai   This is just an exchange of harsh and ugly words.

Sawamura   Mr. Genda, you've been spouting off way too much!

Genda   All I said was that it was strange that the Imai Farm swine were being sent to the alternative processing chamber.

Sawamura   That was the worst thing to say.

Genda   You're always saying yourself that it's more efficient to put the swine on the line.

Sawamura   I don't say anything like that. (*To* **Imai**.) I really don't.

Imai *makes a sour face.*

Sawamura   It's true.

Genda   Who are you trying to flatter?

Sawamura   Really, Mr. Genda.

Genda   That stuff is totally unimportant. We should worry about Yanagi instead.

Sawamura   The cattle team can figure out Yanagi's problems. Fuck, what are we going to do about this?

Anxious about the possible withdrawal of the Imai Farm business, **Sawamura** *sits down with his head in his hands.*

Genda   Sawamura.

Sawamura   I have to make a living. I have my wife and son to think of.

Genda   You'll do fine.

Sawamura   What?

Genda   Sawamura, you'll be OK. You can keep alive eating yakisoba.

Sawamura   What the hell are you going on about? Really.

Genda   The one that's not OK is Yanagi, you see.

Sawamura   Yanagi is not on my mind right now.

Genda   I'm saying he should be. Yanagi's problems are front and center right now. Even if Imai Farm withdraws its business, we still have time on our side, *and* skills as well.

Sawamura   No, we don't.

Genda   Yes, we do. We have more time than Yanagi does.

Sawamura   We need to worry about ourselves, not about Yanagi. I'm young and have a future to build.

Genda   Yanagi is caught between a rock and a hard place.

Sawamura   Yanagi is safe for now.

Genda   If Yanagi is fired, he won't know what to do with himself.

Imai *laughs carelessly.* **Genda** *looks his way.*

Genda   What's funny, eh?

Imai   You're repeating Yanagi over and over again.

Genda   So, what?

Imai   I'm sorry. Honestly, the only one to think it funny is me. Please continue.

Sawamura *pays no heed to* **Imai**.

Sawamura   Yanagi could easily have been the first to be let go at the large-scale firing in autumn.

Genda   So what about that?

Sawamura   I don't know how to answer your question.

Genda   So, are you saying that it would be OK for him to be fired this time round?

Sawamura   No, I don't mean that, but I don't feel I can back him up either.

He prepares to launch on something difficult to say.

Well, you may have had a lot to do with Yanagi during your Osaka period.

Genda (*on the verge of denying having relations with* **Yanagi**, *he changes direction*)   It's not that I didn't have any connection with him.

Sawamura   There you are. You want to help Yanagi because you've known him for a long time.

Imai   Wait, Mr. Yanagi is from the Kansai district, right? Is this a matter of camaraderie.

Genda   Shut up.

Imai   A college friend of mine was like that. He was from Osaka.

Genda   Keep your mouth shut.

Sawamura   Why don't you put an end to making up for your wrongdoings.

Imai   Oh, this is getting interesting.

Genda   If I fuck up this time, I'm in deep shit.

Sawamura   He's almost completely healed, isn't he?

Imai   Healed?

Sawamura   Mr. Genda, you've paid back plenty. This time, if we don't play it well, we'll all be caught up in the mess.

Genda   If it comes to that, I'll be ready.

Sawamura   Please don't rope me in.

Imai   What happened in Osaka?

Sawamura   I'm not involved in that.

Genda   Don't feed me to the dogs.

Imai   Please, don't keep ignoring me. What happened in Osaka?

Genda   Nothing.

Imai   That couldn't be true. What was healed? Did you injure him?

Genda   Hey, Sawamura, have you been dropping hints?

Imai   So he had injuries. What kind?

Genda   Shurrup.

Sawamura   A cow went berserk and Mr. Yanagi was kicked in the belly and arm.

Imai   I see.

Genda   Don't tell him.

Sawamura   It happened when Mr. Genda needed a longer time than usual for the bloodletting.

Genda   Stop it.

Sawamura   You always talk about it when we go drinking. Because you lost sight of where to insert the knife for a moment, Yanagi sustained a complex fracture of his right arm. You say yourself that you destroyed one worker's career.

Imai   So that's it. Then why did you both leave Osaka together?

Sawamura   Yanagi has some after-effects from the injury. Marumoto's work was more subdivided so each part of the work was less demanding. Mr. Genda almost stayed in Osaka, but feeling concern, followed Yanagi to Tokyo.

Genda   You're revealing too much to strangers.

Imai   That's an impressive case of friendship.

Genda   That's not true

Sawamura   Mr. Genda, I understand that you had that kind of a past. I sympathize, too. But Yanagi is pretty close to retirement age. You've provided perfect support, Mr. Genda. What more is there for you to do?

Genda   No, it's not just that. That's, you know, wrong. I've got to help him out.

Sawamura   Of course, there may be a connection I don't know about.

Genda   Come on, Sawamura. I've got to help him.

Sawamura   Honestly, I'm not so close to him. I don't want to go so far as to risk my own neck.

Genda   Sawamura.

Sawamura   Well, what if you find him, what are you going to say?

Imai   Oh, that would be, "Don't do anything foolish."

Genda *glares at* **Imai**.

Imai   Huh, it isn't?

Sawamura   Yanagi is totally out of his mind going off with the slaughter gun. Helping him now may result in something you can't undo.

Genda   Like what for example?

Imai   What does he think he's up to with a brainstem and a gun?

Genda   We don't know yet if Yanagi is behind the missing brainstem.

Sawamura   He's gotta be. He's hiding somewhere with the brainstem as hostage.

Genda   What is a brainstem hostage situation like?

Imai   Imagining it makes me laugh though I don't know what a brainstem looks like.

Genda   Hey, seriously, why don't you just go home?

Imai   I'm basically jumping on the bandwagon here.

Genda *abandons* **Imai**.

Genda   Sawamura.

Sawamura   Don't put matters in my hands. As far as Yanagi's case goes, let's wait until the heat's off. For now, persuading Mr. Imai is the priority.

Imai   You are still harping on that.

Genda   The heat will never be off.

Imai   Don't try to persuade me. That would be a problem.

Sawamura   I seriously don't want our company to go out of business because of the alternative processing chamber.

Imai   There isn't any particular trigger to the proposition.

Genda   Sawamura.

Sawamura   Just cut it out. Yanagi's problems have no connection with the alternative processing chamber. At this point in time, aren't these problems to be resolved separately? His situation is his, and ours is ours.

Imai   Hang on. Whether there will be a withdrawal or not cannot be decided here.

Genda   Come on, these two are no longer separate issues.

Sawamura   Mr. Genda, please be quiet.

Genda   I'm saying they're related.

Heading toward his locker, **Genda** *speaks.*

Genda   It's here.

Sawamura   Huh?

Genda *brings out the nylon bag.*

Imai   Oh, you hid something a while ago.

Sawamura   What is that?

Genda   It's the brainstem.

Sawamura   What?

Imai   Brainstem.

Genda *puts the bag on the table.* **Sawamura** *opens the bag. Surprised to find the brainstem inside, he casts a glance at* **Genda**. *A particular smell floats across the room.*

Imai   It stinks. It's that smell again.

Genda   You're exaggerating.

Sawamura   What's this about?

Genda   This is what it's about.

Sawamura   Why do you have it?

Genda   I snatched it away from Yanagi. I don't know what he was going to do with it.

Sawamura   When?

Genda   I ran into Yanagi on the way to the processing chamber. He was carrying some kind of bag and acting really kind of suspicious. I thought it was weird.

Sawamura   So it was Yanagi.

Genda   I decided not to ask his reason or anything else. I took it and sent Yanagi back to the processing chamber. End of story . . . I took the trouble to make it look as if nothing had happened. Then he had to run away with the slaughter gun. I didn't expect that.

Sawamura   What was he thinking of?

Genda   He probably didn't even know himself. He felt so hounded.

Sawamura   But that doesn't get him off the hook.

Genda   That's right. Because of that, I don't know what to do.

Sawamura   Let's go and return the brainstem.

Genda   No.

Sawamura   Why not?

Genda   What are you going to say when you return it?

Sawamura   Isn't honesty the best policy?

Genda   What'll happen when you tell the truth?

Sawamura   Huh?

Genda   How can we lessen Yanagi's wrongdoing?

Sawamura   What do you mean?

Genda   We have to make it so Yanagi wasn't at fault.

Sawamura   That's impossible. Either way, if we leave the brainstem here, the company will take a hit.

Genda   A head of cattle or Yanagi, which would you save, Sawamura?

Imai   It's not a matter of which.

Genda   Let's do what we can. At least, let's arrange things so that Yanagi isn't responsible for taking the brainstem.

A pause while the two men exchange looks of persuasion and acceptance.

Sawamura   What are you going to do with that?

Genda   That's why I'm stuck.

Sawamura   We can't leave it here.

Noticing a pause, **Imai** *joins the conversation.*

Imai   How about replacing it behind everyone's back?

Sawamura   Huh?

Imai   If the company is in confusion, the cattle processing chamber may be empty.

Genda   No, it's rare that no one's there. Also, on the way there, we're likely to meet someone.

Imai   Still, there'll probably be fewer workers on site than usual. We observe the movement of the enemy, sneak into the site, and leave the bag somewhere.

Genda   You're having a good time, aren't you?

Imai   Excuse me?

Genda   What's the enemy bit about? Is it from a movie? You think you're in a movie, eh?

Imai   I was just delivering a constructive opinion. If it's left here, suspicion will fall on . . .

He looks at the other two.

Sawamura   If it comes to that, I'll blab about Yanagi.

Genda   No!

Sawamura   Why not?

Imai   Wowee. (*Is excited with the development.*)

Genda   What's with you?

Imai   Oh, I think it's best to return the brainstem without being exposed.

Genda   You just shut your face.

Imai   Isn't it a problem to keep it here?

Genda   What'll we do, Sawamura?

Sawamura   Whatever we do, you're the one who brought it here, Mr. Genda.

Genda   I couldn't leave it in Yanagi's hands.

Imai   But at this point, most of the workers believe that Yanagi has it.

Genda   I know that!

Imai   If you want to mitigate Yanagi's wrongdoing, you should casually return the brainstem and say, "Oh, it's here!" Appeal to the other workers.

Genda   If I could be casual, I'd have already done it.

Imai   Nothing ventured, nothing gained.

Genda *suddenly has an idea.*

Genda   Aha.

Imai   Huh?

Genda   You.

Imai *is puzzled.*

I mean you.

Imai   What?

Genda   You take it.

Imai   Excuse me?

Genda   Even if you are stopped by someone, you can pass with your "observer" status.

Imai   It won't work.

Genda   Furthermore, when they find out you are heir to the Imai Farm, matters will be resolved quietly.

Imai   It won't. I'll be in trouble with my father.

Genda   You're the one who recommended sneaking the brainstem back.

Imai   That's not my function.

Genda *won't listen.*

Genda   Alright, let's go, Imai.

Imai   Listen.

Genda   Here take this.

He tries to hand the bag with the brainstem in it to **Imai**.

Imai   Excuse me, I cannot do this.

Genda   You've gone too far to turn back.

Imai   I'm dropping out, right now.

Genda   Too late. Here, hold it properly.

Imai   No, I won't. (*Drops the bag.*)

Genda   Hey, watch out. It's precious.

Imai *keeps his distance.*

Imai   It's too much for me. I mean it.

Sawamura *slowly picks up the bag with the brainstem in it.*

Genda   Here we go, Sawamura. Don't let him escape.

Imai   I won't do it.

Sawamura *does not move from that spot.*

Genda   Sawamura?

Sawamura   Excuse me.

Genda   Huh?

Sawamura   Why don't we think more seriously about this.

Imai   You're right. Please do.

Genda   Huh? I am serious.

While putting away the brainstem into **Genda**'*s locker,* **Sawamura** *speaks.*

Sawamura   I'll put it back into your locker for now. If someone enters and sees it on the table, we wouldn't have a good excuse.

Genda   What can you do with it in the locker?

Sawamura   Let's think of a proper method to handle it.

Genda   This isn't the time for talk.

Sawamura   And I am saying that leaving it out here doesn't help at all.

He closes the locker door, and then sits down on a chair and tries to think with his head in his hands.

Oh no.

Genda   You know, Sawamura, let's go look for Yanagi.

Sawamura   It's impossible.

Genda   What do you mean by impossible?

Sawamura   Mr. Kunimoto and his men are searching for him.

Genda   We have to find him first. We find him first and hear him out.

Sawamura   Why do you want to take this on too? We can't handle any more problems.

Genda   We have to save Yanagi. He has a gun, you know.

Imai   If he uses it to commit suicide, that would be terrible.

Genda   Don't say such things.

Imai   You implied that just now.

Sawamura   Yanagi doesn't have the nerve

Genda   He could do it on the spur of the moment.

Imai   See, he's talking about suicide.

Genda   Shut up. If by chance, we get into a situation that can't be undone, Yanagi's wife . . . (*He stops and cannot continue.*)

Sawamura   Huh?

Imai   What was that? What was that about his wife?

Genda   Why the hell do I have to tell you?

Imai   I'm too far gone to turn back, as you say.

Genda   You're not part of us in the first place.

Imai   Wow.

Genda   A rich boy like you wouldn't understand how many difficulties Yanagi has gone through. Don't ask questions just out of curiosity.

Imai   I had a hard time, too. Right? (*To* **Sawamura**.)

Sawamura *pays no heed to* **Imai**.

Sawamura   His wife's surgery was a success, right.

Imai   What kind of surgery was this?

Genda   Never you mind.

Sawamura   Do his difficulties refer to payment for the operation?

Genda   No, her operation fees were covered by his retirement pay, I hear.

Sawamura   Retirement pay? Yanagi is . . .

Genda   He's not fully employed anymore. He's become a contract worker.

Sawamura   So that's it.

Genda   As Sawamura has said, Yanagi was supposed to be laid off. But the company decided to take his wife's illness into consideration and allowed him to stay on as a contract worker until the end of the fiscal year. The agreement was that he would find other employment by that time.

Sawamura   So that was the arrangement.

Genda   But, just then, his wife's breast cancer spread to the lymph nodes.

Imai   Breast cancer.

Sawamura   Uh-huh.

Genda   What with nursing his wife and all, he wasn't able to do much job-hunting. He asked the director for an extension of his contract, but the company had already given him his retirement payment and has its own financial difficulties . . .

Sawamura   He didn't get it.

Genda *shakes his head.*

Sawamura   Then he gave into despair.

Imai   That really sounds like a scenario for suicide.

Genda   Ever since I unintentionally created the conditions for his injury, he's been out of luck. I . . .

Sawamura   It doesn't even make a good joke—committing suicide with a slaughter gun.

Imai *is surprised.*

Imai   Oh, maybe, in reverse, he's threatening the director.

Genda   Huh?

Sawamura   Pointing the slaughter gun, he says, "Give me cash!" It's certainly possible.

Imai *'s face is glowing with prankish delight. Disgusted with his lack of delicacy,* **Sawamura** *is about to call him out, when* **Genda** *speaks.*

Genda   Cut it out you—

He grabs **Imai** *by the collar.*

Imai   Hey!

Sawamura   Mr. Genda.

Genda (*to* **Imai**)   What the hell are you saying?

Imai   Hey, this is no joke.

Genda   Listening to Yanagi and his troubles, all you can do is think it's funny. You—

Imai   I wasn't, really, I never thought of it like that.

Genda *pushes* **Imai** *energetically towards the grinding machine.*

Imai   Wait, wait. Hey, police.

Genda   Call all you like.

Sawamura   Hey, stop that, Mr. Genda.

Genda *gets* **Imai** *into a headlock position.*

Imai   Wait, what, stop.

Sawamura   Mr. Genda, don't.

Genda   Turn on the switch of the grinding machine.

Sawamura   What did you say?

Imai   Uh.

Genda   I'll sharpen this brat's head.

Imai   What?

Sawamura   What are you saying?

Genda *mercilessly pulls* **Imai** *toward the grinding machine.*

Imai   Hey, you're really strong. Stop it.

Sawamura *holds* **Genda** *from behind.*

Genda   Let me go.

Sawamura   Mr. Genda!

Sawamura *hits* **Genda** *many times.*

Genda   Uggh, uggh.

He and **Imai** *eventually separate.* **Sawamura** *continues to hit* **Genda** *relentlessly.*

Genda   Hey, argh. Stop it, will ya!

Sawamura (*stops hitting* **Genda**)   What on earth are you thinking of?

Imai   Really, I'm shocked. That hurt . . .

Imai *strokes himself where* **Genda** *grabbed.* **Genda**, *in a bad mood, sits on a chair.*

Sawamura   Mr. Genda, what's on your mind?

Genda   Little shit pissed me off.

Sawamura   That doesn't mean you can rough him up.

Imai *straightens himself up.*

Imai   I will sue you.

Sawamura   There you go again. Now you're going too far.

Imai   I'm gonna sue you.

Genda   Go ahead.

Sawamura   Mr. Imai, if you talk that way you are inviting . . .

Imai   That was absolutely a crime of inflicting bodily injury resulting in death.

Sawamura   You're not dead.

Imai   I'm not dead, yet.

Genda   Stupid.

Sawamura   Mr. Genda.

Imai *breathes out through his nose.*

Imai   Just as I thought.

Sawamura   Huh?

Imai   Bunch of savages.

Genda   Whaddaya say?

He is about to stand. **Sawamura** *speaks in a remonstrating tone.*

Sawamura   Mr. Genda. Mr. Imai, too. Come on.

Imai   I wasn't talking about you, Mr. Sawamura.

Genda   What? What do you mean by savages?

Sawamura   Now, let's calm down.

Imai *begins to regain his cool.*

Imai   There were people like that.

Sawamura   Mr. Imai.

Imai   May I tell you of something that happened when I was quite young?

Genda   No.

Imai   I will talk about it.

Genda   No.

Sawamura   Come on, let him tell us, just once.

Genda   No.

Imai   My family used to be ranchers.

Genda   I said no.

Imai   A long time ago, before we developed the Imai premium black swine we kept cattle as well.

Genda   This guy never listens!

Imai *forcefully continues his story.*

Imai   Every month, a truck came to take away some cattle. At our ranch, one or two cows would be loaded. The truckers would lead the cow by pulling on its nose ring. If the cow resisted, things got rough, and the men would pull so hard the cow's nasal septum would tear and bleed a lot. Even so, they'd point a stun gun at the cow's rear end and force the animal into the cargo box on the truck.

Genda   That's their job.

Imai   Whether it's their job or not, it's cruel.

Sawamura   It may look like that to a child.

Genda *looks at* **Sawamura**.

Imai   I was terrified by the men who carried on that way.

Sawamura   I can understand that.

Genda   You can? Sawamura, can you really empathize with him?

Sawamura *responds with an ambiguous look on his face.* **Genda** *gives a clearly negative look.*

Imai   Humans can say it's just work, but cows can't say anything. Even as a kid, I knew what happened to the cows and called those men "Reapers."

Sawamura   I see.

Genda   Don't say stupid things. What feeling is there in a word like reaper?

Imai   But it's really like that. They appear suddenly like gods, take the animal away, and slaughter it.

Sawamura   For cattle, they are reapers of death.

Imai   For me, too, they were reapers.

Sawamura   I agree.

Imai   At times like that, the other cattle cry. They seem to understand that their buddies are going to be killed.

Genda   You think it sounds like that because you raise animals as if they were your pets. It's a matter of subjectivity.

Imai   Is that so? My parents say they feel the same way.

Genda   Your education is totally off track.

Imai   Ethically, it isn't wrong, I think.

Sawamura   That's true.

Genda   Why are you saying, "That's true"?

Imai   What do you think, Mr. Sawamura?

Sawamura   Um.

Imai   Don't they sound afraid of being killed?

Sawamura   Well, sometimes they do.

Genda   Do they? Sawamura, can you take responsibility for what you say?

Sawamura *doesn't answer.*

Imai   Cows shed tears, right? They don't want to die.

Genda   Livestock farmers feed beer to their cattle to soften the flesh. All they are doing is rearing cattle for consumption. Don't give me the touchy-feely talk.

Imai   We don't do such things.

Genda   What do you do? Don't you guys eat meat?

Imai   That has nothing to do with what we are talking about.

Genda   It does. Don't you eat meat?

Imai   We do, but . . .

Genda   See? He eats it.

Imai   That's not the point we are talking about.

Genda   What point are you talking about then?

Imai   About life.

Genda   That again.

Imai   Why do our swine become objects once they are transported beyond the fence of this building? (*Pause.*)

Without listening to **Genda**'*s reply,* **Imai** *continues to speak at the same time.*

Their voices overlap:

Genda   Pigs are pigs. Cows are cows. That's all there is to it.

Imai   It's because the senses of the workers here are paralyzed. If they weren't, they wouldn't be able to take the lives of animals that are crying and screaming.

Pause.

Genda   Enough already. Sawamura, get rid of this brat.

Sawamura *does not move.*

Genda   I don't know what new religion you belong to, but the animals that come here are all livestock. They are products. You eat them, too, right? Without the slaughtering and dressing, you don't get to eat meat.

Imai   Of course, I understand such matters.

Genda   It's because you don't understand that expressions like "taking life" come to your mind.

Imai   As long as one works here, the important point is feeling. The work is to transform life into food. We must value feeling.

Genda   So, then what is it? We butcher them one by one saying we're sorry.

Imai   That's not what I mean.

Genda   Yes, it is what you mean. What'll change by doing that? You just conveniently gloss over the reality.

Imai *looks tired.*

Imai   You said earlier that processing our swine was a real pisser, right, Mr. Genda.

Sawamura   Excuse me?

Genda   Yeah, sure I did.

Sawamura   Wait Mr. Genda, what are you saying? (*To* **Imai**.) It's not as he says. We are properly respecting the life of the livestock you bring us.

Genda   You're full of it.

Sawamura   It's true. At least as far as I am concerned.

Genda   Sawamura, what are you afraid of?

Sawamura   About what?

Genda   When you get fired, you get fired. When you stop being yourself, you lose.

Sawamura *turns to* **Imai**.

Sawamura   I process the Imai black swine with proper respect for their life.

Genda   Just quit it. Sucking up to Imai Farm will be your end.

Imai   It's not lip service. You are handling the lives of the Imai black swine, which we have produced with great care. Of course, we want you to do the processing with proper respect.

Genda   And you're making profit from the business, right. Don't put all the burden of the respect for life on us.

Imai   You're the ones that deal the final blow. I came here concerned about the kind of workers in your employ and found them to be what I feared.

Genda   You little shit, you really want your head shaved, eh?

Imai *keeps a safe distance from* **Genda**.

Imai   See, there you go again. I don't want our swine to be handled by a savage like Mr. Genda.

Genda   I withdraw from any work related to your pigs. They are impossible. Your pigs and staff are all good-for-nothing. All shitty, senile trash.

Imai'*s and* **Sawamura**'*s voices overlap.*

Imai   Hey!

Sawamura   Genda!

He grabs **Genda** *by the collar. Shouts, unheard of in their former relationship, rise in the air.*

Sawamura   Cut it out. Talking off the top of your head. Don't try that shit on me.

Genda   What is it?

Sawamura   All this time, you've . . .

Sawamura, *pushing* **Genda** *roughly away, speaks to* **Imai**.

Sawamura   I apologize, Mr. Imai.

Imai   It's too late.

Sawamura   I see. Mr. Imai, I will request that Mr. Genda be relieved of duty in the alternative processing chamber.

Genda   What?

Sawamura   I will negotiate with the director.

Genda   Sawamura?

Sawamura   Are you satisfied? You'll be released from 'a real pisser' of a job. (*To* **Imai**.) So, you see, please do not withdraw the Imai premium black swine from our business.

Imai   No . . .

Sawamura   Pease accept my sincere apology.

He does a formal dogeza[6] *bow, abasing himself on the floor.*

Genda   What the heck are you doing?

Sawamura   How about you, Mr. Genda? What were you doing while I was away? You were trying to get jobs cut.

Genda   It's the reverse. You were the one trying to betray me.

Sawamura   I can't quit. Absolutely not.

Genda   I know all that.

Sawamura   I only have this one job.

Genda   I'm the same. I can't forgive anyone who puts it down. That's unforgivable.

Sawamura   Mr. Imai is the life line of Marumoto Meat Center and its workers.

Genda   If you rely on a life line that might break at any moment, you're in for a fall.

Sawamura   It won't break. (*To* **Imai**.) Isn't that right?

Imai   So you see . . .

Instead of paying attention to **Imai**'s *words,* **Sawamura** *takes out the knife hanging from his hip.*

Imai   Hey?

Sawamura   I beg you.

Genda   Now, now, Sawamura.

Sawamura   I no longer understand anything.

Genda   What are you doing?

Sawamura   Why do you worry about Yanagi all the time and never think about me?

Genda   I do think of you.

Sawamura   What's going to happen to my life? Are you going to take responsibility?

Genda   Why should I?

Sawamura   It's your fault, Mr. Genda, all your fault.

Genda   Why is it my fault? The mistake was this little shit's arrival.

Imai   Hey, don't blame me.

Sawamura   So which is it? Which of you should I attack?

Genda   What do you mean by "which"? Neither.

Sawamura   I can't draw back now.

Genda   Yes, you can, Sawamura. Calm down, calm down.

Sawamura   Should I attack Genda? Or . . .

Genda   Don't be stupid.

Sawamura   Or Imai?

Imai   Do you realize what you are doing?

Sawamura   No, I don't. But . . .

Genda   No, no. Put it away.

Sawamura   But I have to protect my wife and son.

Genda   I get it. If you use that thing, you won't be able to protect what you have to.

Sawamura   I'm paralyzed. Just like with smell, I've got used to it—cutting meat.

Genda   Stupid, stupid. What are you saying? It's no good, Sawamura. Get a grip on yourself.

Sawamura, *lowers his knife, and stands vacantly . . .*

Sawamura   I beg you. I . . . I . . .

Over time, **Genda** *is able to close his distance from* **Sawamura**.

Genda   We're OK. It's not as if the company is going out of business.

He quietly takes the knife from **Sawamura** *and puts it on the table.*

Imai   This is crazy.

At that moment, the intercom buzzes. It continues for a while and then **Imai** *slowly picks up the receiver.*

Genda   Hey, what are you doing?

Imai *speaks before listening to the other party.*

Imai   The missing brainstem is in the alternative processing chamber. Please come at once.

Genda   What the hell are you saying?

Having said that, **Imai** *puts down the receiver.*

Genda (*to* **Imai**)   Hey you!

Sawamura   This is the end.

Genda   No, it isn't the end.

Sawamura *speaks to the family picture on the front screen of his cell phone.*

Sawamura   Sota, I'm sorry.

Genda   Wait, what are you doing?

Imai *takes the brainstem from the locker.*

Imai   I will reveal everything.

Genda   Whaddaya say?

Imai   About the headlock, about having a knife pointed at me, and about the brainstem.

Genda   You—I'll kill ya.

Imai   Try it. People will come as we speak.

He looks toward the door. **Genda** *also follows* **Imai**'s *glance. Judging that there is no time left,* **Genda** *moves into action.*

Genda   Give it back.

He aims to get the brainstem back.

Imai   No, I won't.

Genda *almost snatches the brainstem away from* **Imai**.

Imai   Oh no!

Genda   What's the "Oh, no!" about?!

Imai   No, don't.

Standing, the two men get into a fight. **Genda** *gets the better of* **Imai**, *and the bagged brainstem gets crushed between their hands.*

Imai   Hold it. What's the point of doing this kind of thing? People are coming very soon!

Genda *presses the bagged brainstem against* **Imai**'s *mouth.*

Imai   H-hey? Hey, that's disgusting.

Genda   Eat it!

Imai   What?

Genda   Eat the brainstem and destroy the evidence.

Imai   Don't be ridiculous. What about BSE?

Genda   Are you stupid? We used to eat it in the old days.

Imai   That's a lie!

Genda   It's true!

The brainstem is pushed against **Imai**'s *mouth.*

Imai   Yuck!

Genda   Eat it!

Imai   Impossible. The nylon bag . . . Hey, someone! Help!

Genda   Shit.

He takes the bagged brainstem away, unties the mouth of the bag, and returns to where **Imai** *is. At that moment,* **Imai** *picks up the knife on the table and points it clumsily at* **Genda**.

Genda   What are you trying to do?

Imai   This is crazy.

Genda   You think you're threatening me?

Imai   That thing. Give it to me.

Genda   Why the hell?

Imai   Never mind, just give it to me. Put it on the table.

Genda *puts the bagged brainstem on the table.* **Imai** *picks it up and then points the knife at* **Genda**.

Imai   Don't try making any stupid moves. I will tell them everything.

Just then, **Sawamura** *snaps a picture of* **Imai** *with his cell phone camera.* **Imai** *and* **Genda** *look toward the sound of the shutter.*

Imai   You know.

Genda   Whaddaya doing at a time like this?

Sawamura *is saving the photo he just took.*

Sawamura   I've saved it.

Genda   Sawamura.

Sawamura   I've saved it.

Imai   What is it? What do you intend to do?

Sawamura   I've put it with my favorites.

Genda   Sawamura, you've really gone crazy.

Sawamura   If you want this pic deleted, you have to promise not to withdraw the Imai black swine.

Genda   What kind of deal is that?

Sawamura   Mr. Imai stole the brainstem and he threatened us with the knife. This is solid evidence.

He raises the cell phone picture.

Genda   Ahh.

Imai   Don't talk such nonsense!

Genda   So that's it.

Sawamura   Mr. Genda, this is OK, right?

Genda   You're real mean, Sawamura!

Imai   Hey.

Sawamura   Please. It would be bad to this industry if a rumor spread, you know. The heir to Imai Farm threatened a business connection with a knife.

Imai   Sheer spite.

Genda   You're the one who's been spiteful all along. Sawamura, upload it on YouTube, why don't you?

Sawamura   It's a still, so.

Genda   Then up on a blog.

Imai   Stop that. Just delete it, please.

Sawamura   Then, will you retract the withdrawal plan?

Imai   Yes, I will.

Sawamura   Huh?

Imai *can tolerate it no longer. He puts down the brainstem and knife on the table and rushes toward* **Sawamura** *to capture his cell phone.*

Imai   Give it here!

Sawamura   No!

Genda   Hey you, wise up.

Imai   Who are you talking to?

As they are fighting over the cell phone, **Genda** *notices someone.*

Genda   Ah.

He stops moving and from the window confirms Yanagi's figure outside on a rooftop.

Sawamura   What?

Genda   Oh no.

Genda *points.*

Genda   Yanagi?

Imai   Huh?

Sawamura *and* **Imai** *follow* **Genda**'*s line of sight.*

Genda   Yanagi is on the rooftop.

Sawamura   Look at his right hand. He does have the slaughter gun after all.

Genda   What's he up to?

At that moment, there is a knock on the door. It is probably Kunimoto. The three turn to look at the door, then, suddenly become aware of the brainstem.

Genda   Brainstem!

Without a plan, they go to get the brainstem when the dry noise of a gunpowder explosion signals that a slaughter gun has been shot.

The three look outside the window.

Next, the door of the room opens.

The three turn their gaze to the door.

A week later.

After 3:00 pm. **Sawamura** *is slurping cup noodles for lunch. With a notebook by him, he occasionally looks at the fine print on the cup and takes notes.* **Genda** *enters in an ill-fitting suit.*

Sawamura   Mr. Genda.

Genda   Oh, shit. The director goes on forever.

Sawamura *stands up in an exaggerated manner and bows his head.*

Sawamura   Thank you for your hard work.

Genda   My hard work refers to what? Oh, I'm beat. What's the time?

Sawamura   It's past 3:00 pm.

Genda   The boss's talk went on for two hours.

Sawamura   This is the first time I've seen you in a business suit.

Genda   I had it made for my coming-of-age ceremony.

Sawamura   You're kidding.

Genda   I am.

Sawamura   What's that?

Genda *notices* **Sawamura**'*s cup noodles.*

Genda   You know, Sawamura.

Sawamura   Yes?

Genda   You're eating cup noodles.

Sawamura   Uh-huh.

Genda   Since when?

Sawamura   Since your official suspension from work.

Genda   Oh, really. What about UFO?

Sawamura   That, well, never mind.

Genda   Uh, why? You loved it to death.

Sawamura   Well, that belongs to the past now.

Genda   What's this? Am I a perfect Urashima Taro?[7] What's this transformation of the landscape about?

Sawamura *is clearly smiling.*

Genda   Hey, hey. What's happened?

Sawamura   I've got news

Genda   Must listen to this.

Sawamura   My boy declared that he wants to open a noodle shop.

Genda   A noodle shop.

Sawamura   A little while ago, I took the family to a new Hakata noodle specialty shop nearby.

Genda   Uh-huh.

Sawamura   Their *tonkotsu*[8] noodles tasted good, And Sota was completely hooked.

Genda   He's a third grader with mature taste.

Sawamura   So to help him build his dream, I've started investigating instant *tonkotsu* noodles. The recent recipes are quite involved.

Genda   And you're even taking memos?

Sawamura   Well, if you're going to do this . . .

Genda   But didn't you tell me once that Sota was put off by your odor?

Sawamura   Come on, Mr. Genda, don't be dense.

Genda   Huh?

Sawamura   Don't you get it after being told this much? My boy's shown a level of understanding for his dad's job, you see.

Genda   How come?

Sawamura (*as if certifying that he has the genuine proof of his boy's acceptance.*) He asked me to bring back good pig bones as he would be opening a *tonkotsu* noodle shop.

Genda   I don't get it.

Sawamura   He wants me to bring back the bones of the swine I butcher.

Genda   So that's it. Well, he's still a third grader. If you take him seriously now, you may be disappointed later on. It sounds like a fickle dream to me.

Sawamura   No way, his eyes were serious. For this Christmas, he wants a hot water colander for draining noodles like this (*gesturing*), the kind with a long handle.

Genda   That's exciting.

Sawamura   Where can you buy colanders like that.

Genda   No idea.

Sawamura *slurps down the last noodle.*

Sawamura   Hmm. That was good. Mr. Genda, do you still have time?

Genda   Sure.

Sawamura   Let me throw away the soup. Oh, would you like to have some coffee?

Genda   Uh, no thanks. I had a can of coffee just a while ago.

Sawamura   Oh really.

He takes the container and the trash to the kitchenette. Meanwhile, **Genda** *looks around the grinding room nostalgically.* **Sawamura** *returns.*

Sawamura (*sitting down on a chair*)   Well, well, well, well . . .

Genda *starts off in a meek tone.*

Genda   Sawamura.

Sawamura, *sensing the change in tone, gets ready.*

Sawamura   Oh, yes?

Genda   I.

Sawamura   Are you going to quit?

Genda   Why do you say that? Do you want me to?

Sawamura   Ohh.

Genda   What does "Ohh" mean? No. I'm going to return to the cattle processing chamber.

Sawamura   Oh, is that right.

Genda   Uh-huh.

Sawamura   Um.

He nods his head as if in assent.

Genda   Huh, aren't you gonna say something?

Sawamura   Something?

Genda   Like "No way!"

Sawamura   No, because it can't be helped. Let off with only a week's layoff and a reshuffling of personnel is the lightest you can expect.

Genda   Why is that?

Sawamura   Why? That's how it is.

Genda   What I mean is how about you Sawamura? How come you weren't chewed out?

Sawamura   Oh, that's because my daily conduct is acceptable.

Genda   Oh, so that's it.

Sawamura   And what happened to Mr. Yanagi?

Genda   *Mr.* Yanagi.

Sawamura   Uh-huh.

Genda   Yeah, *Mr.* Yanagi.

Sawamura   Um.

Genda   *Mr.* Yanagi betrayed me totally.

Sawamura   Huh?

Genda   He told the director that I'd grabbed the brainstem from him.

Sawamura   Really . . .

Genda   An amazing peach tree / Got me by the short and curlies?!

Sawamura   Huh? What's that?

Genda   It's nothing. Oh—why did he say that?

Sawamura   Well, it was factually true.

Genda   Maybe, but he didn't need to give my name. What the fuck did he want to achieve? What was his point in shooting up into the sky with a slaughter gun?

Sawamura   What did you want to achieve by shielding Mr. Yanagi?

Genda   Shut it.

Sawamura   So what is he going to do?

Genda   Oh, he's going back to Osaka with his wife.

Sawamura   Osaka? Oh, really.

Genda   Uh-huh, my wife said she'd go pay them a visit.

Sawamura   Humph. So he was fired. It's a tough world.

Genda   Can't be helped, you know.

Sawamura   Aren't you going to help him?

Genda   There's nothing I can do anymore. Oh hell. It's all that shit's fault.

He is referring to **Imai***.* **Sawamura** *doesn't respond.*

Genda   Yo, did you hear? Sawamura.

Sawamura   Huh?

Genda   Remember he mentioned a meat processing plant in Chiba?

Sawamura   Yeah.

Genda   Now that was him talking off the top of his head all the way.

Sawamura   Uh-huh.

Genda   That really pisses me off. Don't you get angry?

Sawamura   Well, why don't we let it go?

Genda   Why? The Chiba place also argued with Imai about whether to use manual processing or not. It all fell through.

Sawamura   Thanks to that, we get to do business with Imai as usual.

Genda   Not as usual. I've been transferred.

Sawamura   Uh-huh.

Genda   What is that shit doing here?

Sawamura   The only way to deal with this is to think a typhoon is passing through.

Genda   Oh fuck him, I prefer the alternative processing chamber. I can work at my own pace.

Sawamura   What? Haven't you changed your tune?

Genda   Never mind. What I mean is this. Why didn't you send that pic, Sawamura?

Sawamura   Uh?

Genda   It would have clinched it.

Sawamura   Well, he wouldn't confess. If I sent it, we might have been exposed and matters might have gotten out of control. Not a nice conclusion.

Genda   We can't use it?

Sawamura   Come on, let's drop this topic. Here's something else—You don't have any commitments after this, do you?

Genda   Huh?

Sawamura   As I'm on shift A, we could go somewhere, you know. (*Gestures drinking.*) It's been a while.

Genda   I can't.

Sawamura   Why not?

Genda   Employee training starts now.

Sawamura   What's that about? I mean, you hardly need any training, Mr. Genda.

Genda   No, it's the other way round. I'm the trainer. The director told me to take the young ones through the whole line procedure.

Sawamura   Uh-huh.

Genda   It's a total *batsu* game.[9]

Sawamura   It's not a game, it's just punishment. That's all.

Genda   Sawamura, let's do it together.

Sawamura   No.

Genda   I hear that a number of people will come from other plants.

Sawamura   Doubly no.

Genda   What is this? What is this difference between you and me?

Sawamura   Come on, stop going on about it. What time does your training session start?

Genda   3:00 pm.

Sawamura   Geez, you're already late. Get ready. Take off that dirty-looking suit.

Genda   No.

Sawamura   If you ditch this, you really will be fired.

Genda   No.

Sawamura   You've got to go.

Genda   Sawamura, I say no.

Sawamura   Are you throwing a tantrum?

While the two are arguing weakly, the door of the grinding room opens. **Imai***, in a professional white coat, is standing there.* **Sawamura** *and* **Genda** *look at him.*

Sawamura   Huh?

Imai *doesn't change his facial expression and delivers the following message.*

Imai   It's past the start time, please come as soon as possible.

Sawamura   Are you taking part today?

Imai   No, I was told by my father, I mean the president, to see the training site.

Sawamura   Ah.

He looks at **Genda***. After a long pause.*

Genda   Who would teach you?!

Sawamura   Mr. Genda!

Genda   Just kidding. I'm going. Sawamura, you come too!

He overtakes **Imai** *and exits.*

Sawamura   What the . . . (*To* **Imai***.*) Okay, let's go.

Imai   Ah, yes.

Sawamura   Just a moment, Mr. Genda.

Just as **Sawamura** *turns to the door,* **Genda** *comes back in.*

Sawamura   Wow.

Genda*, ignoring* **Sawamura***, turns to* **Imai***.*

Genda   I'll show you a really impressive piece of work that'll blow you away.

Imai *looks at* **Genda** *without responding.*

Genda   What are you looking at? Speak up.

Sawamura   Mr. Genda, please stop this. Let's go. Come on. Let's go.

Looking back at **Imai***,* **Sawamura** *speaks.*

Sawamura   Mr. Imai, you come too, please.

Imai   Excuse me.

Sawamura   Um?

Imai   The swine to be used in today's training isn't one of the Imai Farm's stock, right?

Sawamura *becomes aware at the true meaning of* **Imai***'s question.*

Sawamura   Uh?

In this way, the operation of the meat processing and dressing will continue tomorrow.

The End.

Notes

1. In the context of this play, *buraku* refers to districts where ethnic Japanese of the lowest social status lived in premodern times. Their occupations were restricted to such jobs as abattoir workers and executioners, which were considered sources of defilement according to traditional religious views that abhorred blood shedding and death. The status was officially abolished in the Meiji period (1868–1912). However, the social movement to eradicate discrimination continues, as *buraku* descendants still face prejudice and discrimination in marriage and employment today.
2. Yakisoba refers to instant-fried noodles.
3. Utahiroba refers to a popular karaoke chain called Karaoke Room Utahiroba (song plaza).
4. Kobukuro is a Japanese band, formed in 1998 and made its major label debut in 2001. The name is a portmanteau of the two family names, Kobuchi and Kuroda.
5. *Tei* and the following *Chou* are cries used in martial arts. Together the two words form the word "tetcho," meaning a spirit strong like iron.
6. *Dogeza* is a seated position for making formal apologies by bowing deeply.
7. Urashima Taro is a Rip Van Winkle type of character in a traditional children's story. He is taken to the dragon's palace in the sea by a turtle. After a wonderful visit, he is taken back to land only to find that the short stay was, in human time, many years, and the life he had known was now only a memory.
8. *Tonkotsu* refers to the pig bone used to make the soup.
9. In a *batsu* game, punishment is given to the loser of the game.